Justice and the Meritocratic State

Like American politics, the academic debate over justice is polarized, with almost all theories of justice falling within one of two traditions: egalitarianism and libertarianism. This book provides an alternative to the partisan stand-off by focusing not on equality or liberty, but on the idea that we should give people the things that they deserve. Mulligan argues that a just society is a meritocracy, in which equal opportunity prevails and social goods are distributed strictly on the basis of merit. That gives citizens their just deserts.

In addition to its novel conceptual approach, meritocracy is distinctive from existing work in two ways. First, it is grounded in research on how people actually think about justice. Empirical research reveals that people don't think that social goods should be distributed equally. Nor do they dismiss the idea of social justice. Across ideological and cultural lines, people want rewards to reflect merit. Second, the book discusses hot-button political issues and makes concrete policy recommendations. These issues include anti-meritocratic bias against women and racial minorities and the United States' widening economic inequality.

Justice and the Meritocratic State offers a new theory of justice and provides solutions to our most vexing social and economic problems. It will be of keen interest to philosophers, economists, and political theorists.

Thomas Mulligan is a faculty fellow at Georgetown University's Institute for the Study of Markets and Ethics. Before coming to academia, he served in the U.S. Navy and the Central Intelligence Agency.

Political Philosophy for the Real World
Edited by Jason F. Brennan,
Georgetown University

Justice and the Meritocratic State

Thomas Mulligan

Routledge
Taylor & Francis Group

LONDON AND NEW YORK

First published 2018 by Routledge

2 Park Square, Milton Park, Abingdon, Oxfordshire OX14 4RN
52 Vanderbilt Avenue, New York, NY 10017

*Routledge is an imprint of the Taylor & Francis Group,
an informa business*

First issued in paperback 2019

Library of Congress Cataloging-in-Publication Data
A catalog record for this book has been requested

ISBN: 978-1-138-28380-0 (hbk)
ISBN: 978-0-367-37228-6 (pbk)

Typeset in Sabon
by Apex CoVantage, LLC

To Mom and Dad
for the opportunity

Contents

Acknowledgements

This book is a hugely expanded version of the fourth chapter of my 2015 dissertation, *The Just and Meritocratic State*. Accordingly, my first debt is to my dissertation committee. I thank Eric Mack, my advisor, Jason Brennan, and David Shoemaker. They supported my development of a desert-based theory of justice even as most philosophers (and perhaps they themselves) thought it futile. I wish to acknowledge a special debt of gratitude to Jason, who showed me many professional kindnesses in the subsequent years.

I wrote this book at Brown University's Political Theory Project and the Georgetown Institute for the Study of Markets and Ethics—two research centers which support work that defies common labels, and which still believe, in our divided times, that we can find political solutions through sober, rigorous analysis. I thank John Tomasi and John Hasnas for leading these institutions, and for making them such pleasant places to do philosophy.

Over the past two years, I have presented parts of this work at various fora—the Brown Political Philosophy Workshop, the 2016 Society for Exact Philosophy Conference, the Third International Conference on Economic Philosophy, the Georgetown Institute for the Study of Markets and Ethics Workshop, the Normative Business Ethics Workshop at the Wharton School of Business, and the inaugural Philosophy, Politics, and Economics Society Conference. I thank these audiences for their helpful comments.

Scholars at many institutions, as well as some of my philosophically-minded friends, have influenced this work in myriad ways. I thank Sarah Brosnan, Bruce Brower, Nora Cronin, Kristen Currie, Dan D'Amico, Michael Douma, Bill English, Dave Estlund, David Faraci, Nick Geiser, Jess Guernsey, Gil Hersch, Jesse Hill, Peter Jaworski, Michael Kates, Charles Larmore, Joe Oppenheimer, Govind Persad, Josh Preiss, Kirun Sankaran, Dave Schmidtz, Jesse Shapiro, Steve Sheffrin, Leanne Son Hing, and Carla Yumatle. To those I have failed to acknowledge owing to my forgetfulness, I apologize.

I cannot enumerate the many ways in which the arguments of this book were sharpened in lively discussions with Vanessa Kolb. I thank her.

Huub Brouwer has taught me much about the concept of desert. He and I have co-authored a paper on the distinction between luck egalitarianism and desert-based justice, and I wish to especially acknowledge his influence on §4.6.

Greg Mankiw and George Sher were good enough to provide feedback on a proposal for this book, and to discuss various aspects of the project with me in the months that followed. Without George's path-setting work, no desert-based theory of distributive justice would be possible.

Dick Arneson, John Roemer, and Matt Weinzierl read a draft manuscript and provided extensive notes on it. This final version is much improved as a result. Among many other things, Dick's criticisms led to a conceptual tightening-up of Chapter 7; John helped me make sense of efficient, contribution-based income distribution; and Matt provided guidance on incorporating desert within tax theory.

Finally, I thank my editor, Andrew Weckenmann; his assistant, Allie Simmons; and three anonymous referees for Routledge, who provided valuable feedback. Andrew gave this idiosyncratic idea a home.

Part I
On Justice

1 Meritocracy: The Basics

1.1 Why Meritocracy?

There will be justice in our world, in fact and in sentiment, when people have the things that they deserve. In the economic realm, this is realized through a two-step process: First we establish equal opportunity, and then we judge people strictly on their merits. When this is done—when we live in a *meritocracy*—citizens will have their just deserts, and our unsteady march toward justice will have taken its final step.

Establishing this thesis, and defending it from its critics, is the primary goal of this book.

The second goal is to concretize the concept of meritocracy. Although we have an intuitive sense of what is meant by the term, we still lack a theory of meritocracy. The word itself is a surprisingly recent invention, coined by Michael Young for his 1958 satire, *The Rise of the Meritocracy*. Since then, the concept has been variously regarded: as an implicit feature of a just state; an admirable if impractical ideal; a thinly-veiled excuse for racial or class discrimination; a conservative ideology; and a leftist justification for meddling in free markets. Lacking a theory of meritocracy, these ascriptions were neither true nor false; they were rhetorically useful, or they were not.

As David Miller says, "we don't have a clear understanding of what meritocracy means, so we don't have a proper measuring rod against which to gauge social realities, saying how far they do or do not conform to meritocratic criteria" (1999: 178). And Amartya Sen: "the idea of meritocracy may have many virtues, but clarity is not one of them" (2000: 5). I want to do some conceptual tidying-up.

My third goal is to explain how meritocracy can fix our broken, hyper-partisan politics: by uniting Americans around the common cause of justice. As I survey the public outrage over our politics and our economy, I do not see it spilling forth from a wellspring of egalitarian or libertarian sentiment. As I will explain, it is a result of people not getting what they deserve. Americans left, right, and center want to live in a meritocracy, and that normative agreement can help us reach consensus on policy disputes thought to be intractable, like affirmative action and taxation. Meritocracy can break through the theoretical impasse within the distributive justice debate, and it can cure what ails us politically, as well.

To anyone who is not a political philosopher, that justice and desert are one and the same may seem obvious. But among the professionals, few things are more widely denied. Since the 1970s, desert has attracted little attention, with philosophers polarized between egalitarianism and libertarianism. With the exception of a handful of philosophers who admit desert as merely one of plural principles of justice,[1] it has been paid little heed.

Throughout this book, I shall contrast meritocracy with egalitarianism, in its Rawlsian form, and libertarianism, in its Nozickian form. I do this for a few reasons. First, as noted, these are the two approaches to justice to which most political philosophers subscribe. So any competitor must confront them.

Second, the theoretical polarization mirrors our current political climate. As I argue against the egalitarian I will in the process reject associated leftist policies, and as I argue against the libertarian I will reject associated rightist policies.

Third, just as the meritocratic political position is centrist, meritocracy resides, theoretically, between the egalitarian and libertarian poles. While not a hybrid of these two theories—meritocracy is a distinct, third way of thinking about justice—it does incorporate the best aspects of both.

From the libertarian, we take an emphasis on personal responsibility, individual choice, and unequal outcomes. There is something amiss, as a matter of justice, when the industrious and the lazy are rewarded alike, when the undeserving thrive while the deserving struggle.

From the egalitarian, we take a principle of equality—namely, *equality of opportunity*. Competition for social goods is inevitable owing to scarcity. Justice requires that that competition take place on a level playing field. If a person gets ahead of his peers, it ought to be because he is more meritorious than they are—and not because of his race, sex, or family influence.

We found these ideas on a principle which was obvious to ancient thinkers: People ought to get what they deserve. If meritocracy has an intellectual ancestor, it is Aristotle, who remains, 2,500 years later, the most important proponent of the desert-based approach (§1.2).

The current state of the dialectic about justice is, I think, rather like the Indian tale of the blind men and the elephant. One blind man feels the elephant's tusk, another its tail, another its trunk, and so on. They compare notes and find they disagree wildly about what the thing is. But in fact each has grasped part of the truth. What they ought to do is take a step back, and consider what entity captures all of the features they have individually discovered. This is what we shall endeavor to do with justice.

I ground meritocracy, in Chapters 2 and 3, by appealing to intuition and by pointing out that meritocracy satisfies metatheoretical desiderata. Among these is that meritocracy can surmount the "non-ideal" hurdles which philosophers have erected in recent years (§2.4), and resolve the to-this-point-vexing "equity/efficiency" trade-off (§4.8, §5.11, and §6.11). And meritocracy makes predictions (§9.4).

Part II of the book is devoted to the theory of meritocracy. There are an infinite number of possible desert-based theories, so to talk about "desert-based distributive justice" is to talk about an aspiration. To turn it into a theory, one must specify three things: first, the desert objects that fall under the sphere of inquiry. Second, the relevant desert basis or bases for these objects. And third, any necessary ancillary principles.

One such ancillary principle will be *equal opportunity*. We normally want to say that the fastest runner deserves the medal on the basis of his merit. But this is no longer true if the other runners were hobbled before the starting gun went off. In that case, the winner's just claim on the medal—his claim to deserve the medal—is weakened, if not nullified. And as it goes for races, so too for our collective economic life. Justice is a matter of giving people what they deserve, and that is impossible without equal opportunity

For this reason, each child in a meritocracy enjoys (roughly) equal health care, education, and other forms of social support. No one has a head start because of inherited wealth or nepotism, and none suffers from the persistent disadvantage created by childhood poverty. Each citizen enjoys equal opportunity to develop her merits as she sees fit, in accordance with the plan-of-life she has developed for herself.

The equal opportunity ideal is a popular one, but its connection to desert has remained elusive. In Chapter 4, I argue that the two concepts are intimately linked. I give a transcendental argument: (1) People ought to get what they deserve; (2) economic desert is only possible under conditions of equal opportunity; therefore (3) we ought to establish conditions of equal opportunity. It is thus a matter of conceptual necessity that a robust equal opportunity regime underlies desert-based distributive systems. Structurally, meritocracy is a monistic, desert-based theory which includes a necessary principle of equal opportunity.

The two desert objects that will concern us are jobs and income. In a meritocracy, jobs are distributed strictly on the basis of merit. They are not distributed with an eye toward equal representation (of genders, races, etc.), as an egalitarian might desire. Nor are owners given full liberty to distribute jobs however they like—to family, friends, or members of their preferred race. According to the meritocrat, any factor irrelevant from the point-of-view of merit must be ignored in hiring.

A meritocratic government combats deviations from merit-based hiring. Nepotism and cronyism (which are perfectly legal in the U.S. private sector) are proscribed, as is discrimination on the basis of race or gender (sometimes legal in the U.S. private sector). This is required by justice, but it is also in our economic interest: Efficient economies hire on the basis of merit.

We will then turn to consider income. This should be distributed to citizens on the basis of their meritorious contributions to the economy.

Contrast Steve Jobs, who made *bona fide* contributions to our collective economic life on the basis of his ability, with former Merrill Lynch CEO Stan O'Neal, who mismanaged his firm for years, and then, after posting a $2 billion quarterly loss—the worst in Merrill's history—floated away on a $162 million golden parachute.[2]

We feel that there is a moral difference between these two cases. And there is—but contemporary political theory cannot account for it. For Rawls, what matters is that incomes are distributed with an eye toward the welfare of the least-advantaged class. If it turns out that this is accomplished by enriching incompetent and greedy bankers, then, according to Rawls, justice requires precisely that. That is wrong. Justice is *intrinsically* connected to people's character and contributions.

The libertarian, who protects market exchanges at all costs, also fails to show proper regard for merit—as the above example suggests. Meritocracy dispatches worries about crony capitalism which have plagued libertarian theory, and deals with subtler problems of injustice and inefficiency—such as the passage of corporate power and capital by nepotism.

Now, any good ideology needs an ethos. Meritocracy's ethos is *personal responsibility* (§6.9). An egalitarian society of equal outcomes is a society in which a person does not command his own destiny. Whatever he does, or fails to do, has no effect on the course of his economic life. But a libertarian society of unequal opportunity also ignores personal responsibility. Under libertarianism, the quest for social goods turns on wealth, or class, or race; capricious facts—rather than character, effort, and choice—determine a person's future. Only in a meritocracy is a person wholly responsible for the course of his life. Only in a meritocracy will his successes and his failures turn on his merits alone.

As we proceed through the theory, we will use it to diagnose injustice in our current economy. That our economy is broken is about the only thing that Americans agree on these days. But what exactly is amiss?

Some point to the unequal distribution of income. The bottom 50 percent of Americans receives only 13 percent of national income. Within this group, the average income is $16,000—a figure that has not changed, in real terms, since 1980.

At the same time, the incomes of America's richest have skyrocketed. The top 1 percent receives 20 percent of national income (average income: $1.3 million), and the top 0.1 percent receives 9 percent of national income (average income: $6 million).

Put differently, the bottom 50 percent of our country makes roughly the same as the richest 0.1 percent, even though there are 500 times more people in the former than the latter. The United States now holds the all-time world record for inequality of labor-based income.[3]

The distribution of wealth is even more skewed: The top 0.1 percent of Americans owns 22 percent of our nation's wealth, which is the same share as the bottom 90 percent—a group which is, by definition, 900 times larger. (See Saez and Zucman 2016.)

I agree that these inequalities are worrying. But they are worrying because they are *symptoms* of injustice rather than injustices in themselves. They are symptoms of an economy in which the connection between merit and remuneration has been severed. As I will explain, America's high incomes do not reflect excellence, effort, or economic contribution. They are largely economic rents, and they are inefficient.

Even more worrying is how the meritocratic framework of our country, idealized in the American Dream, has been undermined over the last four decades. Once the source of extraordinary prosperity and civic pride, it has been dismantled, piece by piece, by regressive tax policies, a failure to invest in education, and a cultural disdain for merit.

The single best measure of the health of the American Dream is the intergenerational elasticity of earnings (IEE). This is a measure of the correlation between a person's income and his parents' income.[4] Imagine an aristocratic society, in which a person's socioeconomic position is completely determined by his parents' position. This society has an IEE of 1. A meritocracy lies at the other extreme, with an IEE close to 0 (roughly speaking, it will be positive to the extent that earnings-relevant traits are genetically passed).

Estimates of the IEE in the United States vary, but the mean estimate is about 0.6 (see, e.g. Mazumder 2005). This is among the worst in the developed world, if not the worst (cf. Canada, Finland, and Denmark, with IEEs of 0.2). (See, e.g. Corak 2013.)

For Americans born during the 1940s, approximately 90 percent of them went on to make more money (in real terms) than their parents did (Chetty et al. 2017). This is true of only 50 percent of Americans born during the 1980s. While we do not of course know what the numbers will be for Americans born today, the trend is not promising.

In short, since 1980 we have seen a transformation in the way our economy determines compensation. For a young American entering the labor force today, skill, creativity, diligence, and intelligence are less important than family background or social connections. This is intuitively felt by anyone on the job market, who must contend with an emphasis on pedigree and the overwhelming importance of "networking" (which is nepotism by another name).

Donald Trump is the ultimate manifestation of our failure to maintain the meritocratic structure of society. This is a man who was born into extreme wealth, thus enjoying advantage over his peers. He has been a perennial professional failure, pauperizing his shareholders while enriching himself. He is unlettered and crude. He is devoid of moral fiber. He is a person of low merit. Yet our culture saw it fit to elect him President: a job which he does not deserve, and which, I predict, he will fail to discharge effectively.

The left also bears blame for this state-of-affairs. It constantly celebrates personal characteristics like race, gender, and sexual preference when it should be celebrating intelligence, effort, and creativity. And its ruthless enforcement of silly political correctness norms has impeded the public's ability to assess individuals on their merit.

The left's focus on equality is a tactical mistake on its part. As we shall see, equality is widely regarded as an unjust distributive principle. No surprise, then, that the American left has failed to improve the material condition of the lower and middle classes in recent decades—it has based its policy in and crafted its rhetoric around a moral concept which is rejected even by the poor.

The way to advance progressive social programs is to found them on desert and to argue for them using the language of desert. The Earned Income Tax Credit (to be discussed in §9.3), which is one the largest components of American welfare, is the best example of this.

Over the course of this book, we shall reach roughly the same policy conclusions as the American center-left endorses today, but *via* a very different normative route. We will not, for example, justify anti-discrimination laws on grounds of equality. The real reason a firm ought not to discriminate against a black applicant is because that discrimination deviates from purely merit-based hiring. The most meritorious applicant deserves the job, and race is irrelevant from the point-of-view of merit.

I hope that by turning our attention away from the dominant rhetoric of equality and liberty and toward desert, we can find common ground politically and move our economy in a more just direction. Although other philosophers do not seem to feel this way, I regard the fact that no human beings anywhere—save a handful of academics—want to live in Nozick's nightwatchman state or in Rawls's quasi-egalitarian society as a damning indictment of these two leading approaches. The mission of political philosophy, insofar as distributive justice is concerned, must be to provide a coherent and compelling economic system that people feel is fair, and that serves the common interest by incentivizing productive behavior. These desiderata are satisfied when we treat people for who they are and what they have done—no more and no less. In the end, justice is found in what is simultaneously the most and least likely of places: the venerable but neglected idea that we should give people what they deserve.

1.2 A Brief History of Meritocracy

Although the word "meritocracy" is new, the idea is old, and found in Eastern and Western cultures alike. We find talk about desert in the Bible: "Whatsoever a man soweth, that shall he also reap" (Galatians 6:7).[5] And Confucius (551–479 BC) gave an argument for meritocratic politics which shaped Chinese governance for millennia:

> Meritorious rule is one of the most central ideas in Confucian political thought. The idea, simply put, is that those who occupy positions of power should possess the appropriate virtue and ability. . . . There should be a certain fit between position and virtue.
>
> (Chan 2013: 32)

But *why* should there be a fit between position and virtue? The ancient Chinese gave a consequentialist justification. For example, the Mohists (c. 400 BC)—who developed Chinese philosophy's first systematic approach to ethics and politics—argued for a political bureaucracy filled by "elevating the worthy". Their justification was not that meritorious Chinese deserved these jobs, but that "the utility of the state and society [was] promoted by employing the most qualified candidates, without regard for their social background" (Fraser 2015). This is an early and important distinction regarding the justification for meritocratic distribution (in this case, of political offices): whether it is done on grounds of justice—giving people what they deserve—or of efficiency.[6]

By the Sui dynasty (AD 581–618), China had fully replaced nepotism-driven politics with a system of civil service examinations, which were open to all (see, e.g. Xiao and Li 2013). These so-called Imperial Examinations persisted until the twentieth century, and have played an important role in Chinese culture—for example, its enduring emphasis on education. Although the aim of the system was to produce superior political outcomes, it had the side-effect of increasing social mobility, giving meritorious Chinese from poor families the opportunity to enter the elite classes on the basis of their talent.

Meanwhile, in the West, the meritocratic ideal was being more precisely developed but less successfully implemented. In the *Republic*, Plato famously argues for political rule by "philosopher-kings" (despite the term, Plato does not discriminate—he thinks meritorious women should rule, too). Like the Mohists, Plato justifies meritocracy on consequentialist grounds. His argument goes as follows: Managing a state is hard, requiring specific skills, such as military prowess, a sense of justice, and the power to persuade through public speaking (*Statesman*, 303–304). These skills are not found in common people or among the wealthy. Just as it would be silly to allow anyone to weigh in on medical decisions or the command of a ship, democracy and plutocracy put important decisions in the hands of those ill-equipped to make them. Plato hits a technocratic note when he says that the best political system is one in which "the rulers are not men making a show of political cleverness but men really possessed of scientific understanding of the art of government" (*Statesman*, 293c).

While the majority of his meritocratic arguments are consequentialist in this way, in the *Laws*, Plato does commend a desert-based distributive system:

> By distributing more to what is greater and smaller amounts to what is lesser, it gives due measure to each according to their nature: this includes greater honors always to those who are greater as regards virtue, and what is fitting—in due proportion—to those who are just the opposite as regards virtue and education. Presumably this is just what constitutes for us political justice.
>
> (757c)

This view—that justice is a matter of desert—is most closely associated with Aristotle, and for good reason. Aristotle provided the first—and, to this day, arguably the only—desert-based distributive theory. For Aristotle, the "currency of justice" consisted primarily of political offices and honors (which are not typically considered part of the currency today), and, secondarily, wealth (which most certainly is).

According to Aristotle, justice is done when we give these scarce goods to the people who deserve them.[7] But who among us is this? What is the basis, or bases, on which a person makes herself deserving of some particular good (§4.1)? And, given that goods are heterogeneous (political offices are different than wealth), should their desert bases differ as well?

Aristotle regarded the answers to these questions as uncontroversial: "All agree that the just in distributions must accord with some sort of merit [*axía*]" (*Nicomachean Ethics*, 1131a). Fair enough, but "merit", like "desert", is "thin": We might regard the most intelligent person as the most meritorious, or the most hard-working, or the most virtuous, and so on. Further specification is necessary.

(Note that "merit" is not as thin as "desert" is. To say that justice is a matter of giving people what they deserve, without specifying a basis, is to say almost nothing at all. "Merit" is more limited. There are many possible desert bases—such as Fred Feldman's (2016) "community essential needs"—which are unrelated to merit.)

For Aristotle, we "thicken" the definition of "merit" by looking to the end (*télos*) of the good in question. That tells us who is the most meritorious, and thereby, the most deserving.

> When a number of flute-players are equal in their art, there is no reason why those of them who are better born should have better

flutes given to them; for they will not play any better on the flute, and the superior instrument should be reserved for him who is the superior artist.

(Politics 1282b)

This is not to denigrate wealth, or noble birth, or beauty. They may be merits. But they are relevant to desert in other contexts. Beauty is relevant when we're deciding who should get the tiara, but not when we're deciding who should get the flute.

Suppose, for example, that we come across a baseball glove and decide to give it to one among us. Only one person—Smith—has any interest or skill in baseball; everyone else would simply throw the glove in the closet. It seems obvious that Smith ought to get the glove, and Aristotle's explanation why is that only Smith can ensure that the glove serves its purpose, which is to catch baseballs.

We should, thus, distribute social goods on the basis of merit, and when these goods are divisible, we should distribute them in proportion to merit. Equality is of no fundamental moral relevance. It is just to treat people equally only in the special cases in which they are themselves equal in merit.

Nevertheless, Aristotelian desert does define a sense of equality, known as *proportional equality*. What Aristotle seeks to make equal between persons are the *ratios* of merits to rewards. For example, if A_1 has twice the merit of A_2, then A_1 should receive twice the reward. In general, for a community of size n, a just distribution is equal in the following way:

$$\frac{A_1\text{'s merit}}{A_1\text{'s rewards}} = \frac{A_2\text{'s merit}}{A_2\text{'s rewards}} = \cdots = \frac{A_n\text{'s merit}}{A_n\text{'s rewards}}$$

This construal of equality (which contemporary political philosophers reject as a genuine principle of equality) avoids the problem of explaining how people are equal despite appearances to the contrary. Plenty of ink has been spilt trying to do that; I'll simply say that I regard those efforts as unsuccessful. I agree with John Stuart Mill:

> If it is asserted that all persons ought to be equal in every description of right recognised by society, I answer, not until all are equal in worth as human beings. It is the fact, that one person is *not* as good as another; and it is reversing all the rules of rational conduct, to attempt to raise a political fabric on a supposition which is at variance with fact.

(1859: 23)

Aristotle's view of justice, like all desert-based views, is backwards-looking. Feldman (1995) and Schmidtz (2002) deny that desert is necessarily backwards-looking; I consider and reject their arguments in §4.7). We do not give the flute to the best flute player in order to enrich the community with beautiful music. That is a forward-looking, consequentialist justification. Nor do we give Smith the baseball glove because he, and he alone, would be made happy by it. That is also a consequentialist justification. We distribute these goods as described because it is *fitting* to do so; a great flute fits with a great flute player, as a baseball glove fits on a hand.

After Aristotle, desert lay dormant. (We do find occasional hints of affection for the concept, in, e.g. the work of Leibniz, Kant, Sidgwick, G. E. Moore, and W. D. Ross. But desert is largely incompatible with these thinkers' fully-articulated theories.) By the mid-twentieth century, philosophers no longer took merit, desert, meritocracy, or related concepts seriously. In 1971, John Kleinig wrote that "the notion of desert seems by and large to have been consigned to the philosophical scrap heap" (p. 71).

That scrap heap was promptly set ablaze by the publication of Rawls's *A Theory of Justice*. Rawls purported to show that no one deserves anything at all. Although Rawls's argument is unsound (Chapter 7), it has had a profound impact within political philosophy. To this day, most philosophers regard the quest for a desert-based theory of justice as a fool's errand, on Rawlsian grounds.

This is extraordinary when one recalls that even Marx has warm things to say about desert. In his *Critique of the Gotha Programme*, Marx argues that a form of desert-based distributive justice is a positive step on the road from capitalism to communism.[8] It is a remarkable and true fact that "Marx is more a meritocrat than Rawls, Nielsen, Dworkin, and most contemporary liberal political philosophers" (Pojman 1999: 93).

Of course, Rawls has his detractors. Strikingly, they too deny desert a place in their theories. Libertarianism generally and Robert Nozick (1974) specifically are the exemplars here. That ideology, and that philosopher, are deaf to the demands of desert. What is important for Nozick is that the distribution of social goods accord with principles of acquisition and exchange. So long as we meet those procedural hurdles, then the outcomes are just. It does not matter to Nozick if the evil prosper while the kind suffer; if geniuses are pushed aside to make room for idiots; if the lazy get rich while the industrious live in poverty.

Even as Rawls and Nozick were denigrating desert (Rawls explicitly and Nozick implicitly), they were living in a country which once was but no longer is the best embodiment of the meritocratic ideal.[9] The Founders hoped to establish a nation led by a "natural aristocracy", in which—in contrast to the historical and prevailing hierarchies in Europe—a person's status turned not on "wealth and birth" but rather "virtue and talents" (Jefferson 1813).

Our national ethos is that each of us can enjoy a life of success and prosperity—no matter if we are Brahmin or immigrant—so long as we are willing to work for it.

To every man his chance—to every man, regardless of his birth, his shining, golden opportunity—to every man the right to live, to work, to be himself, and to become whatever thing his manhood and his vision can combine to make him—this, seeker, is the promise of America.

(Wolfe 1940: 432)

Like all dreams, this one was imperfectly realized. Our country has systematically and wrongly denied opportunities to various groups throughout our history—African-Americans, women, homosexuals, et al. And while progress has been made on issues of racial justice and the like, the connection between merit and economic outcomes is perhaps more frayed than ever. But failing to implement an ideal is no reason to abandon the ideal itself. The purpose of this book is, in part, to argue that we should redouble our efforts to make the American Dream a reality.

1.3 Remarks on the Assumptions of This Work

By tradition, philosophy as a discipline was founded by Thales (c. 624—c. 547 BC), a Greek living in Miletus (a city on what is today the western coast of Turkey). Thales is famous for his conjecture that all matter is, despite outward appearances, made of water. Of course, that is wrong. But Thales's underlying claim—that there is *some* unifying structure to things—is, as best we can tell, correct: It is the structure described by the Standard Model of particle physics. That things should have a common structure is not at all obvious—not then, and not now. So Thales's insight was profound.

This is the way philosophy has traditionally been conducted. We investigate foundational questions of existence, knowledge, and value through rigorous *a priori* reasoning and observation. We shall assume that this is the proper mode of philosophical inquiry. Not everyone who calls himself a "philosopher" would agree. One finds, for example, people who appeal to alleged divine revelation for philosophical insight, as well as the "Straussian" school of philosophy (named after the German-American Leo Strauss), which concerns itself with discovering "esoteric" meanings within the great works of philosophy. We assume that these radicals on the right are mistaken.

We shall also assume against radicals on the left. These include postmodernists who deny that there is such a thing as objective truth; "critical theorists" who regard philosophy not as an intellectual enterprise but as a tool for fighting "domination"; and various race-and gender-obsessed partisans who think that studying philosophy amounts to the study of "whiteness" and "maleness". (This camp is especially silly; you are obviously not studying whiteness or maleness—whatever that means—when you study General Relativity, even though that theory was developed by a white man.)

I editorialize here as a plea for unity among the many scholars and members of the public who, though we disagree about moral theory and political practice, believe in the primacy of human reason. Questions of morality and politics are both the most perplexing and the most fervidly debated. The only way to continue to make progress on these questions is to proceed with sober reason and a sense of intellectual humility. Extreme forces on both the left and the right are threatening these shared values.

Sobriety and humility also require that we assess empirical work on its merit—no matter how it makes us feel. When a result imperils a dearly-held belief, the rational reaction is not to reflexively reject the science. It is to put our belief into some doubt. And reason sometimes requires that we ask questions with potentially disquieting answers.

As an example of how we have failed in this regard, consider the plight of Larry Summers, economist and former Secretary of the Treasury, who was forced to resign as Harvard University's President after some incautious comments. In explaining the paucity of women in the sciences, Summers appealed to possible differences in the distribution of IQ: If men display greater variance than women, then even if the average man and the average woman are equally smart, we will find men hired in greater measure. This is because universities don't hire people clustered around the mean but rather those who are several standard deviations above it.

Summers was not making a normative argument but a positive one. He sought to *explain* the state of gender in the academy. This is perfectly compatible with regarding it as unjust. Indeed, an explanation like the one he gave could provide grounds for progressive policy change. Since IQ differences are in part environmentally-derived (§6.5), unequal variance may imply unequal opportunity, and thereby justify economic redistribution.

But in the aftermath of Summers's remarks, no arguments like this were made, and no interest paid to whether what he said was true or false.[10] Indeed, to ask such a question was to put oneself at risk of being regarded as a sexist. That attitude is simply incompatible with honest inquiry. One should be able to express one's best judgment about positive truth without putting one's career on the line. These outcries stunt the search for empirical truth; ruin the solidarity and the culture of academia; and, as explained, interfere with the pursuit of justice.

Although I criticize the academic left here, I do not do so out of any special animus. The right's contempt for rational inquiry is no less profound: climate change skepticism, creationism, religion-based public policy, Fox News and its fellow propagandists, our "post-truth" era, Donald Trump. There is no shortage of foolishness.

Philosophy has long served as the academy's bulwark against sloppy reasoning. It should take up this task with vigor.

Moving on. When it comes to economic matters, we shall assume the wisdom of the mainstream, neoclassical approach. This is the approach of Adam Smith and David Ricardo; members of the marginal revolution like Alfred Marshall and Léon Walras; twentieth-century giants like John Maynard Keynes and Milton Friedman; and, today, liberals like Paul Krugman and conservatives like Gregory Mankiw. Like analytic philosophy, the neoclassical economic approach is widely endorsed. It is the economics taught in high schools and colleges, and the method underpinning the vast majority of economic research.

I note that while the opponents of analytic philosophy are intellectually disreputable, opponents of neoclassical economics are not. They are, in my opinion, simply wrong. They include, on the left, followers of Karl Marx, whose views depart from the neoclassical approach in too many ways to summarize, and on the right, the Austrian School of economics—most associated with Ludwig von Mises and Murray Rothbard—which rejects the mathematics underlying microeconomic theory.

So the general method of this book is to examine normative issues analytically and positive issues through neoclassical models (one exception will be made for economic value, in §6.7). We shall also make the following, specific assumptions.

First, we assume that political authority is justified. Political philosophy has traditionally addressed two questions: (1) Is the state morally legitimate in the first place? Put differently, can the state justly do things to you (force you to pay taxes, imprison you, conscript you into military service), that no individual can? This is the question of political authority. If (1) is answered in the affirmative, the second major question arises: (2) How should we arrange the institutions of government? What laws, regulations, tax-and-transfer policies, if any, ought to exist?

I answer (2) in this book, and so I must assume that (1) is true—that political authority is justified, that we need not be anarchists. There is overwhelming consensus among philosophers that this is the case (Wolff (1970) is the major exception).

Second, we make necessary metaphysical and epistemological assumptions: that the world is roughly the way it appears to us to be through the senses; that we are not brains-in-vats; that we have free will; and so on. Bruce Brower has described these considerations to me as "pragmatic presuppositions of rational inquiry". That is, these are the things that we must assume to be true in order to embark on philosophical investigation within a given domain—which in our case is distributive justice.

Third, and finally, we shall limit ourselves to considerations of justice within a single state. This has been a traditional assumption. According to Hobbes, the possibility of just relations between persons arises when we leave the state of nature and submit to a single sovereign. This view is still dominant, although there has been interest, over the last 40 years or so, in "global justice"—the possibility that citizens have duties of justice to foreigners. We shall not address this possibility.

Notes

1 *Viz.* Feldman (2016) (desert and need), Miller (1999) (desert, equality, and need), Schmidtz (2006) (desert, equality, liberty, reciprocity, and need), and Walzer (1983) (desert, liberty, and need). (Although Feldman's theory is arguably monistic, with need serving as the desert basis rather than an independent principle of justice.)
2 Mankiw (2010) makes a similar point.
3 See Piketty (2014) and Piketty, Saez, and Zucman (2016).
4 The IEE is the percentage difference in a child's income associated with a 1 percent change in his parents' income. The measure is typically made between children and fathers to avoid complexities related to changes in labor force participation by women.
5 On the biblical roots of merit and desert, see Pojman (1997).
6 Fraser (2015) notes that the Mohists "advanced the world's earliest form of consequentialism, a remarkably sophisticated version based on a plurality of intrinsic goods taken as constitutive of human welfare".
7 For a fuller examination of Aristotle's view of distributive justice, see Keyt (1991).
8 As far as I know, Marx did not put things in terms of deserts. But in this phase of Marx's theory, a worker is compensated proportional to his labor contributions to society. That is not far from the meritocratic approach that I endorse in Chapter 6, under which a person's compensation is determined by his meritorious economic contributions. But it will be clear that meritocracy has little in common with Marxian theory.
9 Singapore provides the best example of a meritocratic state now; indeed, meritocracy is (along with incorruptibility and impartiality) one of the foundational values of the state. The Singaporean meritocracy is enabled by extensive public spending on education (20 percent of the national budget), with the result that Singaporean children are the world's best-educated (OECD 2016). And the extraordinary economic growth that has resulted from Singapore's investment in its children is well-known: Its per capita GDP, 87,000 USD, is the fourth-highest in the world (the United States, at 57,000, ranks 14th).
10 Summers presented the evidence fairly. At least as far as mathematical ability is concerned, there is no mean difference in ability between men and women, but men do display greater variance than women (see, e.g. Hedges and Nowell 1995; Hyde et al. 2008). Whether this explains, even in part, the underrepresentation of women is unclear.

1.4 References

Chan, J. 2013. Political meritocracy and meritorious rule: A Confucian perspective. In *The East Asian Challenge for Democracy: Political Meritocracy in Comparative Perspective*, eds. D. A. Bell and C. Li, 31–54. New York: Cambridge University Press.
Chetty, R., Grusky, D., Hell, M., Hendren, N., Manduca, R., and Narang, J. 2017. The fading American Dream: Trends in absolute income mobility since 1940. *Science* 356: 398–406.
Corak, M. 2013. Inequality from generation to generation: The United States in comparison. In *The Economics of Inequality, Poverty, and Discrimination in the 21st Century*, ed. R. S. Rycroft, 107–26. Santa Barbara: Praeger.

Feldman, F. 1995. Desert: Reconsideration of some received wisdom. *Mind* 104: 63–77.

———. 2016. *Distributive Justice: Getting What We Deserve from Our Country.* New York: Oxford University Press.

Fraser, C. 2015. Mohism. In *The Stanford Encyclopedia of Philosophy (Winter 2015 Edition)*, ed. E. N. Zalta. URL = <https://plato.stanford.edu/archives/win2015/entries/mohism/>, retrieved 27 August 2017.

Hedges, L. V. and Nowell, A. 1995. Sex differences in mental test scores, variability, and numbers of high-scoring individuals. *Science* 269: 41–5.

Hyde, J. S., Lindberg, S. M., Linn, M. C., Ellis, A. B., and Williams, C. C. 2008. Gender similarities characterize math performance. *Science* 321: 494–5.

Jefferson, T. 1813. Letter to John Adams, 28 October. Reprinted in *The Adams-Jefferson Letters: The Complete Correspondence Between Thomas Jefferson and Abigail and John Adams* (1959), ed. L. J. Cappon, 387–92. Chapel Hill: University of North Carolina Press.

Keyt, D. 1991. Aristotle's theory of distributive justice. In *A Companion to Aristotle's Politics*, eds. D. Keyt and F. D. Miller, 238–78. Oxford: Blackwell.

Kleinig, J. 1971. The concept of desert. *American Philosophical Quarterly* 8: 71–8.

Mankiw, N. G. 2010. Spreading the wealth around: Reflections inspired by Joe the plumber. *Eastern Economic Journal* 36: 285–98.

Mazumder, B. 2005. The apple falls even closer to the tree than we thought: New and revised estimates of the intergenerational inheritance of earnings. In *Unequal Chances: Family Background and Economic Success*, eds. S. Bowles, H. Gintis, and M. O. Groves, 80–99. Princeton: Princeton University Press.

Mill, J. S. 1859. *Thoughts on Parliamentary Reform.* London: John W. Parker and Son.

Miller, D. 1999. *Principles of Social Justice.* Cambridge: Harvard University Press.

Nozick, R. 1974. *Anarchy, State, and Utopia.* New York: Basic Books.

Organization for Economic Co-Operation and Development (OECD). 2016. *Programme for International Student Assessment (PISA) 2015 Results (Volume I): Excellence and Equity in Education.* Paris: OECD Publishing.

Piketty, T. 2014. *Capital in the Twenty-First Century*, trans. A. Goldhammer. Cambridge: Belknap Press.

Piketty, T., Saez, E., and Zucman, G. Forthcoming. Distributional national accounts: Methods and estimates for the United States. *Quarterly Journal of Economics.*

Pojman, L. 1997. Equality and desert. *Philosophy* 72: 549–70.

———. 1999. Merit: Why do we value it? *Journal of Social Philosophy* 30: 83–102.

Rawls, J. 1971. *A Theory of Justice.* Cambridge: Belknap Press.

Saez, E. and Zucman, G. 2016. Wealth inequality in the United States since 1913: Evidence from capitalized income tax data. *Quarterly Journal of Economics* 131: 519–78.

Schmidtz, D. 2002. How to deserve. *Political Theory* 30: 774–99.

———. 2006. *Elements of Justice.* New York: Cambridge University Press.

Sen, A. 2000. Merit and justice. In *Meritocracy and Economic Inequality*, eds. K. Arrow, S. Bowles, and S. Durlauf, 5–16. Princeton: Princeton University Press.

Walzer, M. 1983. *Spheres of Justice: A Defense of Pluralism and Equality*. New York: Basic Books.

Wolfe, T. 1940. *You Can't Go Home again*. New York: Harper & Brothers.

Wolff, R. P. 1970. *In Defense of Anarchism*. New York: Harper & Row.

Xiao, H. and Li, C. 2013. China's meritocratic examinations and the ideal of virtuous talents. In *The East Asian Challenge for Democracy: Political Meritocracy in Comparative Perspective*, eds. D. A. Bell and C. Li, 340–62. New York: Cambridge University Press.

Young, M. 1958. *The Rise of the Meritocracy*. London: Thames and Hudson.

2   The Metatheory of Justice

2.1 The Scope of Justice

A few words about the goal of this work—what I mean to accomplish and what I do not.

I shall not provide a theory of morality at its most general. For example, I shall have little to say about interpersonal relationships—how friends, or lovers, ought to treat each other, or how parents ought to treat their children and children ought to treat their parents. These are important ethical issues, to be sure, but I owe them consideration only inasmuch as they are relevant to the economic structure of society. And by in large they are not. (The salient exception is the relationship between the family structure and equal opportunity, to be discussed in §4.5.)

Instead, my interest is distributive justice—or economic justice, if you like. The answers I am obliged to provide respond to questions like, "On what bases should job candidates be evaluated?", "How much income inequality is too much?", "Which forms of affirmative action, if any, are morally permissible?", and "Who should pay taxes, and how much should they pay?"

Clearly, these are all normative questions. And so, in contrast to positive questions (e.g. "Who *does* pay taxes, and how much *do* they pay?"), to answer them adequately we must have in mind some moral goal. After all, if I am simply seeking to maximize my own wealth, my answer to "Who should pay taxes?" will be rather different from the answer I would give were I to have some other, less selfish, goal in mind.

But on this matter there is little debate: The thing that we all aspire to is *justice*. We all want an economic arrangement that is just. Of course, we do not all want the same economic arrangement; we disagree about which is in fact just. Egalitarians believe that a just economy establishes some manner of equality among citizens; utilitarians think that it maximizes the general welfare; and libertarians, at least in their Nozickian form, believe that justice consists in protecting free exchanges among citizens. But the "thin" goal—justice—is shared.

The only scholar to deny our shared goal of justice is Friedrich Hayek (1976, 1978), but this is a conceptual error on Hayek's part.[1] He says that "there can be no distributive justice where no one distributes" (1978: 58), but this is mere wordplay. We want to know whether there are moral rules governing economic relations that call for intervention into markets. To say "no", as libertarians do, is not to regard the concept of justice as empty or incoherent as Hayek did. What Hayek really seemed to oppose are *patterned* theories of justice—to use Nozick's (1974) term—and this is a far more plausible target than the idea of justice.[2]

Distributive justice itself, and the philosophical challenge of identifying its content, arise, Hume tells us, "only from the selfishness and confin'd generosity of men, along with the scanty provision nature has made for his wants" (1739: 495, italics removed). That is, were it not for conditions of scarcity (our demand for goods outstrips their supply) and human beings' limited capacity for altruism, there would be no questions of justice. (Hume imposes a third condition, also satisfied: No human being is so powerful that he can dominate all others, living free from fear.)

Rawls approvingly calls Hume's conditions the "circumstances of justice" and founds his theory upon them. And since I largely agree, I shall not tarry on the subject, except to point out one thing: Competition is built into justice. To say that there is scarcity is to say that there are at least two people who want some thing, and that, no matter how the matter is resolved, at least one will walk away unsatisfied. "Meritocracy" has a connotation of competition which some people find off-putting, but I ask these readers to keep in mind that competition is not just socially inevitable—it is *essential* to distributive justice.

While we cannot avoid competition, we can avoid arranging our competitions in ways that are regarded as unfair by their participants. As we shall see, the economic competitions (for jobs, income, etc.) that we feel are fair and those that are required by justice are one and the same. They are meritocratic competitions.

For similar reasons, we cannot eliminate failure, nor the sadness that it brings. But we can eliminate *resentment*. Sadness is an inevitable part of life. It is dignified. But resentment, which is born out of unjust competition, is avoidable and pernicious (§5.6). It should be eliminated.

And, apart from all of that, we should not reflexively regard competition as a bad thing. We might maintain that a world without scarcity would be a better world (though I'm not convinced) while, perfectly coherently, speaking warmly of the value of competition. Among other things, competition stimulates human achievement, recognizes laudable character, and puts resources into the hands of those who can make efficient use of them.

2.2 On the Distinction Between Justice and Morality

A metaethical matter which must be addressed is the possibility of justice coming into conflict with other moral ideals. If we want to say that our economy ought to be arranged in a certain way because that is what justice requires, we must have a sense of what other ideals exist and their economic ramifications. If, for example, we believed that liberty was an important ideal which could come into conflict with justice, then discovering that some theory of justice was true would not get us to our real-world destination. We would be left pondering how our perfectly just economy ought to be modified to accommodate liberty.

This possibility is raised from time to time, but it did not trouble Rawls or Nozick. Rawls begins *A Theory of Justice* with the claim that

> justice is the first virtue of social institutions, as truth is of systems of thought. A theory however elegant and economical must be rejected or revised if it is untrue; likewise laws and institutions no matter how efficient and well-arranged must be reformed or abolished if they are unjust.
>
> (1971: 3)

Rawls rules out the possibility of ideals other than justice playing a role in economic design.

Nozick is more obscure. Unlike Rawls, who draws as I do on the Humean tradition, with just principles and institutions, whatever they be, arising out of the circumstances of justice, Nozick admits from the start that he "does not present a precise theory of the moral basis of individual rights" (1974: xxiv). Still, at least as far as the entitlement theory of *Anarchy, State, and Utopia* goes, Nozick regards the limits and the obligations of the state as coextensive with its responsibilities under justice. Justice requires that the state prevent violence, theft, and fraud in the name of protecting individual rights—and little else.[3]

I do think it is fair to focus on justice—but not so single-mindedly. As we shall see, justice is indeed held in the highest moral esteem, but *efficiency* and *need* are also thought morally relevant to economic life. And, at least conceptually, they can conflict with justice. Rawls is right that justice is the first virtue of institutions—but it's not the only virtue.

How can this complexity be handled? In two ways. First, questions about pluralism may simply be ignored: The theorist can say that he is going to talk about justice, what justice requires of us, and leave aside the possibility of competing ideals. While getting to the truth about justice in this way would be a great victory, the drawback is that it weakens the case for *acting* on the theory, for arranging our institutions in its image.

The second way is to endorse a theory of justice which has, as a side-effect, the promotion of the other identified ideals. If a theory of justice, when implemented, is also (1) efficient and (2) attentive to citizens' needs, then no more conceptual work is necessary. This is the route I take. I shall devote a great deal of space to the efficiency benefits of meritocracy, because the conflict between justice and efficiency is center stage in normative economics. And I address how meritocracy attends to citizens' needs in §6.10. While it's true that, for any given theory of justice, the theory should not be implemented if the efficiency/need trade-offs are too severe, no such worries arise in the case of meritocracy.

We should not underestimate the metatheoretical allure of this feature. If we take a step back to consider what features we expect a true theory of justice to have, one of these is that it be reasonably compatible with efficiency and need. Put differently, it would be odd if the true theory of justice were one which, when implemented, impoverished society. This is a point about justification which I shall discuss further in the next section.

I want to be precise about how I am and am not a pluralist. I am a pluralist when it comes to the morality of economic life—how we ought, *in the broadest possible sense of "ought"*, to set up our economy. The relevant ideals here appear to be justice, efficiency, and need, with justice the most important of the three by far (§3.2).

I am a monist when it comes to justice. Justice is a matter of giving people what they deserve. Nothing more. Of course, explaining what that means, and why that is true, is not simple. I devote the second part of the book to the task.

The finding that justice and morality are not coextensive is important for other reasons. First, it opens the possibility that we might, from time to time, find even a perfectly just system morally unsatisfying. It legitimates these feelings of moral dissatisfaction. To discover the nature of justice precisely and to implement it completely is not to create a utopia, the institutions of which never err morally. And that a theory of justice demands, in some individual cases, something immoral does not prove injustice.

As an example, consider the following "ticking time bomb" case: A terrorist has hidden a nuclear bomb in a city. The terrorist refuses to say where it is. We torture him, but he remains recalcitrant. We also have in custody the terrorist's innocent, 12-year-old daughter. We know that, if we torture her in front of him, he will reveal the bomb's location. Is it morally permissible, perhaps even required, to torture this innocent girl? Many people would say "yes". After all, if the bomb goes off, thousands of innocent children will die. But *nobody*—not even hardcore consequentialists—thinks that it is *just* to torture the girl. Rather, we think it is morally permissible, perhaps morally required, to do something unjust. This is a small conceptual point, but it's an important one.

Second, once we admit that there are competing moral desiderata when it comes to our economy, we should be wary of the single-minded promotion of any ideal, no matter how noble. Implementation costs rise at the margin.

Suppose that we are choosing between two allocations, A and B. Under A, output is \$18 trillion and there is a certain level of justice, j. Under B, output is \$1 trillion and the level of justice is j plus some increment ε.

Rawls would require us to prefer B to A. Efficiency should not concern us a whit, he thinks, if justice is at stake (suppose, i.e. that the worst-off in B has a teensy bit more than the worst-off in A). Many find this intuitively implausible.

Similarly, suppose that we could move from B to A by means of a mild intrusion on liberties (some efficiency-enhancing regulation). Who among us would really insist on the "immorality" of that, *even if* she believed, as Nozick did, that justice is a matter of inviolable side-constraints?

Third, by separating justice from morality, we explain why our government may *tolerate* some unjust conduct. Right or wrong, here in the United States the government tolerates—does not deter, does not punish—all sorts of injustice: hate speech, deceit, and (as decided by the Supreme Court in *Snyder v. Phelps*) the brutalization of the families of dead soldiers, in their hour of grief, by religious zealots. In these cases, we regard the behavior as unjust yet at the same time think that it would be bad if the government curbed it.

This is the essence of tolerance, a difficult concept which I analyze elsewhere.[4] One of the many paradoxes it gives rise to is how allowing bad things to happen could possibly be the right thing to do. A distinction like the one I make here explains things: If the conduct at issue is bad because it is unjust, and if justice is not the only element in the moral calculus, then we have created conceptual space for tolerating injustice.

2.3 Efficiency and Three Requirements of Justice

I shall have a great deal to say about economic efficiency in this book. So it is important to get clear about what is meant by the term.

Put imprecisely, an efficient economy is one in which there is no waste. Resources get put to their best productive uses (doctors practice medicine and lumberjacks log—not *vice versa*), and goods and services are allocated in a useful way (sick people visit doctors, not lumberjacks). One has the intuition that if production and allocation are not so arranged, that is a problem—perhaps one which can be fixed without any ill effects, anywhere.

The intuition is usually made precise in terms of *Pareto efficiency*. A Pareto efficient distribution is one in which it is impossible to make someone better off without making someone else worse off. You distribute a cake in a Pareto efficient way if there are no pieces left over after everyone gets her share. In contrast, if a slice of cake remains after distribution, that is Pareto inefficient: Why throw it away when you could give it to somebody, while, at the same time, not reducing anybody's share?

Pareto efficiency has normative force, but it is clear that it is only a *ceteris paribus* force. Suppose a cake is cut into six slices, and we are choosing between two distributions. Under distribution A, each of five children gets one slice of cake and the sixth slice is thrown into the trash. Under distribution B, one child—the biggest bully of the group—gets all six slices. Now, B is Pareto efficient and A is not—and that is a point in B's favor—but A is morally superior to B. Put differently, we care about efficiency, but not as much as we care about justice.

Although Pareto efficiency is an indispensable theoretical tool, it is not very useful when it comes to analyzing public policy. There are a host of potential laws and regulatory changes that we want to call "efficient", but all of these doubtless make *somebody* worse-off. Consider the exemplar of "efficiency-enhancing" regulation: Taxes on negative externalities, like pollution (to be discussed in §8.3). These taxes are not Pareto improvements; the polluter is better-off without them. But they still reduce waste of *some kind*. Similarly, breaking up a monopoly is not a Pareto improvement—it's bad for the monopolist. But this is still a step we can rightly justify on grounds of efficiency.

For the purpose of evaluating policy, it is more useful to think of efficiency simply in terms of the *total surplus*—the economic gains to consumers and producers, *as measured in dollars*.[5] The difference between what a consumer would pay for a good and what he actually pays (i.e. the market price) is a measure of his economic benefit. The difference between what a producer would sell its good for and the market price is a measure of the producer's economic benefit. Indeed, creating this surplus is often regarded as the *raison d'être* of an economy.

It is clear that efficiency in this sense also has limited normative force. Social planners might increase the surplus by treading on property rights, or transferring resources from the virtuous to the wicked, or reducing the welfare of their society, etc. Increasing the total surplus is desirable, but only *ceteris paribus* desirable.

Now the distribution of cake and economic distribution differ in an important way: When we think about the best way to distribute a cake, we might think of justice and efficiency as going hand-in-hand. Whatever else we ought to do with the cake, we ought to give all of the slices out.

Economic distribution is not like this. For all plausible normative goals (welfare maximization, giving people what they deserve, protecting rights, maximizing the least-advantaged's share, etc.), it is not necessary that the economy be efficient. The distributive system that maximizes welfare (e.g.) might produce fewer welfare-enabling goods than some other, feasible system.

The reason this is so is that we obtain our desired redistribution through taxation and social spending.[6] And as Arthur Okun (1975) memorably puts it, redistribution is akin to carrying water in a leaky bucket: Some potential goods are destroyed by the redistributive process itself. These are the *deadweight losses* associated with taxation and social spending. Those who pay taxes reduce their labor time or otherwise modify their economic behavior as a result of the tax. And the recipients of public funds substitute leisure for work, or leave the workforce completely, when they receive the transfer.

So there is a tension between our normative goal of justice and positive facts about the production and distribution of the resources needed to pursue that goal. The more vigorously we pursue justice, the more we may find ourselves unable to fuel that pursuit. In economics, this is known as the "equity/efficiency trade-off" (or sometimes the "equality/efficiency trade-off"—for those, apparently, who assume that justice is about equality).

Philosophers too often ignore the trade-off.[7] It is widely thought that our job is to identify, *a priori*, the ideally just distributive scheme. Once that is done, the matter is to be passed to social scientists, so that they can develop the necessary institutions, and then to politicians for implementation.

This is too quick. As I shall discuss in §3.2, we seem to grant independent weight to efficiency. And, for the reasons just given, one cannot assume that a theory of justice will not unacceptably tread on efficiency. To be a functional guide for reforming our institutions, a theory of justice must either (1) make precise the efficiency losses that its implementation would create and argue that these are acceptable, or (2) advance a theory that is broadly efficient. I shall endeavor to make clear why (2) is true for meritocracy.

As alluded to in §2.2, this is also a justificatory consideration. It seems that we might deny the truth of a theory of justice on grounds of inefficiency. Again, that a theory of justice would impoverish a society suggests that the theory is false. It is not dispositive, but it is a point against the theory.

While it is hard to know how much inefficiency is too much, I think that the idea can be put adequately thus:

The First Requirement of Justice: A theory of justice should suggest an economy that is reasonably efficient.

Two points here. First, this is a metatheoretical principle because its subject-matter is political theorizing; it serves as a constraint on our political theories, not a constraint on our politics.

Second, I shall not define "reasonably efficient". Again, I do not know where the relevant line here should be drawn. That problem I cannot solve—but I can bypass it. One of main contributions of this book is to show how meritocracy, unique among distributive theories, minimizes trade-offs between justice and efficiency. As economist Roland Bénabou puts it, "the analysis generally validates the common intuition that meritocracy, appropriately defined, is desirable not only on grounds of fairness but also on grounds of efficiency" (2000: 319).

This metatheoretical idea can be taken a step further. We evaluate theories of justice not only with an eye toward their efficiency, but toward their implications for public policy, as well.

Consider taxation. Starting with James Mirrlees (1971), economists have looked at how to maximize the general welfare given the aforementioned disincentives that taxes create. This is the central task of *optimal tax theory* (§8.1). One of the implications of Mirrlees's model is that marginal income tax rates should *decrease* with income; indeed, under suitable distributional assumptions, the top marginal tax rate should be 0%. Why? Because that maximizes the general welfare.[8]

For most people, this is counterintuitive, as evidenced by the fact that income taxes are progressive almost everywhere, including in the United States. We believe that progressivity in the tax code is more just than regressivity in the tax code.

The utilitarian can confront this result in one of two ways. First, he can endorse this policy prescription, its counterintuitiveness be damned. Or, second, he can regard it as reason to revisit his normative commitments. If a perfect utilitarian society is one in which the richer you get, the less your (marginal) income gets taken from you—well, then perhaps the utilitarian ideal is not so just after all. Instead of a *modus ponens* from utilitarianism to regressive income taxes, we have a *modus tollens* which refutes utilitarianism.

Balancing theory and practice in this way should be handled by the standard method of reflective equilibrium, which I shall discuss in due course. This metatheoretical idea may be put in this way:

> **The Second Requirement of Justice:** A theory of justice should suggest morally attractive public policies.

Finally, I suggest a third requirement, related to the *moral opportunity costs* of our justice-mandated public policies. The true cost of anything is what you give up in order to get that thing. Hence the saying, "there's no such thing as a free lunch": You don't have to pay money for it, but you do have to give up *something*—namely, your most-preferred alternative to spending that hour at the diner.

In the same way, there are opportunity costs to implementing justice. To economists, this will seem so obvious as to be hardly worth stating; but surprisingly few philosophers consider either (1) whether the resources spent implementing the policies their theories demand might be spent on more morally-pressing matters, or (2) the incentive effects of these policies, which could reduce (or increase) our overall ability to pursue justice or other moral ends.

Of course, what precisely the most-preferred foregone alternative is depends on one's moral compass. Nevertheless, we can reach consensus on something that is, even if not the worst thing in the world, very nearly so. This is that thousands of children die every day from famine or poverty-related disease—primarily in Sub-Saharan Africa and South Asia. We need not let this happen; it costs about $2,000 to save one of these innocent lives. We ought to keep that in mind when we evaluate the justness of our policy prescriptions. I name this metatheoretical constraint after Peter Singer (1972):

The Third Requirement of Justice: A theory of justice should pass the Singer Test.

At Brown University, where I last taught, the administration has committed to spend $165 million on diversity-related initiatives, including the provision of "safe spaces" for students who feel offended by aspects of campus culture. The moral opportunity cost of this policy is 82,500 dead African children. Brown's administration, whether they were aware of it or not, made a choice: to advance diversity and to let those children die. Does justice require this? Perhaps it does; but that evaluation has to be made with the moral opportunity cost, which in this case is a mortal one, in mind.

Similarly, the American government spent $13 billion to build the U.S.S. *Gerald R. Ford*, an aircraft carrier. It is our 11th. The rest of the world combined has nine aircraft carriers, seven of which belong to friendly nations. The moral opportunity cost of the *Gerald R. Ford* is 6,500,000 dead African children. Surely, with that figure in mind, the military expense seems *less* justified if nothing else.

When evaluating a theory of justice, we must put it to the Singer Test. We must ask if the theory is plausible in light of the moral opportunity costs. Of course, some theorists (utilitarians who pay no heed to national boundaries, like Singer himself) think that these considerations suggest that we simply ought to arrange our economy in the cosmopolitan, welfare-maximizing way. We need not adopt that view. But we must be honest with ourselves about the palatability of our abstract theories.

Consider, for example, the libertarian idea that we ought to protect all parts of a person's income obtained through free contracts. If that is right, then we must protect the trillions of dollars in economic rents received by our highest-income citizens (§6.4). These rents do not reflect value-added to the economy. They are always imperfectly connected to merit, and sometimes utterly unconnected. They may be taxed away without loss of efficiency. They may be taxed away without affecting their possessors' welfare (the marginal utility of rents, since they are obtained by the wealthy, is practically zero).

Yet the libertarian insists that we not confiscate them, which may seem attractive in the abstract but is ludicrous when the moral opportunity cost of protecting them is kept in mind: the death of millions of children (or, more likely given the numbers involved, an end to global poverty).

The idea here is that when we evaluate the justness of some normative principle, we ought to make that evaluation with reference to moral opportunity costs. We *learn* that the right-libertarian is *probably* wrong when we see the extraordinary human suffering that he chooses to perpetuate when he protects the principle of exchange.

Of course, we would like to have a theory of justice that solved all the world's problems, fighting poverty abroad as it establishes justice at home. I am certainly not claiming that meritocracy does this, although there are reasons to think that highly-efficient economies, which meritocracy would produce, help eradicate global poverty—through direct giving, the aid apparatus they enable, and globalization. (See Wenar 2011 for an introduction to some of the empirical issues involved.) I shall seek only to show that meritocratic justice *can* stand up to the Singer Test, in a way that other theories, including libertarianism, cannot.

2.4 Ideal and Non-Ideal Theory

Meritocracy offers an unabashedly utopian vision: of a world in which distinctions of class are not passed between generations; racism, sexism, and other biases wither under society's strict focus on merit; and the economy approaches maximum productivity through sage, efficiency-enhancing regulation. Of course, utopian thinking is nothing new within philosophy, but ever since Rawls (1971) drew a distinction between theorizing under ideal conditions (which for Rawls meant assuming that all citizens would obey identified principles of justice) and theorizing under non-ideal conditions (of more realistic, partial compliance), the traditional approach has come under threat from the non-ideal side of the debate.[9]

It has been claimed, variously, that ideal theory cannot serve as a guide for reforming our institutions; is incoherent for formal reasons; serves to perpetuate unjust social privilege; and is, has been, and will continue to be nothing but a tool for power-hungry politicians to oppress their citizens.

Some non-ideal criticisms are, I believe, sound—or at least plausible enough to take seriously; the ideal theorist must meet them or abandon his project. These I will explicate below, and I will hope to show, over the course of this book, that meritocracy meets the challenge.

Philosophers who deny the importance of *all* non-ideal considerations may skip this section. And do I agree that *some* of these considerations should not move us. For example, consider Charles Mills's claim that ideal theory "is really an *ideology*, a distortional complex of ideas, values, norms, and beliefs that reflects the nonrepresentative interests and experiences of a small minority of the national population—middle-to-upper class white males" (2005: 172).

Mills may be correct, in a limited sense: None of us is so disinterested, such a paragon of logic, that he can divorce his theories from facts about his upbringing, his social class, and so on. It is inevitable that to some degree the content of a theory of justice reflects the character and the experiences of the person who advances it. And it is also true that we can always find a way in which this character or these experiences are non-representative of the population. That is a straightforward consequence of living in a diverse society.

But this tells us nothing about the value of the work itself, which is what should concern us. It is obviously no accident that the majority of feminist philosophers are women. But that says nothing about the intellectual value of feminist thought. To learn that, we must judge the work—not the author.

I do think it is worthwhile to consider perspectives on justice that are absent from the debate owing to the non-representation of race, gender, and class which Mills identifies. The best way to do that is examine how people across lines of race and gender think about justice. We shall do this in the next chapter. The wrong way to incorporate these perspectives is to give special weight to the opinions of, say, black academics—not least because their perspective and ideology is quite different from the perspective and ideology of the black community at-large.

In any case, Mills has something else in mind: "If we ask the simple, classic question of *cui bono?* [who benefits?] then it is obvious that ideal theory can only serve the interests of the privileged, who in addition—precisely because of that privilege (as bourgeois white males)—have an experience that comes closest to that ideal" (2005: 172).

Claims like these are frequent these days, and they are lamentable. Mills commits errors of both fact and logic. He makes a factual error because most ideal theories would not end up serving the interests of the "privileged". Rawls's theory, for example, would impose a relative harm on white men owing to its redistributive demands.

Mills makes a logical error, because the ideal world a philosopher desires may well be different from his socioeconomic experience (even as the theory is *informed* by his experience). In my judgment, it is the poor, not the privileged, whose experience better approximates Nozick's nightwatchman state.

Mills is convinced that Rawls's theory was "constructed to *evade* these problems [of racial justice]" (Pateman and Mills 2007: 258). I doubt that very seriously given Rawls's impeccable character, but in any case I shall confront racial justice head-on.

I shall argue that it is unjust to discriminate against a best-qualified black applicant on the basis of his race, and that justice requires major wealth redistribution in the name of establishing equal opportunity—redistribution which has the net effect (in the United States) of transferring wealth from whites to blacks.

But I will also argue that affirmative action programs that elevate less-qualified blacks over better-qualified whites are unjust (§9.2). And we will take seriously the possibility that blacks are at a genetic disadvantage when it comes to earnings-relevant traits, like IQ (§6.5). Our best evidence suggests that this is not true—but again (§1.3), we will not shrink from uncomfortable possibilities.

I turn to describe the criticisms of the ideal approach that I regard as sound (or at least compelling enough to merit attention). I shall not defend these criticisms—their proponents do a good enough job of that on their own—since if they are unsound then they do not threaten my project.

Non-ideal challenge #1: Theories of justice must be *feasible*.

There must be a way for us to modify our world such that it conforms to our ideal of justice. It is not necessary that this route be easy or short, but it must be passible. We must not be precluded from attaining the ideal because of limitations of resources. These resources could be socio-economic (natural resources, money, political capital), motivational, or something else.[10]

Although some extreme ideal theorists (e.g. Cohen (2003, 2008); Estlund (2011); and Mason (2004)) deny the necessity of feasibility, this challenge has intuitive support and has attracted many defenders. Recently, David Wiens (2015a, 2015b), invoking the language of possible worlds, has provided a perspicuous and powerful defense of the challenge on formal grounds.[11]

Wiens has shown two things. First, if a theorist concedes that his account of ideal justice is infeasible, then we should look to the ideal for guidance only if the social changes that lead to the ideal converge with the social changes that lead to the maximally just *feasible* world. There is no reason to think that this will generally be the case, and so these ideal theorists have a serious gap in their argument.

Second, ideal theorists who do *not* concede the infeasibility of their theories—like me—bear the burden of showing that their ideal worlds are likely in the set of possible worlds that we can reach given current resources. Wiens's point is that, absent such a showing, we are simply unjustified in believing that our principles of ideal justice ought to be implemented. This is neither an impossible nor a trivial standard. It is one that I shall try to meet in this book.

A word above motivational limitations. These may be viewed as simply another type of scarce resource which constrains the possible worlds we might attain (and this is how Wiens views them).[12] But we might also think that a theory's ability to motivate people to comply with its dictates is a merit in itself—especially if this motivation exists across contingent lines of ideology and culture. One reason this is so is that intuition is an important part of our practical reason. To advance a theory that implies that the intuitions of many human beings are wrong is to regard the faculties of practical reason of many human beings as defective. That seems dubious.

Non-ideal challenge #2: Theories of justice must offer policy prescriptions that are sensible.

If a theory of justice fails to provide guidance (laws, regulations, cultural norms) for social reform, it does not live up to its aspiration of making the world a more just place. Or, if the theory does provide guidance, but that guidance is not "sensible"—it has little effect on social development, or, worse, makes society *less* just—it is hard to see what value it has. As Colin Farrelly puts it,

> a theory of social justice that yields impotent or misguided practical prescriptions is a deficient theory of justice. If the collective aspiration to implement the conclusions of a theory would not result in any noticeable increase in the justness of one's society then it fails as a *normative* theory.
>
> (2007: 845)

There is even a case to be made that political philosophers have a professional duty to try to make the world a more just place. If that is true, then excessively ideal theorists act wrongly.

Some ideal theorists, like David Estlund, reject the idea that our theories need to have practical use. Estlund argues for the value of extreme ideal theory by way of comparison with pure mathematics:

> To suggest that the general view that only practically applicable intellectual work has value is difficult to maintain without implausibly implying that even what are widely regarded (not just by mathematicians) as the greatest mathematical achievements have, it turns out, no great value of any kind. If higher math is important, then aspirational theory is not shown to be unimportant simply for being (like much higher math) of no practical value.
>
> (2014: 134)

Reply: This is a bad analogy. It blunts Estlund's point rather than buttresses it. To begin with, pure mathematics admits of proof and most philosophy does not. The various theories of justice on offer are at best coherent conjectures. Their truth or falsity remains open. And many would claim that they are not even that, since every major theory of justice has been subjected to powerful counterexamples and accused of internal inconsistency. We are unable to prove, formally, even the most rudimentary and unambiguous moral facts: We're pretty sure that it is wrong to torture infants for fun, but we cannot prove it. In contrast, there are myriad results in pure mathematics that have been established, beyond doubt, through the method of rigorous proof.

Moreover, even if we concede that they are without practical application, the theorems of pure math and their proofs have intrinsic intellectual value. It is not clear that our current theories of justice—whose mathematical analogues, again, are conjectures, not theorems—have the same value. To be sure, our theories have stimulated much worthwhile discussion, and they are essential steps in the march toward philosophical truth. But those are instrumental grounds of value. And while it is true that *if* some actual theory of justice is true then it is intrinsically valuable, that is a conditional claim—again, unlike the theorems of pure math. What we should ask—the proper analogy—is whether the part of pure math that contains no proven theorems but only conjectures is valuable. That is debatable.

In any case, we should not concede the impracticality of pure math to Estlund. Even the most recherché fields have consistently found relevance. Algebraic geometry has been applied to the making and breaking of codes, and fixed-point theorems from topology are commonly used by economists studying markets. In contrast, so far as I am aware, none of the contemporary work on distributive justice has had any effect on policymaking. How many members of Congress would even recognize the names "Nozick" or "Rawls"? Perhaps I am being too hard on our legislators, but I would wager very few.

Non-ideal challenge #3: Excessively ideal theories are dangerous.

This is a challenge which has been leveled against utopian theorizing by both liberals (especially pluralists like Berlin) and conservatives (Oakeshott 1962) alike. The danger is twofold. First, utopianism often leads to oppression:

> Theories of politics that expect too much of human beings have done even more damage than have those that expect too little. Theories that preach the total malleability of human nature have proved counterfactual and disturbingly open to excess. Faced with resistance, power-holders are wont to assume, not that their goals are unattainable, but rather that they haven't pushed hard enough. So they go further, eventually disregarding all limits.
>
> (Galston 2010: 401)

Second, adherents to the ideal—like True Believers everywhere—think they are justified in resisting any compromise. They alone have glimpsed moral truth, those on the other side of the debate are morally flawed, and so concessions only serve to undermine their purity. Of course, this is bad reasoning—but it does seem like an accurate description of how many people regard their ideological opponents.

Non-ideal challenge #4: Excessively ideal theories are deficient from a justificatory point-of-view.

When a theory fails to delineate the public policies that its principles require, it bypasses an important step in the process we use to evaluate the theory itself: coming to grips with what it wants from us in practice. This point was made in §2.3: Discovering that a theory requires that marginal tax rates decrease with income, as utilitarianism may require, is, for most of us, a reason to doubt the theory itself. To be clear, I am not saying that because some policy makes us morally queasy we ought to abandon the associated theory. Every theory will do this to us to some degree. I am saying that it is a justificatory consideration.

Put differently, the further toward the ideal side of the "spectrum" a theorist is,[13] the more he can get away with. He may simply leave unaddressed the possibility that his theory has, in practice, unseemly consequences. And it is the nature of utopian thinking that we are not inclined to assume the worst. A sufficiently non-ideal theory submits itself to scrutiny; an insufficiently non-ideal theory does not—it may have justificatory flaws, but it keeps them concealed.

These are the non-ideal challenges that, I believe, pose a threat to traditional ideal theory. The onus is on me to show that meritocracy is feasible, that its policy demands make sense, that it will not be exploited, and that it is sufficiently detailed.

If you ask me where meritocracy lies on the ideal/non-ideal spectrum, I think that it is a bit more non-ideal than Rawls's theory, but still within the range that counts, for most philosophers, as "ideal theory". Rawls hopes to find a "realistic utopia" (2001)—and so do I. The theory I offer is more realistic. Its economic mechanisms have been either verified by history or are consonant with our best theory, or both. The public policies necessary to establish justice are given in some detail (in Part III) and are viable. The fundamental principles of meritocracy command widespread intuitive support (Chapter 3), and thus have motivational power.

2.5 Situating Meritocracy in the Debate About Justice

I defend a deontological, desert-based theory of justice, and explore its concepts and its practical implications. As we shall see, this theory suggests a certain economic arrangement, one which is recognizably "meritocratic".

My argument does not preclude the establishment of a meritocracy on other grounds. For example, there are a variety of consequentialist arguments which might be given in favor of some form of meritocracy. Maybe the production of primary goods is maximized when jobs are held by the best-qualified. If that is so, then a Rawlsian will want to establish a meritocracy of sorts—that yields that maximum number of goods available for redistribution to the worst-off. Similarly, there is a utilitarian argument: People are happy when they get good medical care instead of bad medical care, and so there is a moral obligation to hire doctors on the basis of their merit.

But these are instrumental grounds for meritocracy which provide a weaker defense of the ideal than is warranted. I argue for the *intrinsic* justness of meritocracy.

I note, too, that a virtue ethical case for meritocracy could be made. I won't make that case, except to argue (in §6.7) that decisions about how the state should cultivate character in its citizens *cannot be avoided*; they are part and parcel of the policy choices we make, or do not make, about how we should, or should not, regulate our economy.

Meritocracy as I understand it is grounded in two ways. First, it best satisfies the metatheoretical desiderata which I have just surveyed. Second, meritocracy, in contrast to egalitarianism and libertarianism, is intuitively compelling. It harnesses widely shared, common sense ideas about justice, explaining these in a consistent and complete normative theory.

I suspect that many philosophers feel the appeal of desert-based justice. *They want to be desertists.* But they are not convinced that desert-based justice is plausible. Either desert is thought to be conceptually intractable (how could we possibly say what people deserve?) or it is assumed that desert-based justice would lead to reactionary public policies.

In fact, both worries are misplaced. The concept of desert is hard—that I don't dispute—but it is manageable. Our many intuitions about justice yield a consistent and compelling theory. And a desert-based policy regime would be anything but reactionary: At least by contemporary American standards, if we want people to get what they deserve, if we want to live in a meritocracy, we must reform our politics in a progressive direction.

When it comes to policy, meritocracy can motivate change, and in this respect, too, it is different from other theories. Consider the perspective of an educated and thoughtful policymaker alive today, who looks to political philosophy—as I think she should—for normative guidance. She faces an array of theories, all of which are esoteric and starkly at odds with her constituents' desires and her own sense of justice.

In wondering whether people have a moral claim on their income, the policymaker will hear from Rawls that the answer is a resounding "no"—it matters not a whit how hard they worked for it, the value it created for others in the marketplace, and so on. That will strike the policymaker as implausible. But when she turns to Nozick, she finds a view that is no more compelling: that one's moral claim on income is *unbridled*! Cronyism, family influence, and racial preference can all generate a just claim. Surely, the policymaker will say to herself, there is a principled middle ground here.

According to meritocracy, there is. You have a moral claim on your income if you earned it under equal opportunity, and if it reflects your meritorious contributions. The left will say that this leads to too much inequality; the right, that it leads to too little. But I think it's just about correct, and I think our policymaker would agree.

One salient feature of meritocracy is that it admits genetics as a legitimate ground for economic inequality. If Mick and Keith were raised

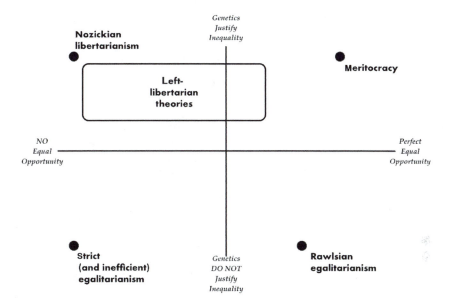

Figure 2.1 Genetics and Equal Opportunity

under conditions of equal opportunity, and Mick is richer than Keith because Mick is a more genetically talented musician, that inequality is just. I say this is "salient" because it is controversial, but it is in fact unimportant: Genetics have a small effect on economic outcomes (§6.5). (Effort is what matters most.)

A diagram may be helpful. Let's identify theories of justice by the extent to which (1) they mandate equal opportunity and (2) they allow genetics to ground economic inequality (Figure 2.1). We plot theories on a plane. A positive y-coordinate means that genetics ground inequality; a negative y-coordinate means that they do not. A positive x-coordinate means that equal opportunity is mandated; a negative x-coordinate means that it is not.

While I have not tried to precisely situate theories, a few useful things can be said. Clearly, Nozickian libertarianism sits at the extreme northwest point. None of the minimal state's few powers are related to equal opportunity, and a person may justly leverage her genetics, like almost anything else in the world, to her economic advantage.

Some left-libertarian theories (e.g. that of Otsuka (2003)) will fall to the east and south of Nozick's theory. How far to the east depends on how strong of an equal opportunity regime is called for, and how far to the south depends on subtle conceptual issues.

To the far southwest, we find a strict egalitarian approach under which nothing justifies unequal outcomes and there is no equal opportunity: People harness their natural talents, social advantages, and everything else, and then it all gets redistributed so that everyone has the same (this may have the incidental effect of equalizing opportunity, but there is no equal opportunity regime). This is not an efficient form of strict egalitarianism, because equal opportunity investments would increase the social product.

Rawls sits in the southeast quadrant: Fair equality of opportunity and denying a role for genetics in just economic outcomes are salient elements of his theory.

Meritocracy is in the northeast quadrant. Note that meritocracy lies farther to the east than Rawlsian egalitarianism does: The meritocratic equal opportunity regime is more robust than Rawls's, proscribing, for example, various forms of family influence which Rawls would not object to.

One might wonder where luck egalitarianism resides. The only thing that can be said, I think, is that it's somewhere in the southern half. It is a treasured luck egalitarian belief that, because you did not choose (or control) your genetics, they cannot justify inequalities. This argument fails for reasons similar to those that doom Rawls (Chapter 7), and the meritocratic approach to justice differs from the luck egalitarian approach in myriad ways besides (§4.6).

Above I distinguished a meritocracy justified on instrumental grounds from a meritocracy justified on intrinsic grounds. We may also distinguish a "weak" meritocracy from a "strong" meritocracy by how it approaches questions of value.

"Meritocracy" connotes excellence. And rightly so, I think: Meritocracy is desirable in part because it fosters achievement in art, music, philosophy, science, athletics, and other fields of human endeavor.

One must take a stand on whether these achievements have the value that they do independent of their being desired. If the answer is "no", then we have no reason to prefer a government that cultivates the music of, say, Justin Bieber over that of Beethoven. If the answer is "no", we may not fret when Bieber is paid 150 times more than the concertmaster of the New York Philharmonic, as is actually the case. If the answer is "no" then we support meritocracy in a weak sense, on the grounds that it creates achievements of great subjective value.

I am convinced, however, that this view cannot hold, and that strong meritocracy—value understood objectively—is what we should defend. The example given is tongue-in-cheek, but as we shall see in §6.7 the problem is a serious one: Any economy that single-mindedly responds to market demand is morally indefensible on grounds of value. When attention is not paid to objective excellence, consumers may be badly hurt by their false beliefs; markets may shape people's preferences in objectionable ways; and nasty behavior, such as racism, may be incentivized.

A consequence of this understanding of value is that meritocracy is a perfectionistic theory: There are objective goods and a just government helps realize them. But meritocracy's perfectionism is atypical.

Perfectionist theories normally proceed by (1) providing an account of the good and then (2) exploring that account's ramifications for politics. In contrast, meritocracy remains *agnostic* about what is good and instead establishes a framework under which the good—*no matter what it be*—can best be pursued. It does this through strict attention to merit.

An example will illustrate what I have in mind. There is an objective truth about what is good music and what is bad music, and a just state fosters the production of the former. But none of us, let alone the state, knows what music is good and what is bad. It might be Bieber's music; it might be Beethoven's. And so the direct promotion of one over the other is unjustified.

What we do know, however, is that good music is produced by good musicians. Therefore, any market behavior that is at odds with merit will impede the production of high quality music. *That* we can have confidence in. We can have confidence that a meritocratic economic framework will, in the long run, lead to achievements of objectively high value. In contrast, if there is anti-meritocratic behavior in the market—if a less-qualified white applicant is chosen for the conservatory over a more-qualified black applicant owing to racism—the quest for musical excellence is impaired. The government cannot justifiably choose a particular musician to promote, but it can proscribe the use of race in college admissions, and thereby, indirectly, promote excellence.[14]

A few brief remarks on perfectionism. First, meritocracy's perfectionism is not entirely humanistic, as many of the goods which meritocracy fosters, like cultural achievement, are unrelated to the development of human nature. In this respect, meritocracy arguably diverges from Aristotelian perfection (and accords with Rawls's understanding).

Second, because meritocracy does not enumerate what the good things in life are, but rather establishes a merit-based framework compatible with many things being good (Bieber, Beethoven, et al.), it may appeal to proponents of neutrality.[15] Indeed, in the face of disagreement over the good life, and given the necessity of choosing between economic arrangements, all of which close off *some* paths-of-life, strict focus on merit may be as neutral as we can get.

Third, as George Sher reminds us, "no government can *avoid* either nonrationally shaping its citizens' preferences or providing them with incentives" (1997: 66). Recent work on "nudging", for example, makes this clear. Even "neutral" governments have a role in preference formation.[16] And even if the role is limited, it seems to have moral features. Meritocracy provides guidance for this limited preference formation; a fully neutral theory does not.

Fourth, for readers wondering "is meritocracy illiberal?", the answer turns on what kind of liberty one has in mind. Meritocracy proscribes racial discrimination in private economic transactions and places (weak) constraints on corporate officer compensation (§8.2). And it redistributes resources, through coercive government, in the name of equal opportunity. In these respects, yes: Meritocracy is illiberal. But of course this is not the sort of liberality we typically have in mind, and nothing about the theory requires regulating private religious, romantic, sexual matters, etc. There is one genuine worry about illiberality, which has to do with meritocracy's interference with the family structure (to be discussed in §4.5). In any event, I shall not defend the liberality of meritocracy but leave the theory to speak for itself in this regard.

A final comment. Contemporary philosophy and economics put welfare and "resources" (i.e. money) at the heart of justice. To a large extent, whether justice requires some institutional change can be determined by looking at the associated impact on social welfare, the lot of the least-advantaged, overall wealth, and similar measures.

We should consider whether the society we would create by such a focus is desirable. It seems to me that these societies—maximally happy, maximally rich ones—would be far removed from the human experience, and awful besides. For most of us, happiness and wealth are important parts of life, but they are hardly commanding. We also want to achieve things that we think are objectively important; to contribute to others, even at the cost of our own well-being; and to have a life which future generations will look back on with respect. Each of us can think of people who have had estimable lives—the sorts of lives we'd like to live. Of these, how many are marked by bliss or riches? Not many, I suspect. What is the story of a life gone well, if not one in which the hero, after enduring chapter upon chapter of failure, misfortune, and terror, takes satisfaction in the meager successes he has had along the way?

For this reason, we should not expect a just political arrangement to simply maximize welfare or resources. We should expect more: a social structure that encourages excellence. And in a just world, as in a good life, there *is* a place for deprivation and suffering—in reasonable measure.

These ubiquitous features of the human experience provide perspective on what is truly meaningful; help us deal with life's travails; and stimulate achievement. We should be skeptical of any theory of justice that would seek to eradicate them, keeping Kant's warning in mind: "The light dove, in free flight cutting through the air the resistance of which it feels, could get the idea that it could do even better in airless space" (1781: A5).

Notes

1 What Hayek rejects, specifically, is the idea of *distributive* justice—he apparently believed that justice can operate in other spheres, like interpersonal relationships.
2 On this point, see Schmidtz (2016).
3 Nozick's later work (1989, 1993) arguably repudiates, to a degree, his libertarian conclusions in *Anarchy, State, and Utopia*.

4 Mulligan (2015). The landmark conceptual analysis of tolerance is King (1976).
5 There are theoretical problems with measuring efficiency in this way (see Boadway 1974) for the most general economies. But as a practical matter, it is an effective measure.
6 The same holds true for libertarianism, which refuses some forms of efficiency-enhancing regulation on the grounds that they violate liberty (for some libertarians, subsidies for producers of positive externalities would be an example).
7 Le Grand (1990) makes some useful comments on the equity/efficiency trade-off.
8 Although Mirrlees's original model is no longer regarded as accurate, much (but not all) contemporary work in optimal tax theory continues to suggest that marginal income tax rates should decrease with income. See Tuomala (1990).
9 See Stemplowska and Swift (2012) and Valentini (2012) for summaries. Phillips (1985) is prescient.
10 The reader, with §2.1 in mind, might wonder whether *all* theories of justice must perforce be non-ideal, given that justice itself—at least on the Humean account—arises only because there is scarcity. That does seem right. The matter is discussed by Estlund (2011: 225–9).
11 See also Sen (2006: 225 n. 11).
12 See also Wiens (2016).
13 While it is often thought that there is a single continuum, running from the ideal (full compliance, no feasibility or motivational constraints) to the non-ideal (constraints on compliance, feasibility, and human motivation defined by what we know about the actual world), these considerations are in fact multidimensional. A theory of justice might be developed, for example, that views compliance and human motivation as irrelevant to the truth of justice, but facts about scarcity as relevant. Such a theory could not be located on a simple line running from the "ideal" to the "non-ideal". (Hamlin and Stemplowska (2012) make a similar point.)
14 Related considerations are discussed by Wilson (2003).
15 Examples here would be Dworkin (1978); Larmore (1987); and Rawls (1993).
16 Some proponents of neutrality, like Dworkin (1978, 2011), recognize this.

2.6 References

Bénabou, R. 2000. Meritocracy, redistribution, and the size of the pie. In *Meritocracy and Economic Inequality*, eds. K. Arrow, S. Bowles, and S. Durlauf, 317–39. Princeton: Princeton University Press.
Boadway, R. W. 1974. The welfare foundations of cost-benefit analysis. *Economic Journal* 84: 926–39.
Cohen, G. A. 2003. Facts and principles. *Philosophy & Public Affairs* 31: 211–45.
———. 2008. *Rescuing Justice & Equality*. Cambridge: Harvard University Press.
Dworkin, R. 1978. Liberalism. In *Public and Private Morality*, ed. S. Hampshire, 113–43. Cambridge: Cambridge University Press.
———. 2011. *Justice for Hedgehogs*. Cambridge: Harvard University Press.
Estlund, D. 2011. Human nature and the limits (if any) of political philosophy. *Philosophy & Public Affairs* 39: 207–37.

———. 2014. Utopophobia. *Philosophy & Public Affairs* 42: 113–34.

Farrelly, C. 2007. Justice in ideal theory: A refutation. *Political Studies* 55: 844–64.

Galston, W. A. 2010. Realism in political theory. *European Journal of Political Theory* 9: 385–411.

Hamlin, A. and Stemplowska, Z. 2012. Theory, ideal theory, and the theory of ideals. *Political Studies Review* 10: 48–62.

Hayek, F. A. 1976. *Law, Legislation, and Liberty, Volume 2: The Mirage of Social Justice*. Chicago: University of Chicago Press.

———. 1978. *New Studies in Philosophy, Politics, and Economics and the History of Ideas*. London: Routledge & Kegan Paul.

Hume, D. 1739. *A Treatise of Human Nature*. London: John Noon.

Kant, I. 1781. *Critique of Pure Reason*. Riga: Johann Friedrich Hartknoch.

King, P. 1976. *Toleration*. New York: St. Martin's Press.

Larmore, C. E. 1987. *Patterns of Moral Complexity*. New York: Cambridge University Press.

Le Grand, J. 1990. Equity versus efficiency: The elusive trade-off. *Ethics* 100: 554–68.

Mason, A. 2004. Just constraints. *British Journal of Political Science* 34: 251–68.

Mills, C. W. 2005. "Ideal Theory" as ideology. *Hypatia* 20: 165–84.

Mirrlees, J. A. 1971. An exploration in the theory of optimal income taxation. *Review of Economic Studies* 38: 175–208.

Mulligan, T. 2015. The limits of liberal tolerance. *Public Affairs Quarterly* 29: 277–95.

Nozick, R. 1974. *Anarchy, State, and Utopia*. New York: Basic Books.

———. 1989. *The Examined Life*. New York: Simon & Schuster.

———. 1993. *The Nature of Rationality*. Princeton: Princeton University Press.

Oakeshott, M. 1962. *Rationalism in Politics and Other Essays*. London: Methuen.

Okun, A. M. 1975. *Equality and Efficiency: The Big Tradeoff*. Washington: Brookings.

Otsuka, M. 2003. *Libertarianism without Inequality*. Oxford: Clarendon Press.

Pateman, C. and Mills, C. 2007. *The Contract and Domination*. Cambridge, UK: Polity Press.

Phillips, M. 1985. Reflections on the transition from ideal to non-ideal theory. *Noûs* 19: 551–70.

Rawls, J. 1971. *A Theory of Justice*. Cambridge: Belknap Press.

———. 1993. *Political Liberalism*. New York: Columbia University Press.

———. 2001. *Justice as Fairness: A Restatement*. Cambridge: Harvard University Press.

Schmidtz, D. 2016. Friedrich Hayek. In *The Stanford Encyclopedia of Philosophy (Winter 2016 Edition)*, ed. N. Zalta. URL = <https://plato.stanford.edu/archives/win2016/entries/friedrich-hayek/>, retrieved 19 August 2017.

Sen, A. 2006. What do we want from a theory of justice? *Journal of Philosophy* 103: 215–38.

Sher, G. 1997. *Beyond Neutrality: Perfectionism and Politics*. Cambridge: Cambridge University Press.

Singer, P. 1972. Famine, affluence, and morality. *Philosophy & Public Affairs* 1: 229–43.

Stemplowska, Z. and Swift, A. 2012. Ideal and non-ideal theory. In *The Oxford Handbook of Political Philosophy*, ed. D. Estlund, 373–89. New York: Oxford University Press.

Tuomala, M. 1990. *Optimal Income Tax and Redistribution*. Oxford: Clarendon Press.

Valentini, L. 2012. Ideal vs. non-ideal theory: A conceptual map. *Philosophy Compass* 7: 654–64.

Wenar, L. 2011. Poverty is no pond: Challenges for the affluent. In *Giving Well: The Ethics of Philanthropy*, eds. P. Illingworth, T. Pogge, and L. Wenar, 104–32. New York: Oxford University Press.

Wiens, D. 2015a. Against ideal guidance. *Journal of Politics* 77: 433–46.

———. 2015b. Political ideals and the feasibility frontier. *Economics and Philosophy* 31: 447–77.

———. 2016. Motivational limitations on the demands of justice. *European Journal of Political Theory* 15: 333–52.

Wilson, C. 2003. The role of a merit principle in distributive justice. *Journal of Ethics* 7: 277–314.

3   What We Think About Justice and Why It Matters

3.1 Human Beings Are Not Selfish

The simplest model of economic motivation treats human beings as single-minded self-interest seekers (i.e. as members of "*Homo economicus*"). For many years, philosophers and economists believed that this was accurate. On this classical model, human beings show compassion to others just in case it is in our interest to do so; we care about "justice" only because that provides a more pleasant society within which to live; and so on.

But over the last 35 years, experimentalists have scrutinized this model and found it wanting. In fact, economic agents do not make decisions, in the marketplace or elsewhere, with an eye toward maximizing their own advantage.

The first work here was done by Güth, Schmittberger, and Schwarze (1982), who developed the *ultimatum game*. In it, one experimental subject, Player 1, is given a sum of money and then charged with offering a fraction of it to another subject, Player 2. Player 2 may accept or reject Player 1's offer. If Player 2 rejects the offer, neither player receives anything. If Player 2 accepts it, she receives the offered amount and Player 1 keeps the remainder.

Under the *Homo economicus* assumption, the correct, game-theoretic solution is for Player 1 to offer the minimum amount possible. And Player 2 will accept this, as it leaves her better off she would be if she rejected the offer (in which case she gets nothing).

But human beings do not play the game this way. Player 2s do not accept any non-zero offer, and Player 1s do not make minimum offers. A sense of justice trumps self-interest. Player 2s respond to what they regard as an unjust, low-ball offer by forgoing all the money, thereby forcing Player 1 to forgo it as well. And Player 1s altruistically give some of the money away. Player 1s typically offer 40 percent of the sum, and these offers are accepted. Offers less than 30 percent are typically rejected.

The *dictator game* is similar in design and obtains similar results. In it, Player 1's "offer" is decisive: He simply decides how much of the money he wishes to keep for himself and how much he wishes to share with Player 2, and then he distributes it, and that is the end of the experiment. Here, Player 1 need not fear that his offer will be rejected. Naturally, the "rational" choice for Player 1 is to keep all of the money. But once again this does not actually happen. Player 1s—who, I stress, have complete control over the distribution—deviate from pure self-interest, giving away, on average, 28 percent of the sum (Engel 2011).

3.2 The Content of Justice

The results just described are thin, in that they demonstrate only that human beings have a sense of justice in distribution which trumps self-interest. They do not themselves provide insight into the particular norm of justice at work. They are compatible with an aversion to inequality, to be sure—and this is how they were originally interpreted—but they are also compatible with a concern for deserts, since in the experiments discussed there were no relevant differences between the players which could give rise to different desert-claims.

More sophisticated experiments show that it is fact desert which motivates players in these cases. For example, Frohlich, Oppenheimer, and Kurki (2004) ran a variant on the dictator game in which players engaged in a productive enterprise (proofreading documents) before the distribution. Strikingly, many of the Player 1s gave their Player 2 *more* than they kept for themselves—*when their Player 2's productive contribution was greater*. In fact, this "just deserts" behavior was the modal response—more frequent than egalitarian behavior, and much more frequent than libertarian behavior. Ruffle (1998) and Konow (2000) report similar results.

Cappelen, Sørensen, and Tungodden (2010) ran an even more sophisticated variant, which allowed for differences during the production phase in (1) working time, (2) productivity (defined as share of total output), and (3) value (as measured by price). This variant allowed the experimenters to test four different distributive norms: strict egalitarianism, "choice egalitarianism" (income in proportion to working time), "meritocracy" (income in proportion to productivity), and libertarianism (under which people were held responsible for all factors affecting their income, including exogenous factors like price). The "meritocratic" norm dominated, preferred by 48 percent of the subjects (strict egalitarianism: 20 percent, choice egalitarianism: 6 percent, libertarianism: 26 percent).

Now, the dictator game is limited in that it has no strategic component. Player 1, when deciding on how he will distribute the money, need not consider what Player 2 might do, since Player 2 cannot affect the distribution. (For this reason, the dictator game is not technically a game.) Real-world economic distribution has an important and obvious strategic component, and so in this respect, at least, it is better modeled by the ultimatum game.

Surprisingly, only recently was the ultimatum game expanded in the necessary way. To wit, Barber and English (Manuscript) report that in ultimatum games, as in dictator games, attention to players' deserts is the driving norm. (See also Lee and Shahriar 2017.)

In the first phase of Barber and English's experiment, subjects earned money for their performance on a spelling test. In the second phase, two of these subjects were paired, their earnings were pooled, and one of them was randomly designated as Player 1. In the third phase, Player 1 made an offer which was either accepted or rejected in the typical way.

Barber and English report three things: First, Player 1s offered more (48 percent of the total wealth, on average) than in the standard ultimatum game, with lower variance in offers. This is consonant with (1) Player 1s recognizing that justice has a role to play in distribution, and (2) Player 1s being guided by a *common* norm of justice.

Second, offers were proportional to earned wealth. That is, if Player 1 earned \$25 from the test and Player 2, \$15, then Player 1 would offer Player 2 \$15 during the distribution phase. *Perfect proportionality* was, in fact, the modal offer. Offers were almost never rejected.

Third, "low earners" (i.e. Player 1s who earned a smaller share of the total wealth) offered more to Player 2 than they kept for themselves. Again, this is at odds with the game-theoretic solution. It illustrates that there is moral psychology at work here which is not captured by standard ultimatum games.

Barber and English's conclusions? That their experiment provides "strong evidence that when money available for redistribution was perceived to be 'earned' this powerfully influenced preferences for redistribution"; that "considerations of 'fairness' influence people's redistributive preferences"; and that fairness is "largely indexed to judgments of desert".

Experimental economics has revealed an affection for desert in other contexts as well. One example is the adjudication of conflicting claims. Suppose that a bank fails, and its remaining assets are to be distributed to depositors—but these assets are insufficient to make everyone whole. How should they be distributed? Herrero, Moreno-Ternero, and Ponti (2010) examine how claimants can reach consensus in cases like this, finding that a desert rule—payment proportional to original asset share— has unique power in reaching consensus.

And when objective observers are asked to select the just distributive rule in a variety of conflicting claims contexts (bankruptcy, estate division, taxation), in *all* contexts, a desert rule is preferred. (See also Bosmans and Schokkaert 2009.)

None of these results from the economics literature come as a surprise to social psychologists, who have, over the last half-century, amassed an enormous literature showing that we are motivated by a sense of desert.

This is the core idea of *equity theory*, which is devoted to studying human beings' ubiquitous urge to proportion the benefits that we receive from a social task to our contributions to it.

Equity theory originated in the work of Stacy Adams (1963, 1965), who noticed that human beings naturally seek to establish an equilibrium between contributions and rewards: If we are underpaid, we get angry; if we are overpaid, we feel guilty (see also Walster, Berscheid, and Walster 1973). We are content only when rewards and contributions are in balance. When they are not, we modify our behavior on both the input side and the output side to reestablish the balance. Desert is the equilibrium condition.

What does this mean in practice? For one thing, our happiness turns on getting what we deserve. While it is true that we feel more distress when we are underpaid than when we are overpaid, we are happiest of all when we receive precisely what we deserve—no more, and no less (Austin and Walster 1974).

The same goes for job satisfaction. If a person believes that he is being paid too little or too much, in light of his contributions, he is less satisfied with his job than he would be were he paid what he thinks he deserves on the basis of his productivity (Pritchard, Dunnette, and Jorgenson 1972). Moreover, inequity leads to bad behavior in the workplace: If pay cuts disrupt the equity equilibrium for some, employee theft rises. Why? Because in the eyes of those whose pay was cut, this restores the just balance (Greenberg 1990).

Human beings are not the only species that has a sense of justice. Other animals feel the drive too, and for them, as for us, justice is desert. Capuchin monkeys who complete the same task revolt when they see a peer get a more desirable reward; they've done the same work, so they want the same reward.[1] (There are amusing videos online of monkeys throwing pieces of cucumber—the less desirable reward—at the faces of unjust researchers.)

The same is true of chimpanzees, who will sacrifice their own interests—refuse a reward—when they see an equally deserving peer receive less.[2] Aversion to inequity has also been observed in dogs (Range et al. 2009), cotton-top tamarins (Neiworth et al. 2009), long-tailed macaques (Massen et al. 2012), and squirrel monkeys (Talbot et al. 2011). This suggests an early evolutionary origin for desert.

To be fair, the evidence supporting justice-as-desert is less robust in non-human animals, owing to difficulties in experimental design. But this is an area of active research; researchers like Sarah Brosnan at Georgia State are developing experiments to test how far members of other species will go to ensure that they and their peers get their just deserts.

Recent neurological research supports the idea that desert has a unique role in human morality. Cappelen et al. (2014) monitored people's brains while exposing them to egalitarian and desert-based economic distributions. No unusual activity was noted in the former case, but when a subject saw people getting their just deserts, his striatum—the part of the brain managing behavior and moral choice—lit up.

The empirical literature on justice generally, and justice-as-desert specifically, is enormous; I can only provide a summary of the main findings here. I do want to caution that specific results turn on subtleties of experimental design, and to say that we are sure that justice simply is desert is too quick. Better to say that it has been conclusively demonstrated that "the concepts of moral desert and justice are deeply connected, and one needs the other for a proper definition" (Rustichini and Vostroknutov 2014).

Despite the dominance of desert, might other moral ideals play a role in our economic life? The answer is yes—but conceptual care is needed.

James Konow—in my view, the world's leading researcher on positive justice—concludes that justice is, indeed, simply a matter of giving people what they deserve. Our guiding norm is what he calls an "accountability principle", which holds that rewards ought to be proportional to productivity (Konow 1996, 2001). This is essentially the meritocratic distributive norm for income.

But, like me, Konow is not an extreme monist about desert. On his assessment, desert is not the *only* thing that is morally relevant to economic distribution for human beings. It is simply the most important thing. Also relevant are (1) efficiency and (2) ensuring that people's minimal needs are met.

This view is consonant with both my conceptual analysis of economic morality and our natural language use. To reiterate, suppose that we are deciding between two distributions, A and B. In A the social product is distributed such that everybody gets exactly what he deserves. In B, there is a deviation from desert, but the social product is greater. It seems to me that if the desert deviation in B got small enough, or the social product difference big enough, we would, eventually, prefer B to A on moral grounds.

Just how strong is our independent attention to efficiency? Within the context of a voting game, Bolton and Ockenfels (2000, 2006) find that it is weak:

> [The] willingness to pay for social efficiency is rather low, and as a social good, equity [i.e. justice] is in greater demand. One way to gauge the magnitude of the difference is to note that . . . an efficiency proposal that benefits two-thirds of the group was overridden by a coalition of the potential losers, together with the potential winners sympathetic to equity.
>
> (2006: 1909)

As an aside, considerations of efficiency appear to play a larger role in the moral calculus of the young and the educated. Therefore, because experiments often use college students as subjects, the literature may overstate the moral relevance of efficiency.[3]

Similarly, if C is more perfect than D from the point-of-view of justice, but C has many more people under the sufficiency line, we might prefer D to C.

A few analytical points. First, it is hard, probably impossible, to know what the precise numbers involved are. How much efficiency should we give up for a given improvement in desert? I have no idea. What we know is that the most important moral consideration is justice, by which we mean giving people what they deserve. Sufficiency is of secondary importance. And efficiency is the weakest part of the moral triad ("even the ostensibly innocuous Pareto Principle loses support when it conflicts with accountability [i.e. desert]" (Konow 2001: 148)).

Second, the sufficiency principle is not a proxy for equality or priority. What is important to us, morally, is that we lift citizens above a minimum distributive floor.[4] If everyone were above this floor, then, *ceteris paribus*, we wouldn't regard the neediest person as having any moral claim on goods. As Konow puts it, "when needs are satisfied, this term falls away as a distributional concern" (2001: 151).

Third, one way to avoid having to come down on how to balance these three moral desiderata is to endorse an economic approach that promotes all of them. Meritocracy does this.

I'll note here that sufficientarian concerns will be far less acute in a meritocracy than they actually are. For one thing, meritocracy rewards productive activity, thus incentivizing people to develop their human capital. And we know from historical experience and economic theory that productivity is ultimately what lifts a society out of poverty.

In addition, establishing equal opportunity goes a long way toward meeting citizens' basic needs. All children will be lifted above the sufficiency line by the definition of equal opportunity. As far as adults are concerned, equal opportunity measures ensure that everyone, save the seriously disabled (who are protected—§6.10), has the necessary human capital to ensure sufficiency for themselves. Only those who fail such self-provision, whether by choice or not, would require public aid. Only this residual could conflict with justice. (See the discussion of the social safety net, in §6.10.)

Fourth, admitting need and efficiency into our moral calculus does not make us pluralists about justice. Need and efficiency *compete* with justice. That is, they compete with desert. This is not merely a linguistic point. It seems to me that some of the normative disputes within the distributive justice debate result from failing to identify the proper domains of the moral principles we think relevant to economic distribution. As Konow observes,

> Efficiency and needs exist as distributional goods distinct from justice, whereas accountability [i.e. desert] represents the distinguishing feature of justice. . . . Although substantial evidence has been

presented in the foregoing sections that efficiency and needs impact and sometimes even dominate experiential justice, some readers view certain scenarios featuring those principles as being rather 'forced' to think of in justice terms, to which I respond: 'Precisely!' They lack the specific sense of justice, and this intuition adds support, I believe, to the contention that accountability [desert] is specific justice, indeed that *accountability [desert] is the quintessence of justice.*

(2001: 156–7, emphasis in original)

We must be pluralists about morality, but most of us knew this anyway. What is surprising is that we need not be pluralists about *justice*. Desert captures what that concept means to us, and everything it means to us.

3.3 Children and Justice

Beginning with the work of the Swiss clinical psychologist, Jean Piaget (1932), researchers have explicated and verified a standard model of moral development in human beings.[5] It goes roughly like this: From birth until age five, children act selfishly—we might say, not entirely fairly, that they act like little libertarians. This selfish norm—which governs behavior across spheres of justice—is replaced by a concern for equality. But as their cognition develops, children gain the concept of desert and replace equality with equity (i.e. reward in proportion to contribution). That process culminates around the onset of puberty, and the desert norm dominates throughout adulthood, as I have described. In this sense, meritocratic distributive justice is a fuller expression of our moral cognition than libertarianism or egalitarianism is.

On top of this, there is evidence that very young children—infants, even—possess a sense of desert-based justice. This is significant because desert is a much more sophisticated concept than self-interest or equality; it requires understanding that people contribute to a process, assessing the size of those contributions, assessing the outputs of the process, and making relevant comparisons. These conceptual demands outstrip the cognitive capacity of young children. Therefore, any sense of desert-based justice which babies do have reflects an innate, culturally independent, genetic basis of human morality. I stress that children continue to behave, broadly speaking, selfishly—as described by the standard model of moral development. But these results are important because they suggest that selfish behavior and, later, egalitarian behavior are really *biases* rather than manifestations of an underlying moral code that changes over time.[6]

For example, Sloane, Baillargeon, and Premack (2012) found evidence of desert-based justice in 21-month-olds. In their experiment, infants watched two people working together (putting away toys) for a reward (a sticker). In the first scenario, the two people divided the work evenly, putting away an equal numbers of toys, and were then both rewarded with a sticker. In the second scenario, one person put away all the toys while the other continued playing, and then, as in the first scenario, both received stickers. Infants visually fixated on the second scenario, suggesting that they found something amiss: "21-month-olds expect individuals to be rewarded according to their efforts: Infants . . . detected a violation when the worker and the slacker were rewarded equally" (p. 202).

Similarly, Baumard, Mascaro, and Chevallier (2012) asked 3- and 4-year-olds to watch two characters, Amélie and Hélène, bake cookies together. These preschoolers were then tasked with distributing cookies to the two characters. When Hélène got bored midway through, stopping work to play with dolls, the preschoolers would give Amélie the large cookie and Hélène the small one. Why? In the words of one child, "because Amélie prepared more".

3.4 Cultural Stability and Support for Redistribution

It is reasonable to worry that our intuitions about justice are mere artifacts of the cultures in which we are raised. After all, the subjects in most of the experiments cited are Westerners—indeed, many are students at Western research universities, which is an unrepresentative demographic. And in these cultures, the argument goes, institutions that may well be unjust—private property, say—shape moral sentiment from an early age. If this is so, then perhaps intuition counts for nothing from the justificatory point-of-view.

I shall discuss the justificatory status of intuition in §3.6. I note, first, that this argument is contradicted by the findings, already discussed, that very young children have a common sense of justice, and by the cited work in neuroeconomics. In a way, the diversity of support for desert is as wide as it could possibly be, given that it appears to include not just human beings but other animals as well.

Nevertheless, it is worth considering what we ought to make of conflicts between intuitions—were it to come to that. We might think, as above, that any such conflicts would reveal that one or more of the intuitions at play is biased for reasons of cultural contingency.

But there is a second way to think about things. Perhaps conflicting intuitions are like conflicting observations in the physical sciences. To regard one or both of them as wrong *simpliciter* is a mistake. Rather, conflicts reveal the need for more fine-grained empirical investigation. Such investigation can produce consensus.

For example, blacks are much more likely to regard affirmative action as just than whites are. The right response is not to assume that bias is present—that this is because blacks are helped by affirmative action and whites are hurt by it—but to investigate more closely this *prima facie* conflict. We might conjecture that blacks and whites actually agree on the underlying moral principle—namely, that a less-qualified black should not be hired over a more-qualified white. We might further conjecture that what they disagree about is a much less serious, purely positive matter—whether real-world affirmative action programs violate that principle. Whites might think it does; blacks might think that affirmative action simply serves to offset anti-meritocratic bias in hiring.

And this is, indeed, what some research suggests. For example, Son Hing, Bobocel, and Zanna (2002) find that among people who care strongly about merit in hiring, support for affirmative action rises with the perception of discrimination in the workplace. People understand that, in these cases, affirmative action ensures that blacks are judged on their merits.

In any event, we find consensus, not conflict, across contexts (intuitions about justice, epistemology, etc.) and across demographic lines (nationality, race, gender, etc.) Let's consider nationality. We are most concerned with economic justice, of course. This is how Konow describes the state of research: "The striking similarity of responses to fairness survey questions among subjects in different countries . . . suggests little variation in notions of fairness across this contextual dimension [nationality], the one across which it would be perhaps most expected" (1996: 15).

My favorite test of the cross-cultural stability of our judgments about justice was conducted during what was arguably the world's most ideologically polarized moment—the Cold War. American citizens, living under free market capitalism, and Soviet citizens, living under socialist central planning (and the Soviet propaganda machine), were interviewed about their views on economic justice. Little difference was found in their normative judgments, despite the huge economic, political, and cultural differences among them. When it came to income, "most Soviet economists appeared to advocate what one might call a meritocratic structure of wages" (McAuley 1980: 242).

Later, after the breakup of the Soviet Union, Alwin, Gornev, and Khakhulina (1995) surveyed citizens of postcommunist nations like Bulgaria, Poland, and Russia; citizens of welfare states like the Netherlands; and citizens of Japan and the United States. Majorities in *every* country opposed equality as the fair principle of distribution. Majorities in *every* country agreed that those who work harder deserve a higher income.

Although my prime concern is the cultural and socioeconomic invariance of moral intuition, it is worth noting that epistemological intuitions are invariant as well. For example, intuitions about Gettier cases (Gettier 1963) are universal—there are no differences across cultures or across socioeconomic strata.[7] And we know that men and women share the same epistemological and moral intuitions.[8]

Here is how Joshua Knobe, experimental philosopher, summarizes things:[9]

> Some commenters seem to assume that it is somehow built into the mission of experimental philosophy as a field that part of its aim

is to show that intuitions vary from one demographic group to the next and that appeals to intuitions are therefore methodologically suspect. As anyone who actually works in experimental philosophy will know, this assumption is wildly incorrect. . . . Consider again the particular case of research on the relationship between philosophical intuitions and demographic factors (ethnicity, gender, age, etc.). It is true that some experimental philosophy studies have suggested that people's intuitions vary with demographic factors, but there have also been a very large number of studies exploring the ways in which people's intuitions *do not* vary with these factors. In fact, my sense is that the majority of experimental philosophy studies on this topic actually come down on this second side, exploring ways in which people's intuitions are surprisingly invariant across demographic variables that one would have thought would make a difference.

Of special interest to us is how economic redistribution is regarded across socioeconomic lines. Implementing any patterned theory of justice, including meritocracy, requires redistribution. And we should like, if possible, to advance a theory whose redistributive demands are broadly acceptable. If they are regarded as too outrageous, they will not be viable (and so perhaps they fail *qua* theoretical principles, for the reasons given in §2.4).

Christina Fong (2001) finds that Americans' socioeconomic status is a poor predictor of their support for redistribution. The strongest predictors of support for redistribution are, instead, beliefs that (1) bad luck, and not effort, is the cause of poverty; (2) *opportunity* is lacking; and (3) good luck, and not effort, produces wealth. That is, redistribution is morally justified when equal opportunity was lacking or goods are obtained on grounds other than merit. This lines up precisely with the conceptual structure of meritocracy.

Alesina and Angeletos (2005) explain cross-national differences in support for redistribution in the same way.

> If a society believes that individual effort determines income, and that all have a right to enjoy the fruits of their effort, it will choose low redistribution and low taxes. In equilibrium, effort will be high and the role of luck will be limited, in which case market outcomes will be relatively fair and social beliefs will be self-fulfilled. If, instead, a society believes that luck, birth, connections, and/or corruption determine wealth, it will levy high taxes.
>
> (p. 960)

People across cultures and socioeconomic lines regard welfare programs as just or unjust by looking at the deservingness of those who benefit from them: "In essence, utilizing a 'deservingness heuristic,' individuals across cultural divides, welfare state regimes, ideology, and political sophistication support welfare benefits for recipients who are perceived as hard-working and reject welfare benefits for recipients who are perceived to be lazy" (Aarøe and Petersen 2014: 685).[10]

This deservingness heuristic has an evolutionary origin: It is an adaptive trait, regulating small-scale interaction (Petersen 2012). It was easier for early humans to obtain food and shelter if they worked together, but there was then, as there is now, a risk of free riding: One might contribute to a shared project in good faith only to watch another abscond with the goods. Thus, it was useful to be able to distinguish the "cheaters" from the "reciprocators".[11]

> The deservingness heuristic is rooted in evolved cognitive categories designed to detect and represent 'cheaters' and 'reciprocators'. . . . The cross-cultural nature of the present evidence supports the view that these categories are not learned. Rather, they are something we as humans naturally come equipped with.
>
> (Petersen 2012, p. 12)

Perhaps most striking—at least from the perspective of a twenty-first century American, observing all the *Sturm und Drang* about economic injustice—is that there actually is consensus among Americans about the structure of a just economy.

Majorities in *all* ideological and economic groups, including Republicans and the wealthy, agree that income inequality is too great. Of course, it appears that their real objection is not to the inequality *per se*, but to what it illuminates: a failure to give people their just deserts. We know that majorities in all ideological and economic groups believe that the government should intervene as a result. We know that majorities in all ideological and economic groups wish to protect equality of opportunity while allowing for differences in economic outcomes. We know, in sum, that everyone wants to live in a meritocracy:

> The public strongly supports educational initiatives to expand opportunity and create a society based on meritocracy in which work and education pay off. . . . In order to provide both genuine opportunity and a measure of economic security—large majorities of Americans favor a number of specific government programs that go well beyond education policy. . . . Support for these government programs comes from all sectors of society: from Republicans, from self-described middle-class and upper-class people, from whites, and from those with high incomes, as well as from Democrats, working-class people, African Americans, and lower-income citizens.
>
> (Page and Jacobs 2009: 22–23)

3.5 Rejecting Rawlsian Justice

The purpose of this book is to construct, not to criticize. I am advancing my own theory of justice, and explain how other theories go wrong only insofar as it serves that purpose.

Nevertheless, I do want to pay special attention to Rawls. Not only was he the most important political philosopher of the contemporary era, he, more than anyone else, is responsible for desert's dismissal from the distributive justice debate. Many philosophers assume that Rawls pretty well killed off the concept in *A Theory of Justice*, but, as we shall see (Chapter 7), this is not so.

Rawls arrives at his distributive rule—the difference principle—*via* a two-stage process. The first stage is normative. Rawls proposes a method by which we may discover the truth about justice. Namely: We identify the principles of justice that citizens *would* choose, *were* they to bargain over these on equal terms and under conditions of very limited information (no information about race, social class, gender—all the things obscured by the veil of ignorance). And those counterfactually chosen principles, whatever they be, are the ones that we actually ought to implement.

The second stage is positive. Rawls claims that suitably situated citizens (i.e. citizens in the original position) would in fact choose (1) equal liberties, (2) fair equality of opportunity, and (3) the difference principle.

As Rawls himself recognized, these two stages are conceptually distinct; one may endorse his normative set-up without endorsing his positive conclusions: "One may accept the first part of the theory . . . but not the other, and conversely. The concept of the initial contractual situation may seem reasonable although the particular principles proposed are rejected" (1971: 15).

Thus, to arrive at Rawlsian egalitarianism, it is insufficient to find his fairness ideal compelling; one must also endorse his positive assessment of contractors' reasoning. Although Rawls does explain why he thinks contractors would choose his preferred principles of justice, that is at base speculation about a purely positive matter.

Some philosophers believe that Rawlsian contractors would not, in fact, select the conservative difference principle; some have suggested that they would instead choose distribution based on desert.[12] Contractors' reasoning might go like this: "While I don't know whom I will be in my new society, however things turn out I want to have the ability to achieve on the basis of my character, effort, and interests. I want to be able to realize my chosen plan-of-life the best that I can. I may face natural disadvantage. But I may enjoy advantage as well. Most probably, like just about everybody else, I will face some combination of the two. I know that since my society will be characterized by fair equality of opportunity and meritocratic selection, whether I succeed or fail will truly be up to *me.* So I don't want an egalitarian distributive scheme. I want only to get what I deserve." This reasoning is perhaps even more plausible if the desert-based theory under contemplation includes a social safety net, which meritocracy does (§6.10).

Ultimately, though, we can conclude little from mere speculation. Rawlsian contractors are very thinly defined and thus ripe targets for manipulation: We know which distributive rule we want, and so we generate a story about how to fill up these empty vessels. As R. M. Hare puts it, "the truth is that it is a wide open question how the POPs [parties in the original position] would choose; [Rawls] has reduced the information available to them and about them so much that it is hard to say *what* they would choose, unless his own intuitions supply the lack" (Hare 1973: 250).

The principled way to investigate this matter is through experiment. We can put human beings into the original position, as best we are able, and then observe their bargaining behavior. Do they choose the difference principle?

Experimenters have done precisely this, and the answer is "no". Not only do contractors in the original position not choose the difference principle, it is among the most unpopular of distributive rules, if not *the* most unpopular.

Frohlich, Oppenheimer, and Eavey (1987) ran an experiment in which subjects were familiarized with four potential distributive rules: maximizing the minimum income (i.e. the difference principle); maximizing the average income; maximizing the average income with a floor constraint; and maximizing the average income with both floor and ceiling constraints.

Subjects were then asked to bargain over the distributive rule that would govern the allocation of actual money to them. This was done under conditions of limited information to simulate the original position. Subjects knew only that (1) if they reached unanimous consensus on a rule, then they would be paid from an allocation that conformed to that rule; and (2) if unanimous consensus was not reached, they would be paid according to an allocation randomly chosen from the full set of possibilities. In this way, these "contractors" were behind a veil of ignorance: They didn't know the "personal facts" that would determine their places within a particular payoff. But they did have the ability to constrain that through selection of a distributive rule.

Of the 44 runs of this experiment, consensus was reached 44 times. So one of Rawls's positive conjectures was verified: "A 'veil of ignorance' permits a group to reach stable decisions in which they have considerable confidence" (Frohlich, Oppenheimer, and Eavey 1987: 628).

But Rawls's other conjecture was *not* verified: The difference principle was not the most popular distributive rule. In fact, it was *never* chosen. Dominant was maximization of average income, subject to a floor constraint. This rule was chosen by 35 of the 44 groups. The experiment was later replicated in Poland (Lissowski, Tyszka, and Okrasa 1991).

Unfortunately, experimental design did not permit the robust test of a desert principle. Although subjects were in theory free to reach consensus on whatever distributive rule they liked, they were strongly primed with the four principles given above: They read a text introducing those principles and only those principles; they then were asked to rank the four; they then read several examples of allocations under those principles; they were then given a test on those principles; and they were again asked to rank them. (See also Frohlich and Oppenheimer 1992.)

So far as I am aware, there have been no subsequent experiments testing this part of Rawls's theory. My prediction is that a suitably designed experiment would show that desert wins the day. Because I reject Rawls's normative set-up, this is immaterial to my argument; but it could bring new adherents to the cause of desert—namely, those convinced by Rawls's ideal of fairness.

An updated, large-scale, and sophisticated test of reasoning in the original principle would be an excellent project for an experimental philosopher to undertake. All that can be said conclusively at this point is that "empirical studies provide almost no support for egalitarianism, understood as equality of outcomes, or for Rawls's difference principle" (Konow 2003: 1199).

3.6 The Importance of Intuition

What is the theoretical relevance of our ubiquitous and deep intuition that justice is giving people what they deserve? Answering this question in a fully satisfactory way would require a separate monograph; the justificatory status of intuition is a complicated matter. Here I only wish to summarize the prevailing wisdom and offer a few new thoughts of my own.

There are skeptics who believe that intuition has no justificatory power whatsoever.[13] These skeptics should skip this section. I note, for the lay reader, that while the skeptical view is a minority one among philosophers, it is not ridiculous.

But it has a principal problem: It requires that we endorse deeply counterintuitive moral results so long as the theories that produced them have desired structural features.

Imagine, for example, a theory of justice that is consistent, complete, elegant—as structurally virtuous as you like. The theory also holds that it is just to torture infants for fun. Now, coming to grips with this theory means either (1) allowing ourselves to be swayed by its structural virtues, and thus endorsing the torture of infants for fun; or (2) viewing that deeply counterintuitive result as grounds to believe that the theory is flawed. These considerations come in degrees, of course—I give an extreme example here—but if we believe that there is *some* point at which intuition can undermine a theory, we cannot be skeptics.

So: Setting the skeptical concern aside, there are five reasons why the intuitive consensus about justice-as-desert is important. First, there is a view of justification, which is admittedly unpopular within political philosophy, and which I regard as erroneous, but which has an estimable pedigree within the analytic tradition and does have adherents.[14] For these thinkers, the task of philosophy is simply to extract and analyze concepts from our intuitions. If that is so, then this chapter decisively establishes the truth of meritocracy; all that is required for political philosophers to do is to provide a more precise definition of "meritocracy".

Second, there is the prevailing view of justification—the view I endorse—which is that our intuitions play a role in a process of reflective equilibrium.[15] We cannot blindly obey the dictates of theory, for that leads to the possibility of engaging in what appears to be plainly immoral conduct, as above. At the same time, pure intuitionism provides no way to systematically resolve disputes that arise when intuitions conflict—as they often do. So we seek a balance: We verify the truth of a theory, to some extent, by comparing it to our intuitions; and in those cases where intuitions clash, we look to theory for help.

Among those who subscribe to the method of reflective equilibrium, there are differences of opinion about how much our theories should defer to our intuitions. I tend to agree with Saul Kripke, who puts it with his characteristic eloquence:

> Some philosophers think that something's having intuitive content is very inconclusive evidence in favor of it. I think it is very heavy evidence in favor of anything, myself. I really don't know, in a way, what more conclusive evidence one can have about anything, ultimately speaking.
>
> (1972: 42)

In any case, intuition has some justificatory power for everyone who subscribes to the method of reflective equilibrium. Why, then, is concrete analysis of intuition so rare in political theory? Nozick pays the matter no mind whatsoever. Rawls does better, in that he at least offers a conjecture about what his contractors would choose from the original position. But he adduces no empirical data for his view, which we now know (§3.5) is erroneous. The luck egalitarian probably does best of all—a typically-cited motivation for luck egalitarianism is to capture our pre-theoretical affection for personal responsibility. But that talk about intuition tends to be hand-wavy; I do not recall a single citation to the empirical literature in any of the foundational luck egalitarian articles.

I think the reason why this is so is that philosophers worry that our intuitions are tainted by cultural contingencies. In this way, philosophers can accept a justificatory role for intuition while devaluing those intuitions that we actually have. This is convenient for them, since our actual intuitions conflict with their theories. But this should only be a concern if our relevant intuitions *are in fact* severely contingent. And we have seen that our intuitions about justice are not.

Third, intuition is relevant for the non-ideal reasons covered in §2.4. Unless we know that citizens would be sufficiently motivated to comply with some theory, we are simply unjustified in believing that it is a guide to justice. So long as that is our goal, intuitions constrain our theorizing. And when the intuitions are deep, and when they are broad—as is the case with our intuitions about desert—these constraints are tight.

Fourth, it is dangerous to violate our meritocratic intuitions. When people feel that the distributive system they live under is unjust, they regard themselves as justified in violating it in the name of justice.

By way of illustration, suppose that Mary, a teacher, gets in a car accident with Chad, an investment banker. And Mary feels, apart from all of this, that teachers make less than they should and investment bankers make more. Although Mary is uninjured in the accident, she lies and says that she is, suing Chad for damages. The lie does not strike Mary as an immoral one, since its result will be, by her lights, to restore the just balance. And that might well be true: Mary's duplicity might lead to a more just distributive pattern.

At the same time, Chad correctly regards Mary as a liar. Perhaps he generalizes this judgment to her profession or gender. The legal system gets clogged with a claim that in some sense never should have been made. Part of the social product is used up in litigation. Class divisions harden. And the social stability is, in the large, undermined. In this way, the more counterintuitive a theory is, the more unstable the political system within which it operates. In contrast, if people feel, intuitively, that a theory is just, then a system based on it can maintain an equilibrium.

Fifth, there is something odd about imposing a distributive pattern, whatever its theoretical virtues, on people who do not want it because they think it unjust. To take the extreme case, imagine a world in which there is perfect consensus on the just distributive principle(s). People live under it, inevitably some win and some lose, but everyone believes that their society is just. Then some clever philosopher among them develops what he believes to be the True Theory of Distributive Justice, and he seeks to implement it. One consequence is that everyone becomes unhappy with the state of justice in their society. It is unclear to me what this philosopher has accomplished, morally. Perhaps he has accomplished something—perhaps the people are being brought to a morally better place, and perhaps they will recognize this in due course. But surely reaching consensus on justice would be a moral victory, not to be given up lightly.

Obviously I think such a consensus has already been reached—on desert-based justice generally and meritocracy specifically. But even more striking is the consensus that competing theories of justice are wrong.

Rawls's theory is the most roundly rejected here (§3.5), but this is only because it has been the most widely tested. I suspect that Nozick's night-watchman state would strike people as even less morally plausible. The simple fact is that no one wants to live under these distributive systems. Blacks don't want to, whites don't want to; men don't want to, women don't want to; the poor don't want to, the rich don't want to. How can we regard this as anything but a flaw, indeed a fatal one?

Notes

1 See Brosnan and de Waal (2003) and Takimoto, Kuroshima, and Fujita (2010).
2 See Brosnan, Schiff, and de Waal (2005) and Brosnan et al. (2010).
3 See Fehr, Naef, and Schmidt (2006) and Pelligra and Stanca (2013). Relatedly, in ultimatum and dictator games, young people and the educated show less interest in considerations of justice and greater attention to self-interest (Bellemare, Kröger, and van Soest 2008).
4 The landmark normative work here is Frankfurt (1987).
5 See, e.g. Damon (1977) and Hook and Cook (1979).
6 See especially Hamann, Bender, and Tomasello (2014) and Kanngiesser and Warneken (2012).
7 See Kim and Yuan (2015); Machery et al. (2017); and Seyedsayamdost (2015).
8 See, e.g. Adleberg, Thompson, and Nahmias (2015) and Sinnott-Armstrong et al. (2008).
9 <http://philosophycommons.typepad.com/xphi/2015/08/what-has-experimental-philosophy-discovered-about-demographic-effects.html>, retrieved 19 June 2017.
10 See also Fong, Bowles, and Gintis (2006) and Gilens (1999).
11 See also Aarøe and Petersen (2014); Petersen et al. (2011); and Petersen et al. (2012).
12 E.g. Daniels (1978); Holmgren (1986); and Sterba (1974).
13 Skeptics about intuition include Singer (1974, 2005) and Williamson (2004).
14 E.g. Audi (2004); Huemer (2005); and Shafer-Landau (2005). The progenitor of intuitionism is Sidgwick (1874).
15 See Goodman (1955) and Rawls (1971).

3.7 References

Aarøe, L. and Petersen, M. B. 2014. Crowding out culture: Scandinavians and Americans agree on social welfare in the face of deservingness cues. *Journal of Politics* 76: 684–97.

Adams, J. S. 1963. Toward an understanding of inequity. *Journal of Abnormal Psychology* 67: 422–36.

———. 1965. Inequity in social exchange. In *Advances in Experimental Social Psychology*, Volume 2, ed. L. Berkowitz, 267–99. New York: Academic Press.

Adleberg, T., Thompson, M., and Nahmias, E. 2015. Do men and women have different philosophical intuitions? Further data. *Philosophical Psychology* 28: 615–41.

Alesina, A. and Angeletos, G.-M. 2005. Fairness and redistribution. *American Economic Review* 95: 960–80.

Alwin, D. F., Gornev, G., and Khakhulina, L. 1995. Comparative referential structures, system legitimacy, and justice sentiments: An international comparison. In *Social Justice and Political Change: Public Opinion in Capitalist and Post-Communist States*, eds. J. R. Kluegel, D. S. Mason, and B. Wegener, 109–30. Berlin: Walter de Gruyter.

Audi, R. 2004. *The Good in the Right: A Theory of Intuition and Intrinsic Value.* Princeton: Princeton University Press.

Austin, W. and Walster, E. 1974. Reactions to confirmations and disconfirmations of expectancies of equity and inequity. *Journal of Personality and Social Psychology* 30: 208–16.

Barber, B. and English, W. Manuscript. Divide our dollars, not divide the dollar: Redistribution, fairness, and the ultimatum game.

Baumard, N., Mascaro, O., and Chevallier, C. 2012. Preschoolers are able to take merit into account when distributing goods. *Developmental Psychology* 48: 492–8.

Bellemare, C., Kröger, S., and van Soest, A. 2008. Measuring inequity aversion in a heterogeneous population using experimental decisions and subjective probabilities. *Econometrica* 76: 815–39.

Bolton, G. E. and Ockenfels, A. 2000. ERC: A theory of equity, reciprocity, and competition. *American Economic Review* 90: 166–93.

———. 2006. Inequality aversion, efficiency, and maximin preferences in simple distribution experiments: Comment. *American Economic Review* 96: 1906–11.

Bosmans, K. and Schokkaert, E. 2009. Equality preference in the claims problem: A questionnaire study of cuts in earnings and pensions. *Social Choice and Welfare* 33: 533–57.

Brosnan, S. F. and de Waal, F. B. M. 2003. Monkeys reject unequal pay. *Nature* 425: 297–9.

Brosnan, S. F., Schiff, H. C., and de Waal, F. B. M. 2005. Tolerance for inequity may increase with social closeness in chimpanzees. *Proceedings of the Royal Society B: Biological Sciences* 272: 253–8.

Brosnan, S. F., Talbot, C., Ahlgren, M., Lambeth, S. P., and Schapiro, S. J. 2010. Mechanisms underlying responses to inequitable outcomes in chimpanzees, *Pan Troglodytes. Animal Behaviour* 79: 1229–37.

Cappelen, A. W., Eichele, T., Hugdahl, K., Specht, K., Sørensen, E. Ø., and Tungodden, B. 2014. Equity theory and fair inequality: A neuroeconomic study. *Proceedings of the National Academy of Sciences* 111: 15368–72.

Cappelen, A. W., Sørensen, E. Ø., and Tungodden, B. 2010. Responsibility for what? Fairness and individual responsibility. *European Economic Review* 54: 429–41.

Damon, W. 1977. *The Social World of the Child.* San Francisco: Jossey-Bass.

Daniels, N. 1978. Merit and meritocracy. *Philosophy & Public Affairs* 7: 206–23.

Engel, C. 2011. Dictator games: A meta study. *Experimental Economics* 14: 583–610.

Fehr, E., Naef, M., and Schmidt, K. M. 2006. Inequality aversion, efficiency, and maximin preferences in simple distribution experiments: Comment. *American Economic Review* 96: 1912–17.

Fong, C. M. 2001. Social preferences, self-interest, and the demand for redistribution. *Journal of Public Economics* 82: 225–46.

Fong, C. M., Bowles, S., and Gintis, H. 2006. Strong reciprocity and the welfare state. In *Handbook of the Economics of Giving, Altruism and Reciprocity*, Volume 2, eds. S.-C. Kolm and J. M. Ythier, 1439–64. Amsterdam: North-Holland.

Frankfurt, H. 1987. Equality as a moral ideal. *Ethics* 98: 21–43.

Frohlich, N. and Oppenheimer, J. A. 1992. *Choosing Justice: An Experimental Approach to Ethical Theory*. Berkeley: University of California Press.

Frohlich, N., Oppenheimer, J. A., and Eavey, C. L. 1987. Choices of principles of distributive justice in experimental groups. *American Journal of Political Science* 31: 606–36.

Frohlich, N., Oppenheimer, J. A., and Kurki, A. 2004. Modeling other-regarding preferences and an experimental test. *Public Choice* 119: 91–117.

Gettier, E. L. 1963. Is justified true belief knowledge? *Analysis* 23: 121–3.

Gilens, M. 1999. *Why Americans Hate Welfare: Race, Media, and the Politics of Antipoverty Policy*. Chicago: University of Chicago Press.

Goodman, N. 1955. *Fact, Fiction, and Forecast*. Cambridge: Harvard University Press.

Greenberg, J. 1990. Employee theft as a reaction to underpayment inequity: The hidden cost of pay cuts. *Journal of Applied Psychology* 75: 561–8.

Güth, W., Schmittberger, R., and Schwarze, B. 1982. An experimental analysis of ultimatum bargaining. *Journal of Economic Behavior and Organization* 3: 367–88.

Hamann, K., Bender, J., and Tomasello, M. 2014. Meritocratic sharing is based on collaboration in 3-year-olds. *Developmental Psychology* 50: 121–8.

Hare, R. M. 1973. Rawls' theory of justice—II. *Philosophical Quarterly* 23: 241–52.

Herrero, C., Moreno-Ternero, J. D., and Ponti, G. 2010. On the adjudication of conflicting claims: An experimental study. *Social Choice and Welfare* 34: 145–79.

Holmgren, M. 1986. Justifying desert claims: Desert and opportunity. *Journal of Value Inquiry* 20: 265–78.

Hook, J. G. and Cook, T. D. 1979. Equity theory and the cognitive ability of children. *Psychological Bulletin* 86: 429–45.

Huemer, M. 2005. *Ethical Intuitionism*. New York: Palgrave Macmillan.

Kanngiesser, P. and Warneken, F. 2012. Young children consider merit when sharing resources with others. *Plos One* 7: 1–5.

Kim, M. and Yuan, Y. 2015. No cross-cultural differences in the Gettier car case intuition: A replication study of Weinberg et al. 2001. *Episteme* 12: 355–61.

Konow, J. 1996. A positive theory of economic fairness. *Journal of Economic Behavior & Organization* 31: 13–35.

———. 2000. Fair shares: Accountability and cognitive dissonance in allocation decisions. *American Economic Review* 90: 1072–91.

———. 2001. Fair and square: The four sides of distributive justice. *Journal of Economic Behavior & Organization* 46: 137–64.

———. 2003. Which is the fairest one of all? A positive analysis of justice theories. *Journal of Economic Literature* 41: 1188–239.

Kripke, S. A. 1972. *Naming and Necessity*. Cambridge: Harvard University Press.

Lee, K. and Shahriar, Q. 2017. Fairness, one's source of income, and others' decisions: An ultimatum game experiment. *Managerial and Decision Economics* 38: 423–31.

Lissowski, G., Tyszka, T., and Okrasa, W. 1991. Principles of distributive justice: Experiments in Poland and America. *Journal of Conflict Resolution* 35: 98–119.

Machery, E., Stich, S., Rose, D., Chatterjee, A., Karasawa, K., Struchiner, N., Sirker, S., Usui, N., and Hashimoto, T. 2017. Gettier across cultures. *Noûs* 51: 645–64.

Massen, J. J., van den Berg, L. M., Spruijt, B. M., and Sterck, E. H. 2012. Inequity aversion in relation to effort and relationship quality in long-tailed Macaques (Macaca fascicularis). *American Journal of Primatology* 74: 145–56.

McAuley, A. 1980. Soviet attitudes toward redistribution. In *Income Distribution: The Limits to Redistribution*, eds. D. A. Collard, R. Lecomber, and M. Slater, 238–61. New York: John Wiley & Sons.

Neiworth, J. J., Johnson, E. T., Whillock, K., Greenberg, J., and Brown, V. 2009. Is a sense of inequity an ancestral primate trait? Testing social inequity in cotton top tamarins (Saguinus oedipus). *Journal of Comparative Psychology* 123: 10–17.

Page, B. I. and Jacobs, L. R. 2009. *Class War? What Americans Really Think about Economic Inequality*. Chicago: University of Chicago Press.

Pelligra, V. and Stanca, L. 2013. To give or not to give? Equity, efficiency and altruistic behavior in an artefactual field experiment. *Journal of Socio-Economics* 46: 1–9.

Petersen, M. B. 2012. Social welfare as small-scale help: Evolutionary psychology and the deservingness heuristic. *American Journal of Political Science* 56: 1–16.

Petersen, M. B., Slothuus, R., Stubager, R., and Togeby, L. 2011. Deservingness versus values in public opinion on welfare: The automaticity of the deservingness heuristic. *European Journal of Political Research* 50: 24–52.

Petersen, M. B., Sznycer, D., Cosmides, L., and Tooby, J. 2012. Who deserves help? Evolutionary psychology, social emotions, and public opinion about welfare. *Political Psychology* 33: 395–418.

Piaget, J. 1932. *The Moral Judgment of the Child*. London: Kegan Paul, Trench, Trübner & Co.

Pritchard, R. D., Dunnette, M. D., and Jorgenson, D. O. 1972. Effects of perceptions of equity and inequity on worker performance and satisfaction. *Journal of Applied Psychology* 56: 75–94.

Range, F., Horn, L., Viranyi, Z., and Huber, L. 2009. The absence of reward induces inequity aversion in dogs. *Proceedings of the National Academy of Sciences* 106: 340–5.

Rawls, J. 1971. *A Theory of Justice*. Cambridge: Harvard University Press.

Ruffle, B. J. 1998. More is better, but fair is fair: Tipping in dictator and ultimatum games. *Games and Economic Behavior* 23: 247–65.

Rustichini, A. and Vostroknutov, A. 2014. Merit and justice: An experimental analysis of attitude to inequality. *Plos One* 9: 1–19.

Seyedsayamdost, H. 2015. On normativity and epistemic intuitions: Failure of replication. *Episteme* 12: 95–116.

Shafer-Landau, R. 2005. *Moral Realism: A Defence*. New York: Oxford University Press.

Sidgwick, H. 1874. *The Methods of Ethics*. London: Macmillan and Co.

Singer, P. 1974. Sidgwick and reflective equilibrium. *Monist* 58: 490–517.

———. 2005. Ethics and intuitions. *Journal of Ethics* 9: 331–52.

Sinnott-Armstrong, W., Mallon, R., McCoy, T., and Hull, J. G. 2008. Intention, temporal order, and moral judgments. *Mind & Language* 23: 90–106.

Sloane, S., Baillargeon, R., and Premack, D. 2012. Do infants have a sense of fairness? *Psychological Science* 23: 196–204.

Son Hing, L. S., Bobocel, D. R., and Zanna, M. P. 2002. Meritocracy and opposition to affirmative action: Making concessions in the face of discrimination. *Journal of Personality and Social Psychology* 83: 493–509.

Sterba, J. P. 1974. Justice as desert. *Social Theory and Practice* 3: 101–16.

Takimoto, A., Kuroshima, H., and Fujita, K. 2010. Capuchin monkeys (Cebus apella) are sensitive to others' reward: An experimental analysis of food-choice for conspecifics. *Animal Cognition* 13: 249–61.

Talbot, C. F., Freeman, H. D., Williams, L. E., and Brosnan, S. F. 2011. Squirrel monkeys' response to inequitable outcomes indicates a behavioural convergence within the primates. *Biology Letters* 7: 680–2.

Walster, E., Berscheid, E., and Walster, G. W. 1973. New directions in equity research. *Journal of Personality and Social Psychology* 25: 151–76.

Williamson, T. 2004. Philosophical "intuitions" and skepticism about judgement. *Dialectica* 58: 109–53.

Part II

A Meritocratic Theory of Economic Justice

4 The Foundation of Meritocracy

4.1 The Concept of Desert

The first step in developing the theory of meritocracy is to get clear about the concept of desert. John Hospers says that "justice is getting what one deserves; what could be simpler?" (1961: 433), but in fact, almost anything is simpler: Desert is a rich and labyrinthine concept which has defied easy analysis for millennia. That said, progress has been made—by, especially, Joel Feinberg (1963); Kleinig (1971); and Sher (1987).

To begin with, desert-claims come in the form "X deserves y on the basis of z". While the language used can vary—"by virtue of z" and "for z" are common—and while elements of the claim are often left implicit ("You deserve it!")—in all cases, a *bona fide* desert-claim has these three components.

That is, a *bona fide* desert-claim includes, first, a *desert subject*, X, which is typically a person but need not be (we may also say that a manuscript deserves to be published and that the Grand Canyon deserves its reputation (Kleinig 1971)). Second, a *desert object*, y, for which there are an almost infinite number of examples: one can deserve an award, deserve punishment, deserve a piece of blueberry cobbler, deserve to have one's manuscript published, deserve to be happy, and so on.

It is sometimes said that when it comes to *personal desert* (i.e. cases in which the desert subject is a human being), the desert object must be either beneficial or injurious to the desert subject. But this is not correct.

Consider Lance Armstrong, who was stripped of his Tour de France titles in the face of doping allegations. Let us stipulate that he deserved this treatment. But suppose their loss had no effect on Armstrong; he just didn't care, one way or another, whether he had those titles. That does nothing to imperil the claim that Armstrong did not deserve them.

So desert is about more than just rewarding or punishing; it is also about *making things right*—in this case, ensuring that the record books reflected Armstrong's duplicity. As Feinberg puts it, "to say that a person deserves something is to say that there is a certain sort of propriety in his having it." (1963: 71). A notion of propriety, often "fittingness", is ubiquitous in the literature on desert.

The third component of desert-claims is the *desert basis*, z. A physicist deserves the Nobel Prize on the basis of his discoveries; a criminal deserves jail on the basis of his crimes; and I deserve a piece of cobbler because I baked the thing. Here the issue of fit arises, as there must be a proper connection between the desert basis and the desert object. One can deserve the Nobel on the basis of one's scientific discoveries, but no one could ever deserve that prize on the basis of his crimes, or because he baked a cobbler.

There is, thus, a conceptual connection between X and y (the Grand Canyon can never deserve a job), and between y and z, as just described. There is also a connection between X and z—between the desert subject and the desert basis—which is of critical importance moving forward.

Philosophers have debated the nature and the strength of the connection. Some say that desert subjects must be *responsible* for their bases.[1] But this is wrong, or at least too quick: A sick child, not responsible for his sickness, may well deserve our sympathy.[2]

In any case, I shall rely on the weakest, and uncontroversial, construal of the connection—sometimes known as the "aboutness principle" (Feinberg 1963). To wit: To be *bona fide*, desert bases must be *about* the desert subject. Tiffany cannot deserve the tiara on the basis of Jennifer's beauty. Frank cannot deserve to go to jail on the basis of Phillip's crimes. And so on.

Next, we must take care to differentiate desert from *entitlement*, which is sometimes what people mean when they talk about "desert", but which is conceptually distinct from true desert.

Imagine that a man has committed a murder, is known to have committed the murder, and is put in jail. Yet because of a procedural error, the evidence collected against him cannot be used. Prosecutors must let him go free.

This man is entitled to his freedom. That is, within the rules of criminal law he ought to be let go. And one might, and some do, carelessly say that this man "deserves" his freedom, as a sort of synonym for "proper under the rules". But that use of "desert" refers to something else. This man does not *really* deserve his freedom; quite the opposite, justice was not served. What the man deserves is a prison cell.

So when I talk about "desert" in this work I mean true desert—not entitlement. Entitlement is sometimes regarded as a "post-institutional" notion and desert a "pre-institutional" notion, which is a reasonable way of looking at things. Rawls, for example, while rejecting desert as a principle of justice, accedes to what he calls a person's "legitimate expectations" under the government. (Perhaps this is Rawls's attempt to accommodate moral intuitions about desert.)

There are two more features of the concept of desert to cover. First, desert is *retrospective* (or "backwards-looking") in the sense that desert bases must lie in the past. If an individual deserves a certain mode of treatment now, it is on the basis of contributions he's made, or the actions that he's taken, or the character that he's formed, etc. Walton cannot deserve punishment on the basis of future crimes. Only if Walton actually commits those crimes will he thereby deserve to be punished. Although this view of desert as purely backwards-looking is widely held, there are dissenters. I devote §4.7 to responding to them.

Second, it is sometimes wondered whether desert is a *comparative* or a *non-comparative* notion. If desert is non-comparative, then figuring out what someone deserves can be done by scrutinizing that person alone, by asking: Does she possess the relevant desert basis in the proper measure? If, on the other hand, desert is comparative, this cannot be determined without reference to how other people are faring.

Issues of comparative and non-comparative desert quickly become complex and quite technical (Kagan (2012) discusses them in extreme detail.) But desert within distributive justice is standardly understood to be comparative in nature (see, e.g. Olsaretti 2004). Whether Joe deserves a job depends at least in part on the qualifications of the other applicants. (Joe might also fail to reach a non-comparative standard of merit, rendering him undeserving of the job, even if he is more meritorious than everyone else.)

The reason the distributive justice debate is fundamentally comparative is because of scarcity. In contrast, consider criminal justice: There is no hurdle to each person receiving the punishment that he non-comparatively deserves, since there is no shortage of punishments we might mete out.

But even if there were a non-comparative way to determine what income Sarah deserves, deciding how much Sarah ought actually to be paid, given those deserts, requires contact with others. Sarah may deserve a $50,000 salary if she is working in the United States, but not if she moves to Mali, where the average yearly income is $700. Maybe there are ways around this (perhaps what Sarah deserves, non-comparatively, is some share of national income), but these are abstractions which are irrelevant to the matter at hand—which is how to *actually* respond to people's economic deserts.[3]

To summarize, then: A person deserves a job, or income, just in case she possesses the relevant desert basis (which may but need not be different for these two desert objects) in the relevant measure. The desert basis must not be a product of institutions. That is, she doesn't deserve the object because that's what the rules say; the rules ought to be written so that people get the objects that they deserve. And in all cases the desert basis must be *about* that person. This is the conceptual schema to be filled in.

4.2 The Connection Between Merit and Desert

Justice cannot simply be a matter of responding to people's merits. Suppose we wish to hire a new art teacher. The fact that *A* is a more meritorious artist than *B* is a good reason to think that justice demands that the job go to *A*. But it is insufficient to establish this. If *A* is Adolf Hitler, then it is unjust to give him the job, no matter how talented a painter he be.

This is a simple point, but it's an important one conceptually, since it suggests that if merit has a role to play in justice, it's by virtue of the relation it has to something of more fundamental moral importance. Standing in conceptual isolation, merit is not a plausible principle of justice.

The thing that is of fundamental moral importance is, of course, desert. Merit serves as the basis for our most important and powerful desert-claims. If justice is about getting what one deserves, and if one deserves on the basis of one's merits, then we have connected merit to desert, merit to justice, and merit to morality.

This ground has been traveled before. William Galston notes that the idea that the best should be chosen is "one of the historically and conceptually most important desert-claims" (1980: 176). And the first definition of "merit" in Merriam-Webster's dictionary is a surprisingly sophisticated one: "The qualities or actions that constitute the basis of one's deserts".[4]

Here a question arises: If merit is just one desert basis among many, how can it control distributive decisions? It would be a sorry sort of meritocracy, if merit were constantly defeated by other, more compelling bases when determining people's deserts.

The answer is that it is rare for a non-merit desert basis to overcome merit. The above Hitler-as-art-teacher is an example: The negative desert basis (genocidal lunacy) is so strong that it swamps considerations of merit.

Moreover, often desert bases thought to be independent of merit in fact are not. Suppose *A* is not Hitler but a run-of-the-mill jerk. One might believe that, because of this, he does not deserve the teaching job. However, this judgment comes from making a reasonable inference about his pedagogical skill from his character. One is judging this man undeserving on the basis of his merit. If we knew that *A*, despite being a general jerk, was friendly in the classroom, and thereby truly a better teacher than *B*, we would insist that *A* deserves the job.

Consider a familiar scenario in which these considerations arise: academic hiring. In today's slack market, search committees receive hundreds of applications for each tenure-track job. The applicants differ in merit, as that term is defined and interpreted by the committees. But the applicants also differ in non-merit bases: Some are alumni of the schools doing the hiring; some are donors to these schools; some have done charity work; some are veterans; some have family members who require care near the schools; and so on. These are all facts that could, conceptually, render a person deserving, none of them related to merit. And wouldn't we find it odd, indeed unprofessional, if a committee chose a less meritorious applicant over a more meritorious applicant on the basis of them? I think so.

Now, a non-merit basis might justly be used as a tie-breaker between two equally meritorious applicants. If a committee simply cannot distinguish between *A*'s merits and *B*'s merits, but *B* is a veteran, then perhaps *B* deserves the job. But if we heard that a committee had decided that *A* was the more meritorious applicant, but then chose the less meritorious *B* on the grounds that *B* was a veteran, I think that choice would strike us as faulty and morally wrong. *Maybe* there is an extreme case in which *B* would deserve the job—if, for example, he were a Medal of Honor winner— but I don't think so.

So these cases—economic desert turning on a non-merit basis—are rare, if indeed they exist at all. I don't want to devote more space to this conceptual analysis (for that, see Mulligan 2015), except to make the following point.

Owen McLeod describes meritocracy like this:

> One view is that merit is a quite specific kind of desert: A merits x if and only if x is a position, and A would perform excellently in x. This might be the notion that 'meritocrats' have in mind when they urge that positions be assigned on the basis of merit only.
>
> (1999: 67)

While this is close to correct, McLeod makes two small errors.

First, meritocrats do not urge that positions be assigned on the basis of merit only. That would produce outrageous results like Hitler-as-art-teacher. Meritocrats, rather, urge that positions be assigned on the basis of *desert* only. It happens to be true that almost always the most meritorious applicant is the most deserving.

Second, it may be the case that the most meritorious candidate for some position will *not* perform excellently in it. Dysfunctional external factors can and often do intervene to cleave merit apart from performance. Imagine a factory in a racist society which seeks to hire a new widget maker. The best-qualified candidate, Matt, is black. The meritocrat says that Matt ought to get the job: He is the best widget maker, and so he deserves it. Yet suppose it is also known that, if he is hired, the other workers, who are racist, will sabotage Matt's work and cause him to underproduce. (This is a case of taste discrimination, to be discussed in §5.9.) Here, the most meritorious candidate will not perform excellently. To the meritocrat, that is irrelevant: Matt still deserves the job.

That said, except in these cases, merit does have a powerful *predictive* quality: It tells us not only who is more excellent now but who will perform better in the future. This is a consideration of efficiency.

So we value merit for its own sake (and not, e.g. its instrumental power in promoting the general welfare). In so valuing merit, a worry may arise:

It is a short move from the claim that effort is valuable, or skill is valuable, or beauty is valuable—as I believe—to the claim that those who possess these merits are valuable, and, more worrying, more valuable than those who are not meritorious.

Providing a fully-developed theory of value is outside of the scope of this book. It will suffice to show that the above implication does not hold.

It is true that it is better to be hard-working than lazy; better to be talented than inept; and better to be beautiful than ugly. And it is true that these features of a person constitute the person himself. But it is a simple fallacy of composition to say that the whole person is valuable because his parts are. (The sorry history of some rock and roll "supergroups" provides an analogy: Individual virtuosity does not guarantee group virtuosity.)

In this way, the meritocrat is not committed to the idea that a society composed of highly-skilled people is more valuable than a society of the unable. It is the *merits themselves* that have value. A person or a society is excellent not to the extent to which they are meritorious, but to the extent to which they develop, promote, and apply merit.

This is important for two reasons. First, it thwarts dystopian attacks against meritocracy; for example, the charge that a meritocratic society demonizes the unskilled. That simply does not follow from meritocratic principles. That Daryl is more meritorious than John does not imply that we ought to hold Daryl in greater esteem.

Indeed, John is more estimable if he shows better attention to developing and applying his more meager merits than Daryl shows to his. In a similar way, a poor society that seeks to improve its lot by developing excellence in its citizens is superior to a wealthy society that has become contented and decadent.

Second, this is relevant for the role that natural traits should play in economic distribution. Since Rawls, they have been regarded as "arbitrary from a moral point-of-view" and therefore unable to justify economic inequalities. I shall argue at length in Chapter 7 that that is wrong—we cannot escape these traits, they define our identity in part, and thus we must respect them politically and allow them to influence distributive decisions.

But another objection to the Rawlsian view, which has been raised by Elizabeth Anderson (1999) and Jonathan Wolff (1998), is that compensating people for natural flaws violates a norm of equal respect. While I don't think there is such an equality norm, I do believe that people are owed respect and that this respect does not turn on their natural capacities. Meritocrats can maintain this position because, as explained, we have no *per se* reason to value a disadvantaged person less than an advantaged person.

The meritocrat accepts the natural diversity of persons without celebrating or lamenting it. He recognizes that natural traits play a role in the way a person develops and pursues a plan-of-life. And he recognizes that respect for that plan-of-life requires respect for the natural traits on which it is based.

In contrast, respect is not shown by the egalitarian, who feels compelled to erase natural differences through the homogenizing power of equal outcomes. Respect is also not shown under libertarian *laissez-faire*; there, the extent to which a person may exploit or mitigate his natural traits is under the partial social control of others (e.g. the wealthy). But respect *is* shown to the individual in a meritocracy, through the provision of equal opportunity and strict attention to merit. Demonstrating this requires explaining the essential relevance of equal opportunity, a task to which I now turn.

4.3 No Justice Without Equal Opportunity

The metaphor most frequently used to explain equal opportunity is that of a race.[5] Suppose that the rules for a race include the provision that all black runners get a minute added to their finishing times. William, who is white, goes around the track in 4:30. Brian, who is black, goes around in 4:00. William's finishing time gets recorded as 4:30 and Brian's as 5:00. And so, under the rules, William is entitled to the medal. We say that this competition lacks *formal equality of opportunity* (Formal EO). Why? Because the competitors were not judged meritocratically; they were judged, in part, on the basis of their race.

Formal EO is thus tantamount to a meritocratic distributive rule. The meritocrat holds the above result to be unjust; Brian deserved the medal since he was the faster runner. (Again: Desert is pre-institutional.) Other theories of justice may not arrive at this result: If society is racist, the general utility may be served by giving the medal to William. And the libertarian holds that there was no injustice if Brian agreed to the rules when he decided to race. The meritocrat disagrees: Brian was the best, and so he deserves the medal, and that is all there is to it.

Yet Formal EO is only a necessary, and not a sufficient, condition for ensuring that the most deserving runner receives the medal. Suppose that this society is in fact racist: Blacks are malnourished and lack health care while whites have access to elite trainers and facilities. Then, even if the race is judged only on the basis of merit (i.e. even if Formal EO prevails), Brian faced hurdles to becoming meritorious which William did not. In this society, it is not really true to say that each runner had an equal opportunity to win the race—no matter what the rules say. A deeper, substantive sense of equal opportunity—*fair equality of opportunity* (Fair EO)—was lacking. As a result, William's moral claim to the medal—his claim to deserve the medal—is undermined.

There has long been a sense that meritocracy and equal opportunity are connected.[6] It is intuitive. I want to make the intuition precise.

The meritocratic argument for equal opportunity is a transcendental one, going as follows:

(1) We should give people what they deserve.
(2) Economic desert requires Fair EO.
THEREFORE, we should establish Fair EO.

This is a valid argument. There are both metaphysical and epistemological issues involved here. Metaphysically, if Fair EO is perfectly implemented and Formal EO prevails, then everyone gets her economic deserts. When Fair EO is lacking, on the other hand, the degree to which this happens—the degree to which the world is just—is diminished.

Epistemologically, absent Fair EO, one cannot have confidence that the outcome of a meritocratic process is just. Indeed, even if a hobbled runner like Brian happens to win, his desert-claim on the medal is mitigated by the possibility that another hobbled runner might have won instead, were the race conducted under Fair EO.

The precise connection between Fair EO and desert is found in the aboutness principle (§4.1). When conditions of Fair EO are lacking, the putative desert basis is in part about people *other than* the desert subject. And, once again, it is conceptually impossible to deserve something on the basis of who someone else is or what someone else has done.

Take a run-of-the-mill economic example: Daisy and Myrtle are competing against each other for a place at Yale. Daisy attended an elite high school and as a result is more meritorious than Myrtle. Daisy attended this school because her parents, in contrast to Myrtle's, were rich. And Daisy's parents were rich either as a result of their own merits or because they enjoyed a bequest which they passed along to Daisy in the form of elite education.

Thus, when Daisy, the more meritorious applicant, is admitted rather than Myrtle, it is not *her* merits, in full, that control the distributive decision. Her parents' merits (or her grandparents', etc.) control it too. These historically-grounded components of Daisy's merit are not really *about* Daisy; they cannot ground her desert-claim here. And Daisy appreciates this if she is self-reflective; she takes limited pride in her achievement, understanding that the competition for the scarce admissions slot was not conducted on level terms. This reduces Daisy's sense of desert.

Now, this account may be objected to in two ways. First, it might be said that Daisy's merit in its entirety is still "about" her—after all, she is the one, and the only one, with the merit. But this does not satisfy the aboutness principle, which means something different. Suppose that Anna slips a mind-control drug into Veronica's drink, thereby inducing Veronica to commit some crime. We ask whether Veronica deserves to be punished. The answer is "no". Punishing Veronica would violate the aboutness principle, even though the crime is "about" her in some weak sense. What the aboutness principle seeks to do, rather, is limit the moral judgments made about a person to admirable or objectionable facts about her—and her alone. As Sher puts it, "how better to capture the moral importance of the differences between persons than to say that each person uniquely deserves things for precisely what he does, and for precisely what he is?" (1987: 211)

Plainly, stronger principles than aboutness yield the relevant result, too. Veronica is not *responsible* for the crime, and therefore cannot deserve on the basis of it. The same may be said about Daisy.

When Formal EO is lacking, merit no longer determines who gets what, and so people do not get their just deserts. When Fair EO is lacking, *other people's* merits influence individual distributive decisions, and so people's desert-claims lose force. Merit, the heart of justice, comes alive under equal opportunity.

This explains, I think, why philosophers have been so skeptical that merit has a role to play in justice: Because opportunities have been unequal, we find out there in the world many meritorious but undeserving people. It is wrong to conclude from this that merit should not matter. It's quite the opposite: Merit should matter, and we should establish equal opportunity so that it can serve its central function in distributive justice.

The second conceptual objection may be disposed of easily. It says that because equal opportunity can never be perfectly established (which I concede), it is impossible for anyone to deserve anything. This objection would only be sound only if *any* inequality of opportunity nullified desert-claims *in their entirety*. But there is no reason to think that this is true. And consider this: Suppose someone comes from relative disadvantage (there is no Fair EO), yet through her extra efforts becomes meritorious and receives the good at stake on the basis of her merit. She certainly deserves it, no? But that verdict would be impossible to deliver if this objection were sound. The meritocrat's point is that as equal opportunity is better implemented, desert-claims gain more and more force, and the world becomes a more and more just place.

I close this section by considering two objections to equal opportunity. Despite its broad political appeal—or perhaps because of it—objections have been leveled by scholars on both the left and the right. Equal opportunity has been variously regarded as the harbinger of socialism, a means to discriminate against minority classes, a means to provide unjust advantage to these classes, and an invitation for the government to meddle in private affairs. My all-time favorite bit of alarmist rhetoric comes from John Schaar, who warns that equal opportunity

> opens more and more opportunities for more and more people to contribute more and more energies toward the realization of a mass, bureaucratic, technological, privatized, materialistic, bored, and thrill-seeking, consumption-oriented society—a society of well-fed, congenial, and sybaritic monkeys surrounded by gadgets and pleasure-toys.
> (1967: 231)

It is hard for me to see how, for example, efforts to ensure that the best-qualified candidate is not excluded from a job on the basis of his race put us in danger of becoming pleasure-toy-wielding monkeys, but that is an example of the sort of scaremongering that one sometimes hears from critics of equal opportunity (and of meritocracy more broadly).

The first objection I consider is also one of Schaar's, and it is rather more sober. Schaar says that equal opportunity "promises that the doors to success and prosperity will be opened to us all yet does not imply that we are all equally valuable or that all men are really created equal" (1967: 229).

Reply: That is correct. Meritocracy takes no stand on those questions of deep equality between persons. True or false, claims about people having equal value, or being "created equal"—whatever that means— are compatible with meritocracy. To my mind, it is a weakness, not a strength, of a theory of justice that it requires that one or both of those propositions be true.

Richard Arneson gives a second objection to Fair EO—namely, that it is overbroad:

> One sign that [equal opportunity] overreaches is that it not only for-bids Christian heterosexuals . . . from excluding gays from the vast bulk of desirable employment opportunities, but also and equally forbids a few gays who want to form a communal workplace from establishing a single business in which all employees are gay.
>
> (1999: 88)

Reply: Gays who arrange a workplace like this act unjustly. Sexual orientation cannot justly be used in employment decisions, neither as a benefit nor a burden. And it certainly must not be used as a decisive fac-tor in hiring, as the homosexuals here wish to do. The fact that a group has been treated unjustly in the past does not legitimate its own unjust conduct now.

4.4 Elaborating Equal Opportunity

In a meritocracy, we would find a sharp distinction between state inter-vention into the lives of children, which would be significant, and state intervention into the lives of adults, which would be small.

When it comes to adults, the government's principal economic respon-sibility is to ensure that citizens are not discriminated against on grounds irrelevant from the point-of-view of merit. The state enforces Formal EO.

When it comes to children, the government is driven by concerns about Fair EO. A just state ensures that each person, upon reaching moral agency, has had a *de facto* equal opportunity to pursue the economic goals that he sets for himself. This requires ensuring that no person is disadvantaged by substandard health care, lackluster education, or the like during her childhood.

But what, exactly, does Fair EO demand of us? Clearly, the state must invest more in the human capital development of children born into disadvantage. But just how much more? And for what, precisely, are we trying to equalize opportunity? What should count as "disadvantage"?

I first address the question of proper outcomes. The two economic goods I concentrate on are income and jobs. These are the foci of the philosophical and popular debates, and in my view exhaust almost the whole of economic justice. (Wealth is merely a stockpile of income, and, in a meritocracy, a person's wealth is a result of his justly-received income.) As a practical matter, we may concentrate on equalizing opportunity for income. There are a few reasons for this.

First, owing to the heterogeneity of jobs it is hard to know what it would mean to equalize opportunity for employment *simpliciter*, beyond those protections provided by Formal EO. (Note, too, that establishing Formal EO has a Fair EO effect: Young people who know that they will have no formal barriers to future employment will be more inclined to make the necessary human capital investments.)

Second, preferences for particular jobs are shaped during childhood in myriad ways, and more acutely than the general preference for income which we share. It is not clear that it is possible or desirable to intervene against these influences (e.g. to prevent a child born to a happy lawyer to develop her own interest in law). More on that in the next section.

Third, equal opportunity for employment is likely to be achieved instrumentally, through equal opportunity for income. Human capital specialization in preparation for a particular job happens after reaching adulthood. Fair EO regimes, with future income in mind, provide the broad preparation necessary for adults to have many employment paths open to them.

Next, we must clarify *how* equal opportunity will be achieved. Education has traditionally been considered the most important means—and I agree—but it is not sufficient. Disadvantaged children must also have access to health care, for example. Implementing that is comparatively simple: A system of universal health care suffices. There must also be intervention into some family affairs, which I discuss next. And, it should be noted, state action alone cannot establish Fair EO; there must also be a degree of cultural "buy in"—a shared adherence to the meritocratic ideal—to sustain the equal opportunity framework and discourage subtle violations of it.

The next question is where the so-called "responsibility cut" should be made. Must unequal opportunity that arises from birth into poverty be nullified? To be sure. But what about race? What about IQ, insofar as it is environmentally obtained? Insofar as it is genetic?

For egalitarian philosophers, including luck egalitarians, the answer is "yes" to all of the above: Facts about an individual's family, location of birth, IQ however obtained, genetics, and more cannot justly play a role in determining economic outcomes. (Note, however, that luck egalitarians are not typically asking where to make the responsibility cut for the purpose of establishing equal opportunity; they seek to equalize outcomes—typically, welfare.) These philosophers follow Rawls's anti-desert argument: Because we do not deserve our traits, natural or otherwise, we do not deserve that which we might obtain through them.

Clearly, the meritocrat does not reject this idea *in toto*, but the meritocrat does reject the idea that natural traits cannot justly influence economic outcomes. Economic outcomes should not turn on family wealth, location of birth, parental education, and that portion of IQ due to environmental factors. But they can justly turn on one's adult efforts, IQ genetically obtained, one's native social skill, and one's personality.

Chapter 7 is devoted to justifying this idea. I will simply note here that the meritocratic responsibility cut accords with intuition. People find economic inequalities that derive from social advantage, like elite schooling, unjust, but we are not disturbed when a person becomes wealthy as a result of her natural skill (Goya-Tocchetto, Echols, and Wright 2016).[7]

With the normative structure of meritocratic equal opportunity now fixed, how can it be implemented? John Roemer (1998, 2003) provides the necessary formalism. He suggests the following. First, we make the responsibility cut, separating *circumstances* (which ought not to play a role in determining one's economic outcomes) from *abilities* (which should).[8] Second, we define a *type* as a class of people who share the same circumstances. We then distribute resources so that the incomes of each type are in some sense equal,[9] but the incomes within types are not. In this way, income is a function of ability but not circumstances.

Although I disagree with Roemer about where to make the responsibility cut—like most luck egalitarians, he views natural traits as inadmissible—his model is a good one and the best tool we have to turn vague claims about equal opportunity into concrete policy recommendations.

What might such a policy look like in practice? This depends on the elasticity of income with respect to educational investment for each type. In theory, equal opportunity could require big differences in public spending on poor children versus public spending on rich children. This could be the case if elasticities are roughly equal across types (see Betts and Roemer 2007). However, recent work (*viz.* Jackson, Johnson, and Persico 2016) finds that elasticities are not equal—the elasticity for poor children is roughly double that of "non-poor" children—and that mitigates inequality of public investment.

In any case, the philosophically important question is this: Suppose the state really did have to invest 10 times more (e.g.) in the education of poor children in order to establish equal opportunity. Would the meritocrat really insist on such an unequal investment?

Yes. This is required by theory. It is, however, a result that neither the right nor the left will be keen to accept. It is unpalatable to libertarians for categorical reasons: Redistribution, even to poor children, violates putative rights.

But it is also unjustifiable to egalitarians who believe in "equal respect" and "equal concern" (§4.2). Massive differentials in the way children are treated by the state, on the basis of socioeconomic status, plainly violate equal concern, because there is no equal concern: The state shows more concern for the development of poor children. And equal respect is violated because, according to the egalitarian, no poor person could maintain his self-respect in the face of such public spending. These arguments find no purchase with the meritocrat. If equal opportunity requires spending much more on poor children than rich children, that is what we are morally obligated to do.

One final reason why equal opportunity is important. While economic competition between adults is not only inevitable but admirable, there is little more viscerally nasty than the sight of children being forced to compete against each other for future advantage. But this is precisely what is happening in the United States today: Elite jobs go to those with elite higher education; but admissions to elite universities are hyper-competitive; and so children are pitted against each other in an unpleasant but necessary battle to earn a place on the path to prosperity. With every passing year, the competition begins earlier and earlier in life; for elite preschools, parents solicit letters of recommendation on behalf of their *toddlers*.

As William Deresiewicz (2014) puts it,

> wealthy families start buying their children's way into elite colleges almost from the moment they are born: music lessons, sports equipment, foreign travel ('enrichment' programs, to use the all-too-perfect term)—most important, of course, private-school tuition or the costs of living in a place with top-tier public schools.

I am not sure what to say about this state of affairs except that it is morally horrible and inefficient and should be eradicated through equal opportunity.

4.5 Equal Opportunity and the Family

One apparent obstacle to equal opportunity is the family. Plainly, a person's prospects are shaped not only by broad social circumstances and by genetics, but also by the particular family environment in which he is raised. Socioeconomic status aside, it is a huge boon to be raised by loving parents; it is a disadvantage, sometimes an irrecoverable one, to be raised by bad ones.

This is a perennial worry about equal opportunity, best advanced by James Fishkin (1983), who argues that we face a trilemma: We must either give up Formal EO, or we must give up Fair EO, or we must give up the autonomy of the family. We cannot have all three.

Fishkin's argument is in fact unsound, in part because he relies on the mistaken empirical claim that Fair EO can only be established by leveling down advantaged children: "Strategies of leveling up are either so paltry in their efficacy or so utopian in their expense that they cannot be expected to provide a solution to our problem" (p. 66).

In the 30-plus years since Fishkin wrote his book, the efficacy of leveling up policies has been demonstrated. And the charge of utopianism is wrong in light of the efficiency gains associated with Fair EO (§4.8).

But the general worry Fishkin raises persists, and so it is fair to ask: Which leg of the trilemma should we kick out? I answer that we should limit the autonomy of the family. Now, to some this might seem an impossible case to make. Fishkin thinks so:

> It would not be an exaggeration . . . to conclude that the portion of the private sphere of liberty that is least controversial and of greatest importance to most of us is, without doubt, the part singled out by the autonomy of the family. . . . Were this portion of the private sphere of liberty to be sacrificed, the realm of negative liberty remaining would be mutilated virtually beyond recognition.
>
> (pp. 42–3)

Fishkin overstates things. While establishing equal opportunity does reduce the negative liberty of parents, the reduction is modest, and it comes with an enormous expansion of the positive liberty of children. Because equal opportunity is an essential feature of a just state, at some point protecting the negative liberty of parents comes at the expense of justice. That is a trade-off that cannot be avoided.

It is uniformly accepted that parents have a moral obligation to their children. Even philosophers who regard children as mere property (e.g. Narveson (1988)) concede that this is so. It is also accepted that this standard of care includes attention to a child's future ability to flourish. Feinberg (1980), for example, argues that children have a "right to an open future" which limits parental autonomy.

With this obligation in mind, we must attend to a subtle but critically important point: Parents' responsibility is *not* to promote their children's future ability to flourish by the means that they believe to be best. Their responsibility is to *act* in a way that is maximally likely to promote their children's future ability to flourish.

An example will illustrate the difference here. Suppose that Darlene is trying to decide whether or not to have her child vaccinated. Darlene is intelligent, educated, and has a perfectly good will; she is doing the very best she can to make good decisions about her child's health. After her due diligence, Darlene decides that vaccines cause autism, and so she does not have her child vaccinated.

Has Darlene fulfilled her responsibility to promote her child's future ability to flourish? Does it suffice to do one's best to understand vaccine safety and then to act on that understanding? The answer is "no". It is one thing to have a maximally justified belief about vaccine safety—let's stipulate that Darlene has this—but is another thing to *act* in a maximally justified way.

What Darlene must do, to fulfill her responsibility to her child, is step outside of her own reasoning about vaccine safety and engage in a virtual collective decision-making process. For the purposes of determining how she ought to act, Darlene must consider not only what she believes about vaccine safety, but what other people believe as well. And she must (in a technical way which I won't get into here) weight these beliefs in an appropriate way—in proportion to the competence of those that hold them. And the virtual collective decision-making process regarding vaccination is unambiguous: If you want your child to be healthy (which you must, that is your duty), you should vaccinate your child. This is the consensus belief, and the overwhelming consensus of experts; it is the justified action yielded by the process.

Note that the virtual collective decision-making process does not tell Darlene *what to believe* with respect to vaccinating her child, but *how to act* with respect to vaccinating her child. These can come apart. I call this the principle of *epistemic modesty*: When a morally important goal, like a child's future ability to flourish, hangs in the balance, one must act with an eye toward maximizing the probability that that goal is realized, even if that means acting in a way that one believes is wrong.[10]

For some, this will have the appearance of paradox: How can the right thing to do be that which you believe will result in the wrong outcome? In fact, there is no paradox. There is only the appearance of paradox, a result of generally-accepted but false views about the connection between belief and action. In fact, to do the right thing, it is neither necessary nor sufficient that you believe that what you are doing is right.

It is not sufficient because, it if were, then many of history's worst moral monsters would be exonerated. Some Nazis were simply insane, but others honestly believed, using their best judgment, that by killing Jews they were making the world a better place. Of course, that these Nazis acted "in good faith" in this way changes little if anything about the immorality of what they did. They should have known that they were acting wrongly. Their beliefs were badly contradicted by prevailing moral sentiment, by the implicit collective decision-making process that had taken place.

It is also not necessary that one act in accordance with the moral view that one believes to be correct. This was explained above: Darlene might truly believe, and might be justified in light of the evidence that she has, that she will harm her child through vaccination. But that belief does not change how she is morally obliged to act.

In this way, the folk notion that you should "follow your conscience" is deeply flawed. Obeying such a maxim can and often does lead one into moral error.[11]

Epistemic modesty is counterintuitive, and can only be made perspicuous through technical explanation (I refer the interested reader to my Manuscript-A). I'll just mention two things. First, this distinction between justified belief and justified action *cannot* be resolved by the epistemology of disagreement. No matter how Darlene ought to modify her beliefs in light of the beliefs of others, the possibility that she is justified in *acting* in a way contrary to her belief persists.

Second, for the purposes of this book, the technicalities are unimportant. Parents must be circumspect about their own epistemic limitations and act accordingly. Epistemic modesty thus provides a new justification for intervening into family affairs. The government is justified in intervening against parents if they are (1) not meeting the standard of care *simpliciter* (by, e.g. not feeding their children) or (2) not meeting the standard of care owing to violations of epistemic modesty (e.g. by refusing to vaccinate because they think it harmful).

Whatever the good motivations of vaccine-denying parents be, they are acting to fulfill their *own* plans-of-life at the expense of their children's. Whether they appreciate it or not, for these parents it is more important that they get the thing that they want (*viz.* raising a child in the way that they desire) than that their children be healthy.

The state should enforce epistemic modesty by mandating vaccination. If it did, it would reduce parents' negative liberty but it would hugely increase positive liberty: Some children will live rather than die. This is good. "Liberty" is a poor excuse for hurting another to satisfy one's ego.

In a similar way, religious education should probably be proscribed, or at least heavily regulated—to ensure that children born into religious households are not disadvantaged, or, worse, brainwashed. This is already a concern: In New York City, the yeshivas that cater to Orthodox Jews have been criticized for failing to provide rudimentary secular education (writing, arithmetic, etc.) to boys, who spend their days studying the Talmud and the Torah. The fact that some Orthodox parents believe that focused religious study is of prime moral and religious importance is irrelevant. It is fine to make decisions about oneself on these bases, but when the decisions affect another—and especially a child—epistemic modesty must be practiced.

We should also be wary of homeschooling. While doubtless there are parents who homeschool because they correctly judge their local schools to be inadequate, many seek to inculcate their own religious or political views. In doing so, they promote their own plan-of-life, which includes indoctrinating their progeny, at the expense of their children's future.

All of that said, we must be attentive to the ways in which clumsy regulation can do more harm than good. If unrestricted homeschooling better promotes the future abilities of children to flourish than any viable regulatory regime, we should permit unrestricted homeschooling. That is a positive matter, to be sorted out by the relevant experts (§9.1).

A few more points. First, we should not overestimate the effect of the family on economic outcomes. Bruce Sacerdote points out that "while educational attainment and income are frequently the focus of economic studies, these are among the outcomes least affected by differences in family environment" (2007: 120). Sacerdote finds that family environment explains only 11 percent of variance in income.

Second, I suspect that equal opportunity will turn out to be more a matter of satisfying a minimal standard of care rather than establishing strict equality. The goal is not to raise every child under identical circumstances, but to ensure that each is cared for in such a way that, upon reaching adulthood, she can compete against her peers for scarce social goods on a more-or-less level playing field.

In a meritocracy, there would be more government oversight of family matters than is typical today. But there would be no dystopian invigilation. If a parent wants to inculcate in her child an interest in ballet, there is no bar of justice to that. After all, some hobbies are necessary—to ensure that childhood time is not wasted, and to get a sense of what hobbies are and how they can contribute to a life of meaning. It does not violate equal opportunity when a parent chooses a hobby arbitrarily, or, indeed, on the basis of her own preference. That promotes filial bonding.

The moral violation occurs when the child is able to consciously reject the hobby and does so. At that point, it no longer promotes her future flourishing—she will not be practicing ballet as an adult—and it wastes time that might be spent on *bona fide* personal development. There are complications here, but the basic point is intuitive, I think. We can spot when the activities a parent chooses for her child—even if they're not loved by the child—promote that child's development. And we can spot when they are burdens on the child, serving only the parent's own interests.

Third, meritocratic equal opportunity policies work with and not against the incentives of parents. It is increasingly clear from research that inequalities of opportunity arise early on in life—and so public intervention must take place in early childhood.[12] To that end, a meritocratic government might subsidize preschool, or offer it directly as a public good. That would be attractive both to altruistic parents and to those seeking time for work or leisure.

Fourth, there need not be leveling-down in a meritocracy. Brighouse and Swift (2008), for example, suggest abolishing "elite private schools" as a step toward establishing Fair EO (and they feel such an abolition would not violate parental liberty).

While I find these schools distasteful (§4.4), Brighouse and Swift misdiagnose the problem. Especially when it comes to higher education, elite institutions do not provide significantly better human capital development than, say, good public institutions. If your sole interest is getting smarter, you're as well off at UMass as at Harvard. What elite schools provide is an interpersonal advantage in the form of pedigree and personal connections. Put differently, by attending elite schools, one can later extract rents from the economy. In a meritocracy, neither pedigree (a non-existent or poor proxy for merit) nor nepotism may be used as a hiring criterion. In a meritocracy, the advantages that these schools provide are limited to their actual educational superiority. And so Brighouse and Swift's worry about their potential damage to Fair EO is eliminated.

4.6 On the Difference Between Luck Egalitarianism and Desert-Based Justice

That meritocracy differs radically from egalitarianism is, I hope, clear. Among other things, meritocracy does not require equal outcomes or even take them as presumptive; egalitarianism has no conceptual mechanism for rewarding merit for its own sake; and egalitarians typically give little attention to economic efficiency.

Nevertheless, it might be thought that desert-based justice is similar to a variant of egalitarianism which has attracted attention in recent years: namely, luck egalitarianism. Some philosophers seem to think so; Nicholas Barry says that luck egalitarianism is "both an egalitarian and a desert-based theory" (2006: 201). And Arneson describes luck egalitarianism as "a response to conservative critics of the welfare state and egalitarian redistributive policies who assert that they erode personal responsibility, *reward the undeserving*, and *punish the deserving*" (2011: 28, my emphasis). So a few words about how luck egalitarianism and desert-based justice differ are worthwhile.[13]

The central claim of luck egalitarianism, which was first proposed by Ronald Dworkin (1981a, 1981b) is that it is unjust when some people are worse off than others owing to bad luck. This principle has two ambiguous features, and how to interpret these two features constitutes much of the luck egalitarian literature.

First, there is the question of what "worse off" means. This is the question of the currency of justice. Dworkin holds the currency to be resources. Others (e.g. Arneson (1989, 2000)) prefer welfare. Still others (e.g. Cohen (1989)) think that it is both.

Second, it must be said what is meant by "bad luck". All luck egalitarians (save one—Segall (2010)) reject the view that all inequalities arising from bad luck are unjust. After all, Joe might choose to bet some money on the favorite in a football match. And Joe might—unlucky for him—lose. This produces an inequality, but it hardly seems an unjust one. On the other hand, if Joe has the bad luck of being robbed while walking to the bank, making him worse off than his peers, that is more plausibly an unjust inequality, in need of repair. A distinction is thus made between inequalities due to *option luck* (i.e. inequalities due to a person's *choices*, or which he *controlled*), which demand repair, and inequalities due to *brute luck*, which do not.

To see why meritocracy and luck egalitarianism are hopelessly at odds, consider the following scenarios:

(1) Ross has religious views which are unpopular. He is the best-qualified applicant for a job, but, owing to religious prejudice, he does not get it.
(2) Emily is running for political office. Emily's sexual tastes are found distasteful by the electorate. Emily is the best candidate for office but because of her sexual tastes she is defeated.
(3) Sarah is pro-life and an outstanding worker. The company she works for is owned by ardent leftists. Sarah is up for a bonus but does not get it because her company's owners dislike her views on abortion.

In all three scenarios, the meritocrat diagnoses injustice: Jobs ought to go to best-qualified applicants, and income ought to turn on merit.

This diagnosis is unchanged if we stipulate that Ross was fully aware of his community's religious prejudice; Emily knew that the electorate would find her sexual tastes problematic; and Sarah had freely chosen, with full knowledge of her bosses' moral views, to work for her company. According to the meritocrat, that is irrelevant: In (1)-(3), merit is not recognized, and so justice is not done.

In contrast, those conditions render (1)-(3) morally unproblematic in the luck egalitarian's eyes. The inequalities of employment and income therein are not matters of brute bad luck. After all, Ross could have chosen to adopt different religious views; Emily could have chosen to engage in different sexual activities or to have kept her tastes private; Sarah could have chosen to work for pro-lifers rather than pro-choices. All three knew the economic risks when they made the choices that they did.

We have, I think, the sense that injustice remains in (1)-(3), and the luck egalitarian cannot reinterpret the examples to consist of something other than free choice (or control). To say, for example, that we have no choice over our sexual practices is to abrogate the commitment to personal responsibility which is luck egalitarianism's *raison d'être*.

To press the case, suppose that Emily's "problem" is simply that she is a lesbian and the electorate is prejudiced against homosexuals. This is a perfectly plausible scenario, and I presume the luck egalitarian agrees about the existence of injustice here. If that is so, he must identify the relevant source of bad luck. What would this be?

The most obvious contender is Emily's sexual orientation. Just as it's bad luck to be born with serious physical defects (a typical example of bad brute luck which, the luck egalitarian says, requires recompense), it's bad luck to be born homosexual.

That will strike some people as ludicrous. It strikes me that way. And, in any case, isn't it simpler, and more compelling, to say that it's unjust to discriminate on the basis of sexual preference? That is the meritocrat's response. In contrast, the luck egalitarian refocuses the source of injustice to the very person who suffered unjust harm (i.e. to Emily, who had the alleged bad luck of being born a lesbian).

Maybe there are other ways for the luck egalitarian to put it. Maybe Emily's bad luck was being born into the world that she was. But now things are getting tortuous, and that explanation fails to account for cases in which the sexual preference is not inborn but chosen: Suppose Emily has a taste for bondage. I don't see any difference in injustice between discriminating against Emily because she's a lesbian, and discriminating against her because of her taste for bondage. The meritocrat explains why simply: Justice requires that the most meritorious candidate be chosen. Period.

Kasper Lippert-Rasmussen makes precisely this mistake when he attempts to identify the source of unjust inequality in Apartheid-era South Africa:

> In the bad old days of Apartheid most black South Africans were much worse off than most white South Africans. This was so, not because black South Africans were less hard-working than white South Africans or anything of that sort. It was . . . due to the fact that, under Apartheid, South Africans lived in a society in which being born black meant being subjected to all sorts of unjust restrictions. . . . While being born black is not in itself an instance of bad luck, under Apartheid it was an instance thereof.
>
> (2016: 2)

The claim here is that while being black is not necessarily bad luck, it was bad luck for blacks in Apartheid-era South Africa. There are two problems with this claim. First, because one is black owing to one's genes, and having the genes that one does is a matter of metaphysical necessity, it does not make sense to talk about a person's race in terms of luck (see Chapter 7). Second, it seems wrong—some might say offensive—to go to a black South African and say, "Sorry about the injustice you've faced! What bad luck, you happen to be black." No. Luck has nothing to do with it. The injustice is the bigotry.

Finally, I note that desertists' and luck egalitarians' analyses of the currency of justice are quite different. Luck egalitarianism is a fully liberal theory; the individual is the unit of moral measure, and the distribution question turns wholly on what the individual is morally entitled to (welfare, resources, opportunity for welfare, etc.) In contrast, desert-based theories contain a communitarian element.

Imagine a race in which Elaine comes in first and Tori, second. Elaine deserves the gold medal and Tori deserves the silver medal. But suppose Elaine hates gold and loves silver, and her welfare would be improved if she were to get the silver medal and Tori, the gold. Would the desert theorist then say that Elaine ought, morally, to get the silver medal? No. What if the currency of justice were different? What if silver somehow provided Elaine more opportunity for welfare? Or more "capabilities to function" (Sen 1985)? None of that matters. The community has decided that excellence is recognized by gold, not silver. Elaine was the most excellent, she deserves the gold medal, and that is what she ought, morally, to get.

Of course, typically the gold medal redounds to the winner's advantage, as a source of psychic utility if nothing else. But for the desertist, considering how the individual will fare, in light of some proposed distribution, is insufficient. Incentive effects are also relevant. So is symbolizing great achievement. And so on. Insofar as we think that a theory of justice ought to be able to promote communal values like these, we must prefer desert-based justice.

4.7 Desert Is Never Forward-Looking

I have said that desert is, as a matter of conceptual necessity, backwards-looking: If a person deserves something, it's on the basis of who she is or what she has done. (While "who she is" may sound like a contemporaneous claim, the moment of desert must be preceded by the formation of the character that makes the person deserving.)

This was the accepted wisdom for decades, and it largely still is. However, Feldman (1995) and David Schmidtz (2002) argue against it; they believe that desert sometimes can be forward-looking. Although tangential to the main argument of this book, I wish to make a few comments about why they are mistaken.[14]

In support of forward-looking desert, Feldman offers the following example (pp. 70–71): A soldier volunteers for a suicide mission. Before embarking on it, he is feted for his bravery—there is a ceremony, he receives a medal. We may think that he deserves these honors, even though the desert base—which Feldman says is the sacrifice—has not yet occurred. If that is right, then desert is sometimes forward-looking.

To get at the truth of the matter, we must thicken the thought experiment. Consider, first:

(SM1) Master Sergeant Schaefer, a 25-year Army veteran, volunteers for a suicide mission. Schaefer is decorated, widely respected, and renowned for his courage and loyalty. On the helicopter, en route to his final operation, he receives a medal for his upcoming sacrifice. Schaefer deserves that medal.

To be sure. But what if we thicken the thought experiment in a different way?

(SM2) Private Buckwheat, fresh out of boot camp, volunteers for a suicide mission. Despite knowing little about Buckwheat, Army officers sign him up (they're happy to have gotten a volunteer). The mission is scheduled to take place five months later, but Buckwheat is given the medal now. Buckwheat deserves that medal.

This is dubious. There is an intuitive difference between SM1 and SM2. It appears to be epistemological: We know that MSG Schaefer deserves the medal, but we do not know this of PVT Buckwheat.

Also, it appears that the relevant knowledge is not, *pace* Feldman, whether the sacrifice will in fact be made; it is whether Schaefer and Buckwheat are *disposed* to make the sacrifice. Suppose that, against all odds, Schaefer emerges from the mission unharmed. Do we believe that we committed an injustice when we awarded him the medal? Do we believe now that he didn't deserve it after all, because he did not in fact sacrifice? No. This is because the medal served to recognize laudable facts about Schaefer's character, like his loyalty and courage.

Feldman is aware of this argumentative line. He considers it a "desperate manoeuvre", giving the following putative counterexample (p. 71): Two sick children are in the hospital. Both have suffered equally, but doctors are confident that one will recover while the other will die. The Make-a-Wish Foundation is able to grant a wish to only one of them. It is plain, Feldman says, that the terminal child deserves that benefit, and that he deserves it on the basis of what will happen to him in the future.

I agree with Feldman that the terminal child deserves to have his wish fulfilled. But this is not a case of forward-looking desert, because the child's unhappy future is not the desert basis.

Instead, this is an archetypical case of moral desert. The desert subjects are the two children. The desert object is the welfare that wish fulfillment provides (observe that we would not insist that the terminal child deserves his wish if we knew that it would reduce his welfare). The desert basis is something like virtue, and by design of the thought experiment, the two innocent children do not differ in this way (if we knew the terminal child to be evil and violent, we would no longer regard him as deserving). And proportional equality (§1.2) tells us that when two desert subjects possess a desert basis in equal measure, they deserve equal desert objects.

But this is impossible; one child is terminal. We can, however, get closer to moral parity—do a better job of giving the children what they deserve—by granting the terminal child's wish. It is not that he deserves this on the basis of future suffering. Instead, our knowledge of that suffering helps us maintain the moral balance.

Claims about forward-looking desert rest on mistakes related to the epistemology of the cases under consideration. This is true for Schmidtz's view, as well. He asserts that "a person who receives opportunity X at t_1 can be deserving at t_1 in virtue of what she will do if given the chance" (2002: 781), and gives the following example:

> Two students receive scholarships. One [June] works hard and gets excellent grades. The other [Madison] parties her way through her first year before finally being expelled for cheating. Does their conduct tell us *nothing* about which was more deserving of a scholarship?
>
> (p. 779)

Of course it does. Admissions committees want to give their scarce scholarships to diligent, intelligent, and honest high schoolers. But committees cannot precisely determine who has these qualities from the scanty information an application provides. Mistakes get made. It is not that Madison's moment of desert gets undone by her subsequent indolence and plagiarism; rather, those things illuminate unhappy features of her character, and demonstrate that she never deserved the scholarship in the first place.

Suppose, for example, that, at the moment of award, the committee *knew* that June's and Madison's merits were equal and awarded them the scholarships. Subsequently, Madison undergoes a change of personality and starts ignoring her studies and cheating on tests. Would we say that Madison did not deserve her initial scholarship as a result of this change? I do not think so. We would say that Madison does not deserve to have her scholarship renewed, but justice was done when it was awarded to her the first time around.

Now, Schmidtz thinks that no explanation of this kind will work:

> Can we defend the convention . . . [that] the students' conduct is relevant only because it reveals what they were like before receiving the award? It would appear not. When we look back at the expelled student's disgraceful first year, our reason for saying she did not deserve her award has nothing to do with speculation about what she did in high school. We may agree that both students were equally qualified for scholarships qua *reward*.
>
> (p. 779)

This misunderstands the nature of the desert object. A scholarship is not a reward—or, at least, it is much more than that. A scholarship is also an object that looks to future achievement. And one can deserve on the basis of traits that support future achievement—*but those traits must already exist*. That is the requirement of backwards-looking desert.

To illustrate, imagine a third applicant, who had an unambiguously better record than either June or Madison, but who, tragically, suffered brain damage after graduating from high school. We do not think that that applicant deserved a scholarship, no matter his record. This is because merely recognizing high school achievement is not what scholarships are for.

Similarly, Schmidtz wonders what we would say were we to discover that June and Madison were "equally unqualified . . . chosen via clerical error" (p. 779). In his view, June, given her subsequent performance, deserved the scholarship. Madison did not.

I do not agree. We are certainly pleased that June turned out as she did, but this does not make her retroactively deserving. Suppose Tyler, who lost out on the scholarship owing to the error, confronts us about our choice. It would be odd to respond to him in this way: "Tyler, had we not made a mistake, we would have known that you deserved the scholarship and given it to you. But we gave it to June, and in fact she ended up deserving it, because she made good use of it." I find that confusing.

A more plausible response is this: "Tyler, you deserved that scholarship. We thought that June did, but we made a mistake. You were the better applicant. Maybe you would have done better in college than June, maybe not. All we can do is take solace in the fact that June didn't squander her undeserved opportunity." That sounds right.

I should say that Schmidtz's purpose in proposing forward-looking desert is to justify the moral relevance of "natural and positional advantages" (p. 786). As discussed, since Rawls, philosophers have typically assumed that these advantages undermine the possibility of desert. Thus, anyone who wants to admit desert as a moral principle, which a pluralist like Schmidtz does (see his 2006), must explain how the two are compatible. Schmidtz's "promissory desert" provides a way: We can "come to deserve" our advantages on the basis of what we do with them.

As I have argued, that is wrong. But I do agree with Schmidtz that (1) the existence of *some* advantages do not undermine the possibility of desert, and (2) demonstrating why this is so is a necessary task for the desert theorist.

Schmidtz and I disagree in the following two ways: First, I believe that "positional advantages" (e.g. receiving a large inheritance) do indeed undermine desert; Schmidtz does not. Second, I recover desert by grounding desert-claims in the metaphysics of personal identity (Chapter 7) and requiring equal opportunity (§4.3); Schmidtz appeals to promissory desert.

4.8 The Justice/Efficiency "Trade-Off", Part 1

It is sometimes thought that there is an inevitable tension between justice and efficiency; that improvements in one must come at the cost of the other. For some, this is a truism of public economics.

Taxation provides the classic example: If we construe "justice" as utility maximization, as economists almost always do, or about equality, as philosophers often do, then we must keep Okun's leaky bucket (§2.3) in mind: Any redistribution in the name of justice reduces the surplus owing to the deadweight loss of taxation. Each step we take toward justice is a step away from an efficient economy.

In fact, there need not be a trade-off between these two moral goals. Some public policies are efficiency-enhancing, and if one's preferred theory of justice calls for these, then we may satisfy the moral demands of justice and of efficiency at the same time.

Here and in two subsequent sections (§5.11 and §6.11) I explain how meritocracy's principal features—equal opportunity, merit-based hiring, and income-responsive-to-merit—are efficiency-enhancing. Thus, I give more careful attention to efficiency than either Rawls or Nozick. And this is necessary for metatheoretical reasons (§2.3).

Public policy is not discussed in detail by Rawls, and so the efficiency losses associated with his theory (and everyone agrees there will be loss) were and largely still are unknown. As for Nozick, the public policies (lack thereof, really) are clear enough, but the results are opaque. Waking up in the nightwatchman state would be to wake up in Cockaigne or present-day Somalia—I'm not sure which.

Meritocracy does not suffer from this defect. We have good evidence—microeconomic and macroeconomic, theoretical and empirical—that its public policies are efficient. In this section, I discuss the equal opportunity component of the theory, and explain in particular why publicly-funded education provides economic gains. There are three reasons.

First, education improves workers' human capital, and thereby their productivity—and, as Paul Krugman reminds us, "productivity isn't everything, but in the long run it is almost everything. A country's ability to improve its standard of living over time depends almost entirely on its ability to raise its output per worker." (1994: 11). Further, human capital improvement has a spill-over effect: When we educate a worker, W, he becomes more productive—and so do W's peers, through their subsequent interactions with W.[15]

Second, education enables a wider range of jobs, making it easier for a person to find work and recover from layoffs. This, in turn, reduces his incentive to engage in criminality and other forms of socially damaging behavior. (Education may also cultivate a moral disquietude toward crime.) Lochner and Moretti (2004) estimate that a 1 percent increase in the high school graduation rate for men saves $1.4 billion in social costs (property loss, incarceration expenses, etc.) These certainly must be taken into account when considering the "cost" of education.[16]

Third, education cultivates a respect for the truth, rational decision-making, and a reliance on evidence over emotion—in short, all those traits that we educators hope to instill in our students. I know of no way to even begin to estimate the positive externalities associated with these virtues, but they might be enormous.

Public education also solves various forms of market failure. One example involves an imperfection in credit markets: We should like for parents to be able to finance their children's education by borrowing against their children's future earnings, which get increased by education. But this is not generally possible, not least because the relevant contract cannot be enforced: The child did not sign the contract—his parents did.

Glenn Loury (1981) gives a model in which parents divide their incomes between consumption and providing education to their children. Owing to decreasing marginal returns to education, it is in everyone's interest for rich parents to transfer some of their income to poor parents so that it can be invested in education. But this cannot be done privately for the reasons given above. Loury shows that redistribution, in the name of universal public education, can leave *all* parties, including the taxed rich, better off.

Fernández and Rogerson (1997, 1998) present a model of this class and calibrate it using data from the United States They estimate that moving from purely private education to a public system would produce a welfare gain equivalent to 3 percent of national income (over $500 billion today).

Bénabou summarizes the lesson of these models in this way: "The long-run gains from redistributing resources (either directly or through income transfers) toward educational investment by poor families or communities could be quite large, amounting to several percentage points of GDP" (2000a: 328-9).[17]

Macroeconomic work also suggests that public investment in education is efficiency-enhancing. One approach, pioneered by Mankiw, Romer, and Weil (1992), examines cross-country economic data to determine the relationship between education and economic growth.

Robert Barro (1991) finds that a 1 percent increase in primary (secondary) school enrollment is associated with 2.5 percent (3.1 percent) increase in the per capita GDP growth rate. Murphy, Shleifer, and Vishny (1991) obtain a similar result for primary school enrollment—a 2.2 percent increase in the growth rate. And Levine and Renelt (1992) obtain a similar result for secondary school enrollment—a 2.5-3.7 percent increase.[18]

I note that a new focus on educational investment would be in keeping with American tradition. The United States was the first nation to provide secondary education to all young citizens (although African-American children did not initially share in this good). This was a surprisingly recent innovation, ushered in by Progressives at the beginning of the twentieth century. Until then, high school had largely been limited to the children of the wealthy. In 1900, 10 percent of children attended high school; 50 years later, after massive public investment, 76 percent did.[19] Educational attainment continued to rise until roughly 1980. Since then, it has stagnated. Some economists believe that this explains, in part,

America's historical prosperity and recent economic challenges; as Goldin and Katz (2008) put it,

> that the twentieth century was both the American Century *and* the Human Capital Century is no historical accident. Economic growth in the more modern period requires educated workers, managers, entrepreneurs, and citizens. . . . Because the American people were the most educated in the world, they were in the best position to invent, be entrepreneurial, and produce goods and services using advanced technologies.
>
> (pp. 1–2)

I want to mention, in conclusion, that it would be hugely inefficient (not to mention impossible) to try to *perfectly* implement any principle of justice—and that includes equal opportunity. No one is suggesting that. What we ought to concern ourselves with is the impact that viable, justice-mandated public policies have on our economy. For some theories of justice (e.g. strict egalitarianism), the associated public policies are known to be hugely inefficient. For others (e.g. luck egalitarianism), the necessary policies are unclear. In contrast, the public policies, like equal opportunity, that meritocracy calls for are straightforward, and known to be efficient.

Notes

1 Pojman (1997) and Rachels (1978) think so.
2 This rejection of the responsibility principle, given by Cupit (1996a, 1996b) and Feldman (1995), has come under attack by Smilansky (1996a, 1996b), who thinks that alternate forms of the principle can handle these counterexamples.
3 Interested readers may see Hurka (2003) for further discussion.
4 <www.merriam-webster.com/dictionary/merit?utm_campaign=sd&utm_medium=serp&utm_source=jsonld>, retrieved 3 August 2017.
5 The metaphor may have first been used by Lyndon Johnson, in a 4 June 1965 address at Howard University: "Imagine a hundred-yard dash in which one of the two runners has his legs shackled together. He has progressed ten yards, while the unshackled runner has gone fifty yards. At that point the judges decide that the race is unfair. How do they rectify the situation? Do they merely remove the shackles and allow the race to proceed? Then they could say that 'equal opportunity' now prevailed. But one of the runners would still be forty yards ahead of the other. Would it not be the better part of justice to allow the previously shackled runner to make up the forty-yard gap, or to start the race all over again?"
6 See, e.g. Arneson (2015) and Daniels (1978).
7 See also Weinzierl (2016).
8 What I call "ability", Roemer calls "effort"—confusing, given that diligence (i.e. what we typically think of as "effort") is only one part of what we intuitively believe should affect economic outcomes.
9 There is no obviously right way to compare ability across types, given that, generally, each type will see a different distribution of it. Roemer suggests that

we equalize quantiles across types; e.g. those in the top 1 percent of ability in type *A* should have the same economic outcomes as those in the top 1 percent of ability in type *B*, etc.

10 I discuss epistemic modesty in my 2015, Manuscript-A, and Manuscript-B.

11 On the moral irrelevance of conscience, see Foot (2002); Schueler (2007); and Wilcox (1968).

12 See, e.g. Cunha et al. (2006); Heckman (2013); and Heckman and Krueger (2003).

13 I limit the exposition I give here for reasons of space. Huub Brouwer and I have a paper which analyzes the differences in detail (Brouwer and Mulligan Manuscript).

14 See also Celello (2009) for a reply to Feldman and Schmidtz.

15 See, e.g. Moretti (2004) and Rauch (1993).

16 There are other possible social returns to education which I exclude for reasons of space. For example, the more education a woman receives, the less she smokes and the more attentive she is to prenatal care—to the benefit of her child (Currie and Moretti 2003).

17 See also Bénabou (2000b, 2002); Gradstein and Justman (1997); and Saint-Paul and Verdier (1993).

18 Some caution is in order: There is uncertainty about the size of the effect; there are unexplained differences between the returns on education for men and for women; and some evidence suggests that quality of education, rather than quantity, is the real driver of economic growth. See Sianesi and Van Reenen (2003) for a discussion of these issues, and of the econometrics involved.

19 See the National Center for Education Statistics' *Digest of Education Statistics*, at <https://nces.ed.gov/programs/digest/d15/>, retrieved 6 August 2017.

4.9 References

Anderson, E. S. 1999. What is the point of equality? *Ethics* 109: 287–337.

Arneson, R. J. 1989. Equality and equal opportunity for welfare. *Philosophical Studies* 56: 77–93.

———. 1999. Against Rawlsian equality of opportunity. *Philosophical Studies* 93: 77–112.

———. 2000. Welfare should be the currency of justice. *Canadian Journal of Philosophy* 30: 497–524.

———. 2011. Luck egalitarianism—a primer. In *Responsibility and Distributive Justice*, eds. C. Knight and Z. Stemplowska, 24–50. Oxford: Oxford University Press.

———. 2015. Equality of opportunity. In *The Stanford Encyclopedia of Philosophy (Summer 2015 Edition)*, ed. E. N. Zalta. URL = <https://plato.stanford.edu/archives/sum2015/entries/equal-opportunity/>, retrieved 19 August 2017.

Barro, R. J. 1991. Economic growth in a cross section of countries. *Quarterly Journal of Economics* 106: 407–43.

Barry, N. 2006. Defending luck egalitarianism. *Journal of Applied Philosophy* 23: 89–107.

Bénabou, R. 2000a. Meritocracy, redistribution, and the size of the pie. In *Meritocracy and Economic Inequality*, eds. K. Arrow, S. Bowles, and S. Durlauf, 317–39. Princeton: Princeton University Press.

———. 2000b. Unequal societies: Income distribution and the social contract. *American Economic Review* 90: 96–129.

————. 2002. Tax and education policy in a heterogeneous-agent economy: What levels of redistribution maximize growth and efficiency? *Econometrica* 70: 481–517.

Betts, J. R. and Roemer, J. E. 2007. Equalizing opportunity for racial and socio-economic groups in the United States through educational-finance reform. In *Schools and the Equal Opportunity Problem*, eds. L. Woessmann and P. E. Peterson, 209–37. Cambridge: MIT Press.

Brighouse, H. and Swift, A. 2008. Putting educational equality in its place. *Educational Policy and Finance* 3: 444–66.

Brouwer, H. and Mulligan, T. Manuscript. An argument for desert and against luck egalitarianism.

Celello, P. 2009. Against desert as a forward-looking concept. *Journal of Applied Philosophy* 26: 144–59.

Cohen, G. A. 1989. On the currency of egalitarian justice. *Ethics* 99: 906–44.

Cunha, F., Heckman, J. J., Lochner, L., and Masterov, D. V. 2006. Interpreting the evidence on life cycle skill formation. In *The Handbook of Economics of Education*, Volume 1, eds. E. Hanushek and F. Welch, 697–812. Amsterdam: Elsevier.

Cupit, G. 1996a. Desert and responsibility. *Canadian Journal of Philosophy* 26: 83–99.

————. 1996b. *Justice as Fittingness*. Oxford: Clarendon Press.

Currie, J. and Moretti, E. 2003. Mother's education and the intergenerational transmission of human capital: Evidence from college openings. *Quarterly Journal of Economics* 118: 1495–532.

Daniels, N. 1978. Merit and meritocracy. *Philosophy & Public Affairs* 7: 206–23.

Deresiewicz, W. 2014. Don't send your kid to the Ivy League: The nation's top colleges are turning our kids into zombies. *New Republic*. URL = <https://newrepublic.com/article/118747/ivy-league-schools-are-overrated-send-your-kids-elsewhere>, retrieved 4 August 2017.

Dworkin, R. 1981a. What is equality? Part 1: Equality of welfare. *Philosophy & Public Affairs* 10: 185–246.

————. 1981b. What is equality? Part 2: Equality of resources. *Philosophy & Public Affairs* 10: 283–345.

Feinberg, J. 1963. Justice and personal desert. In *NOMOS VI: Justice*, eds. C. J. Friedrich and J. W. Chapman, 69–97. New York: Atherton.

————. 1980. The child's right to an open future. In *Whose Child? Children's Rights, Parental Authority, and State Power*, eds. W. Aiken and H. LaFollette, 124–53. Totowa, NJ: Littlefield, Adams, and Co.

Feldman, F. 1995. Desert: Reconsideration of some received wisdom. *Mind* 104: 63–77.

Fernández, R. and Rogerson, R. 1997. Education finance reform: A dynamic perspective. *Journal of Policy Analysis and Management* 16: 67–84.

————. 1998. Public education and income distribution: A dynamic quantitative evaluation of education-finance reform. *American Economic Review* 88: 813–33.

Fishkin, J. S. 1983. *Justice, Equal Opportunity, and the Family*. New Haven: Yale University Press.

Foot, P. 2002. Moral relativism. In *Moral Dilemmas: And Other Topics in Moral Philosophy*, ed. P. Foot, 20–36. New York: Oxford University Press.

Galston, W. A. 1980. *Justice and the Human Good.* Chicago: University of Chicago Press.

Goldin, C. and Katz, L. F. 2008. *The Race between Education and Technology.* Cambridge: Harvard University Press.

Goya-Tocchetto, D., Echols, M., and Wright, J. 2016. The lottery of life and moral desert: An empirical investigation. *Philosophical Psychology* 29: 1112–27.

Gradstein, M. and Justman, M. 1997. Democratic choice of an education system: Implications for growth and income distribution. *Journal of Economic Growth* 2: 169–83.

Heckman, J. J. 2013. *Giving Kids a Fair Chance: A Strategy That Works.* Cambridge: MIT Press.

Heckman, J. J. and Krueger, A. B. 2003. *Inequality in America: What Role for Human Capital Policies?* Cambridge: MIT Press.

Hospers, J. 1961. *Human Conduct: An Introduction to the Problems of Ethics.* New York: Harcourt, Brace & World.

Hurka, T. 2003. Desert: Individualistic and holistic. In *Desert and Justice*, ed. S. Olsaretti, 45–68. New York: Oxford University Press.

Jackson, C. K., Johnson, R. C., and Persico, C. 2016. The effects of school spending on educational and economic outcomes: Evidence from school finance reforms. *Quarterly Journal of Economics* 131: 157–218.

Kagan, S. 2012. *The Geometry of Desert.* New York: Oxford University Press.

Kleinig, J. 1971. The concept of desert. *American Philosophical Quarterly* 8: 71–8.

Krugman, P. 1994. *The Age of Diminished Expectations: U.S. Economic Policy in the 1990s.* 3rd ed. Cambridge: MIT Press.

Levine, R. and Renelt, D. 1992. A sensitivity analysis of cross-country growth regressions. *American Economic Review* 82: 942–63.

Lippert-Rasmussen, K. 2016. *Luck Egalitarianism.* London: Bloomsbury.

Lochner, L. and Moretti, E. 2004. The effect of education on crime: Evidence from prison inmates, arrests, and self-reports. *American Economic Review* 94: 155–89.

Loury, G. C. 1981. Intergenerational transfers and the distribution of earnings. *Econometrica* 49: 843–67.

Mankiw, N. G., Romer, D., and Weil, D. N. 1992. A contribution to the empirics of economic growth. *Quarterly Journal of Economics* 107: 407–37.

McLeod, O. 1999. Contemporary interpretations of desert. In *What Do We Deserve? A Reader on Justice and Desert*, eds. L. P. Pojman and O. McLeod, 61–9. New York: Oxford University Press.

Moretti, E. 2004. Workers' education, spillovers, and productivity: Evidence from plant-level production functions. *American Economic Review* 94: 656–90.

Mulligan, T. 2015. *The Just and Meritocratic State*, doctoral dissertation.

———. Manuscript-A. Epistemic modesty and political participation.

———. Manuscript-B. Social choice or collective decision-making: What is politics all about?

Murphy, K. M., Shleifer, A., and Vishny, R. W. 1991. The allocation of talent: Implications for growth. *Quarterly Journal of Economics* 106: 503–30.

Narveson, J. 1988. *The Libertarian Idea.* Philadelphia: Temple University Press.

Olsaretti, S. 2004. *Liberty, Desert and the Market: A Philosophical Study.* Cambridge: Cambridge University Press.

Pojman, L. 1997. Equality and desert. *Philosophy* 72: 549–70.

Rachels, J. 1978. What people deserve. In *Justice and Economic Distribution*, eds. J. Arthur and W. Shaw, 167–96. Englewood Cliffs, NJ: Prentice-Hall.

Rauch, J. E. 1993. Productivity gains from geographic concentration of human capital: Evidence from the cities. *Journal of Urban Economics* 34: 380–400.

Roemer, J. E. 1998. *Equality of Opportunity*. Cambridge: Harvard University Press.

———. 2003. Defending equality of opportunity. *Monist* 86: 261–82.

Sacerdote, B. 2007. How large are the effects from changes in family environment? A study of Korean American adoptees. *Quarterly Journal of Economics* 122: 119–57.

Saint-Paul, G. and Verdier, T. 1993. Education, democracy and growth. *Journal of Development Economics* 42: 399–407.

Schaar, J. H. 1967. Equality of opportunity, and beyond. In *NOMOS IX: Equality*, eds. J. R. Pennock and J. W. Chapman, 228–49. New York: Atherton.

Schmidtz, D. 2002. How to deserve. *Political Theory* 30: 774–99.

———. 2006. *Elements of Justice*. New York: Cambridge University Press.

Schueler, G. F. 2007. Is it possible to follow one's conscience? *American Philosophical Quarterly* 44: 51–60.

Segall, S. 2010. *Health, Luck, and Justice*. Princeton, NJ: Princeton University Press.

Sen, A. 1985. Well-being, agency and freedom: The Dewey Lectures 1984. *Journal of Philosophy* 82: 169–221.

Sher, G. 1987. *Desert*. Princeton: Princeton University Press.

Sianesi, B. and Van Reenen, J. 2003. The returns to education: Macroeconomics. *Journal of Economic Surveys* 17: 157–200.

Smilansky, S. 1996a. The connection between responsibility and desert: The crucial distinction. *Mind* 105: 485–6.

———. 1996b. Responsibility and desert: Defending the connection. *Mind* 105: 156–63.

Weinzierl, M. Forthcoming. Popular acceptance of inequality due to brute luck and support for classical benefit-based taxation. *Journal of Public Economics*.

Wilcox, J. T. 1968. Is it always right to do what you think is right? *Journal of Value Inquiry* 2: 95–107.

Wolff, J. 1998. Fairness, respect, and the egalitarian ethos. *Philosophy & Public Affairs* 27: 97–122.

5 On the Distribution of Jobs

5.1 Meritocratic Hiring: Whetting the Intuition

None of the prevailing theories of distributive justice demands, categorically, that the best-qualified applicant be hired. The utilitarian requires this only if it maximizes the general welfare. But it is conceptually possible and sometimes true in practice that the general welfare is served by hiring a less-qualified applicant on the basis of an irrelevant feature, like race (§5.9). A similar claim may be made against Rawls (see Arneson 1999).

Libertarians, on the other hand, reject any constraints on how firm owners or their agents ought to behave when hiring. If owners/agents wish to hire a less-qualified person because he is a relative, or a friend, or a member of their preferred race, according to the libertarian there is nothing unjust about that.[1]

We should reject merely instrumental arguments for meritocratic hiring. Justice demands that the best-qualified applicant be hired as an intrinsic matter. She deserves the job.

To bring out the intuition, let's consider a context which will be familiar to many readers: academic hiring. This context is beset by claims of injustice: Women claim that since a CV is regarded more highly when it has a male name on it than a female name, women face an unjust hurdle.[2] Men claim that, owing to strong pressure on committees to hire women, male candidates must have much stronger CVs than their female peers to be competitive for the very same job.[3] Graduates of "unpedigreed" institutions wonder why, despite publications in top journals, they are passed over in favor of Ivy Leaguers who have produced nothing.[4]

Set aside the question of whether these claims are true or not to note that *none of them* is an objection to merit-based hiring. In fact, it's just the opposite: All of these claims are objections to the justness of the job market made *on the grounds of merit*. The female candidate says that she's the better philosopher but is denied the job owing to implicit bias; the male candidate says that, despite being more meritorious, he loses out because of affirmative action; and the unpedigreed candidate argues (correctly—see, e.g. Burris 2004) that the publication record, not pedigree, is a better proxy for merit.

Indeed, there is an inevitability to accepting merit as our distributive criterion. My friends on the left typically respond to my call for meritocratic hiring like this: "Tom, don't you know that minority applicants are at a disadvantage, since hiring committees don't prize the unique qualities that they possess?" Perhaps so. But what if we repaired that distortion? What if committees had a better definition of "merit"? They continue: "There would still be problems of implicit bias—committees unconsciously regard minority applicants as inferior to white applicants." Fine, but what if that distortion were repaired as well? What if we continued in that vein? What will ultimately satisfy us? The answer, it is agreed all around, is merit.

Consider another real-world example. In 2003, firefighters in New Haven, Connecticut took a civil service examination for promotion to Captain and Lieutenant. Ten white firefighters were found eligible for promotion to Lieutenant. Seven white firefighters and two Hispanic firefighters were found eligible for promotion to Captain. No African-American firefighters were found eligible. The City of New Haven refused to certify the exam results as a result. The white and Hispanic firefighters sued, and, after appeal, the Supreme Court ruled in their favor (*Ricci v. DeStefano*).

Let us analyze the case from the meritocratic point-of-view. To begin with, the white and Hispanic firefighters have a plausible moral objection to the city's action. We can imagine being one of those firefighters, having studied hard and competed in a fair examination in pursuit of promotion. Yet after coming out on top, we are told that the job is not ours after all—*because of our race*. A very natural reaction would be to throw up our hands at the injustice of it and ask: What does *race* have to do with anything? What else could I have done?

However, the existence of injustice is predicated on several things. First, was "merit" properly defined? If the exam was all that mattered for promotion (it wasn't), and, as things turned out, the winners were all rookies who happened to be expert test-takers, then our intuitions shift—perhaps the result is not just after all. But we do not dispute that merit is what counts; we only think that "merit" was misdefined.

Second, perhaps the test was not fair. If we find out that the exam's essays were graded by white supremacists, then the "losers" are perfectly reasonable in their complaints. Why? Because they might in fact have been the more meritorious candidates, and their scores did not reflect their merit.

Indeed, although the question facing the courts was a legal, not a moral, one, supporters of the city's decision frequently relied on merit-based arguments: "Other firefighters spoke against certifying the test results. They described the test questions as outdated or not relevant to firefighting practices" (*Ricci v. DeStefano*, 557 U.S. 557 (2009), pp. 7–8).

Even in these highly controversial cases involving race, there is something deeply compelling about recognizing a person's merit. Again, this is typical: One finds that "anti-meritocratic" arguments are really arguments *for* merit. The objectors want merit to be recognized; they just think that the extant process fails to do this.

Let us push things. Suppose that the African-American firefighters were in fact less meritorious, and that this was because they had been saddled with extra duties while white firefighters had time to study. Then the intuition shifts: An injustice has been done. We now know why. The white firefighters, despite being more meritorious, do not deserve their promotions. Equal opportunity was violated.

Finally, suppose that all of the firefighters had an equal opportunity to compete for the positions, and suppose that the white and Latino candidates did, indeed, win on the basis of their merit. Then they deserve those positions. One might still think that the city of New Haven has a legitimate worry. We can imagine the mayor saying something like this: "We simply can't have a state-of-affairs in which a minority group which has faced discrimination and which continues to contend with serious social challenges is unrepresented in the civil service leadership. Maybe it is unjust for me to take a few jobs from more qualified white applicants and give them to less qualified African-American applicants. But I don't have a choice. I have practical consequences to consider in making these judgments."

Regardless of whether one is swayed by such an argument—I am not—meritocratic theory explains how it gets made. To wit, one concedes that justice demands that the white and Hispanic applicants be hired, but then claims that there are overriding consequentialist considerations.

This view of the supremacy of merit is supported by empirical research. Although controversial from a legal point-of-view, affirmative action programs "designed to increase the number of black and minority students on college campuses" enjoy strong support with the public. (Republicans are almost evenly split in response to this question.)[5]

However, if polling questions make clear that these programs will violate meritocratic standards—that is, that they will provide an advantage to less-qualified black or female applicants (rather than just, say, encouraging blacks or women to apply in the first place)—things change. When put in this way, these programs are overwhelmingly rejected—by Democrats, Independents, and Republicans.[6]

5.2 Why Should We Hire on the Basis of Merit?

In this section, I want to explore the core conceptual justification for the idea that the most meritorious candidate deserves the job. Later on

(§§5.5–5.8), I will advance other justifications for merit-based hiring: that it is a fair social framework; that it minimizes resentment in the labor market; that it provides second chances to people; and that it best satisfies fiduciary duties.

One might wonder how those justifications differ from the one given in this section. This is connected to an objection which has occasionally been leveled against desert itself (by, e.g. Lamont (1994)): Namely, that on its own, desert has no moral content; it is only a rhetorical tool, laid upon more fundamental moral notions.[7] Thus, (the argument would go), what we should concern ourselves with is creating a fair social framework, minimizing resentment, etc. Then, to say that people ought to get what they deserve is just to say that they ought to get what is required by the fair social framework, that which minimizes resentment, etc. There is no deeper sense of desert.

This is a mistake. The way to look at the admirable features of meritocracy that I describe in §§5.5–5.8 is—in keeping with general justificatory structure of this book—as *grounds to believe* that the theory is correct. Just as it would be odd, *a priori*, if the true theory of justice were a disaster from the point-of-view of efficiency, it would be odd if just hiring were widely regarded as unfair. Meritocracy avoids this fate.

So that is the strategy. One still wishes to have an answer to the question, "What's so special about merit?" Here I shall critically survey three answers which have been given and add two of my own.

First, the power of merit is sometimes put in terms of "appraising attitudes". The act of awarding the gold medal to the fastest runner is a kind of universal expression of an attitude we all feel—namely, admiration. And we express that attitude and others (gratitude, respect), when we award goods, including jobs, on the basis of merit. This view has an estimable history, going back to Smith (1759).[8] Indeed, some philosophers think these attitudes essential to the concept of desert; as Miller puts it, "if we did not adopt these attitudes towards one another, we would not and could not use the concept of desert" (1976: 89).

I find that view problematic. Imagine a society in which prevailing attitudes are reversed: Skill is shunned, stupidity is applauded; Justin Bieber is considered a virtuoso and Beethoven a rank amateur. One thing you might say about such a world is that, there, the inept and the stupid, and Justin Bieber, are deserving. That is a consequence I am unwilling to accept.[9]

Second, there is Aristotle's argument (§1.2) for a natural fit between desert objects and merit. Michael Sandel argues along these lines: "Suppose a Stradivarius violin is for up sale [*sic*], and a wealthy collector outbids Itzhak Perlman for it. The collector wants to display the violin in his living room. Wouldn't we regard this as something of a loss, perhaps even an injustice—not because we think the auction is unfair, but because the outcome is unfitting?" (2009: 189).

It does seem that there is injustice here which goes beyond the fact that the world will be deprived of good music if the collector gets the violin rather than Perlman, but I'm not sure how widely shared the natural fit intuition is.[10]

More promising is, third, the argument given by Sher (1987) (who finds the natural fit idea lacking), explaining the moral importance of merit-based hiring by its connection to autonomous action:

> When we hire by merit, we abstract from all facts about the applicants except their ability to perform well at the relevant tasks. . . . We treat them as agents whose purposeful acts can make a difference in the world. . . . Selecting by merit is a way of taking seriously the potential agency of both the successful and the unsuccessful applicants.
>
> (p. 121)

The argument goes like this: A person is constituted by his traits and the choices he has made. Thus, when he sets his sights on a job and prepares himself to do that job, he is, in a very real sense, changing his identity. If he is not judged on his merits then that autonomy is violated—he has lost control over the development of his life and, indeed, his identity.

I believe that is correct. The interested reader can consult Sher's book for the detailed argument. Here I want to suggest two other possible grounds for merit-based hiring.

Let us consider criminal desert for a moment. What has happened when a person in the criminal context gets what he deserves? Two things, certainly. First, he has been convicted and punished for what *he* has done—not what someone else has done. This, recall, is the aboutness principle (§4.1): A person cannot deserve punishment on the basis of another's crimes.

Second, the punishment must fit the crime. It is unjust to hang someone who jaywalked, and this is true no matter the consequences of that crime (imagine it caused a fatal car accident).

It *always* seems unjust to punish an innocent person, even in those cases in which it seems morally necessary. Consider H.J. McCloskey's famous example:

> Suppose that a sheriff were faced with the choice either of framing a Negro for a rape that had aroused hostility to the Negroes (a particular Negro generally being believed to be guilty but whom the sheriff knows not to be guilty)—and thus preventing serious anti-Negro riots which would probably lead to some loss of life and increased hatred of each other by whites and Negroes—or of hunting for the guilty person and thereby allowing the anti-Negro riots to occur. . . . In such a case the sheriff, if he were an extreme utilitarian, would appear to be committed to framing the Negro.
>
> (1957: 468–69)

Excepting hard-core Kantians, there comes a point for all of us at which utilitarian considerations control: If the consequences of failing to punish the innocent man are severe enough (imagine millions will die, somehow), we accede, morally, to the punishment. But we *never* view that as a just action. (A similar point was made in §2.2.)

The situation is analogous with distributive justice. Suppose we hire a less-qualified person in order to achieve some consequence (e.g. diversity). When we do this, we sever the aboutness connection: No longer is the basis for awarding the job, in its entirety, the applicant's character. This alone negates desert. Just as the innocent man cannot deserve punishment on the basis of another's crimes, no applicant can deserve a job on the basis of other people's performance (which, the argument goes, gets enhanced by diversity).

Similarly, when we select a person based on facts about him but which are unrelated to the job, we sever the fitness connection. It is unjust to hang someone because he jaywalked, no matter how wicked he be; and it is unjust to give a person a job when he is not the most meritorious applicant, no matter his other virtues.

If these considerations are correct, then the concept of desert—and, in particular, the aboutness and fitness principles—itself contains the grounding for distributing jobs on the basis of merit. And it does no good for the skeptic to try to push matters, asking *why* aboutness and fit are relevant. This is akin to asking why it is unjust to punish a person on the basis on another's crimes. There is no "why". This simply *is* our concept of justice and desert.

A final idea: While Sher's argument for merit-based hiring may be interpreted as an appeal to the dignity of the potential recipients of jobs, it may also be that the *conferrers* of jobs find *their* dignity undermined when they deviate from merit-based hiring. It speaks well of a person when he recognizes that Beethoven is more meritorious than Bieber and acts accordingly, selecting the former for admission to the conservatory. And by advancing a system under which the distribution of scarce goods, like university slots, depends only on relevant facts about individuals' character, a person supports his own future potential to be treated with dignity.

5.3 How Do We Hire on the Basis of Merit?

I propose the following distributive rule:

> (Meritocratic Hiring Principle) When hiring, it is unjust to discriminate against an applicant on grounds irrelevant from the point-of-view of merit.

I shall elucidate this principle, which is the second of the three core features of meritocracy (equal opportunity being the first), over the course of this chapter. It may be understood easily enough. Its call for a strict focus on merit is simply a generalization of what we know to be true in specific cases. We know that it is unjust to deny an African-American man an office because of his race. We know that it is unjust to pass a woman over for a Nobel Prize on account of her gender and to give it to a less deserving man instead. Those are salient and obvious cases of injustice, but they are salient and obvious for contingent, historical reasons; not because race and gender have a special moral status. The world could have gone such that, say, brunettes faced prejudice that precluded their being judged on their merits. Or people with bushy eyebrows. Or whatever. What all these cases have in common is irrelevance from the point-of-view of merit.

But what, exactly, do we mean by "merit"? Here there is no single answer, since merit is clearly a contextual concept. What constitutes merit in a baseball player is quite different than what constitutes merit in a physicist. And even within those contexts, more fine-grained definitions may be found: What makes a third baseman meritorious is quite different from what makes a pitcher meritorious.

Nevertheless, once a context is fixed, it is usually plain what constitutes merit. Once a team decides it wants a third baseman, there is no dispute over what traits it should look for: quick reflexes and a powerful arm; hitting ability; discipline; an understanding of the game; and a first-rate work ethic.

Work ethic is almost always the most important element of merit.

Of course, there will be lively dispute about how these various elements of merit should be weighed. Notice that the meritocratic hiring principle does not constrain that debate. It is not unjust, although it might be quite stupid, for the team to make its decision purely on the basis of fielding prowess. That way of discriminating between prospects complies with the meritocratic hiring principle.

There will be other disputes: over, for example, the epistemic relevance of past performance and the use of proxies, like 60-m dash time. But these are not debates over the definition of merit; these are debates over whether some prospect is in fact meritorious.

Still, we need a *practical* way to define merit. In particular, compliance with the meritocratic hiring principle requires knowing which features of a person are *irrelevant* from the point-of-view of merit—so that we do not use them. I suggest the following heuristic: In a given hiring context, no applicant should be judged on the basis of a characteristic C if it is the case that a reasonable person, familiar with the hiring context, regards C as irrelevant from the point-of-view of merit. Put differently, hiring committees should only appeal to characteristics which *all* reasonable authorities believe are relevant from the point-of-view of merit.

So, when hiring a new faculty member, a physics department may consider their applicants' intelligence, pedagogical skill, creativity, etc.—for all reasonable people who are familiar with physics research and teaching agree that these are relevant traits. But skin color, sexual preference, hobbies, appearance, political views, religious beliefs, and the like will fail to enjoy universal acclaim—and so they must be ignored.

This is a stringent rule. Some *bona fide* elements of merit are likely to be excluded. But history tells us that broadness in assessing merit, not narrowness, is typically our sin—and so that is what we must guard against.

Once upon a time in the United States (and still, in some parts of the world) a homosexual applicant would have been denied a job owing to his sexual preference. And arguments were given for the relevance of sexual preference to merit. Some of these arguments would have been beyond the pale, even then ("God punishes those who employ sodomites"). But others would have won acclaim from some reasonable people ("homosexuality is a mental illness, and we do not want unstable people around students"). (*N.B.* homosexuality was not removed from the *Diagnostic and Statistical Manual of Mental Disorders* until 1987.) Of course, these arguments are now, rightly, regarded as unsound. And they would have been ruled out in the past, had committees obeyed the meritocratic hiring principle.

What guidance might the meritocratic hiring principle provide us now? Let us consider contemporary examples involving sexual behavior. Suppose a firm is hiring, and has a *prima facie* best-qualified applicant whom it also knows: (1) enjoys bondage, or (2) is a former pornographic actor, or (3) has sex with kangaroos? Can any of that behavior, all of it weird and some of it arguably immoral, be held against the applicant?

No. The fact that behavior is weird carries no weight whatsoever. And when the moral dimensions of behavior are unclear, as they are here, we should be *very* skeptical that they speak to a person's merits.

For (1) and (2), this is clear. I happen to think there's nothing immoral about either of these behaviors. A reasonable person might; but that judgment is inadmissible, as some reasonable people disagree. Facts (1) and (2) cannot justly be regarded as demerits.

Now, (3) is tougher because the case for immorality is stronger. (To avoid complications, assume the behavior is legal.) Nevertheless, I think we should remain committed to meritocratic hiring. That a person was convicted of theft is a good reason to believe that he lacks moral character. But we should not adduce sexual behavior as a demerit if doing so requires telling a complicated story that relies on propositions (about, e.g. the moral status of animals) of debatable truth.

One wonders how far such a principle should go. Should a former pornographer, open about her penchant for bondage, *really* be hired as a schoolteacher, to be put in front of innocent and impressionable children?

The answer is yes—if she is meritorious. That is the one and only thing that matters from the point-of-view of justice.

Now there will come a slew of objections: People with these sexual tastes are more likely to abuse children; no one with such a background

could possibly be a good role model; the aspiring teacher will try to inculcate promiscuity in the children; etc.

The rejoinder is simple: These are positive claims, and rationality
requires that we believe positive claims only with sufficient evidence. The
objector bears the burden of showing that these considerations are in fact
true. *Obviously* no one wants a teacher who is abusive or promotes promiscuity; *obviously* we want a teacher to be a good role model. No one
disputes this. These are hugely important elements of merit. But treating
people justly means not drawing unreasonable inferences about them on
the basis of shoddy empirical claims.

Indeed, hiring schoolteachers who have, shall we say, a checkered
past might be good in itself, as it would help children develop a respect
for merit. We should like each young person to grow up confident that
the personal choices she makes will not damage her ability to shape her
life as she sees fit. Scenarios like these make us queasy precisely *because*
we do not live in a meritocracy. When the world is a more just place,
a schoolteacher's pornographic past will no more disturb us than her
stamp-collecting hobby.

5.4 Conceptual Complexities

I turn to the task of tidying up conceptual loose ends. To begin with,
it should be clear that our justification for hiring the best-qualified is
backwards-looking. Indeed, it must be, if it is to be a true desert principle
(§4.7). It has the happy side-effect of being efficient (§5.11), but that is
only a side-effect.

This is not a trivial point, since one sometimes finds arguments for
"meritocratic" distributive schemes that are forward-looking. Norman
Daniels (1978), for example, endorses a "Productive Job Assignment
Principle" in which the "most qualified" applicant is the one who will
maximize overall productivity. This may require denying jobs to best-
qualified applicants in a particular case:

> Jack and Jill both want jobs A and B and each much prefers A to B.
> Jill can do either A or B better than Jack. But the situation S in which
> Jill performs B and Jack A is more productive than Jack doing B
> and Jill A (S'), even when we include the effects on productivity of
> Jill's lesser satisfaction. The PJAP selects S, not S', because it is attuned
> to macroproductivity, not microproductivity, considerations.
>
> (p. 210)

This is a consequentialist justification; as Daniels admits, it is not responsive to desert. While the meritocratic theory of justice I endorse would be
better from the point-of-view of efficiency than the status quo, it is not
optimally efficient.

Next, let us consider some remarks by Feinberg, who denies what I have argued to be true—namely, that desert "represents uniquely the claim of justice" (1963: 90). Feinberg adduces the following example:

> [Consider a] contest between two leading candidates for the master-ship of a Cambridge college. Candidate *A* is, on the whole, more fit for the function (considered simply as a function). He is a better administrator, a tireless worker, a clever money-raiser, and has a cooler head. . . . Candidate *B* is a rather older man, past his peak in all respects, but on the basis of his previous scholarly achievement much more distinguished than *A* and also better liked.
>
> (p. 89)

Feinberg views this as a case of desert against desert on the grounds that the mastership can be regarded as either (1) a prize (in which case it would go to *A*) or (2) a reward (in which case it would go to *B*). If that were so, then both men deserve the job, and so (this seems to be the logic) we need another principle of justice to adjudicate between them—desert cannot not do so.

But this is not a case of desert versus desert; it is a case of desert basis versus desert basis. The fact that *B* is better-liked and more scholarly are decisive for determining *B*'s deserts in some contexts (e.g. the awarding of emeritus status), but *A* seems to be more meritorious here, and that carries the day. Jobs are not rewards, nor are they prizes. They have a unique ontological status and they must be filled on the basis of merit. We need not look outside of desert to answer these questions of justice.

That said, we can conjure up a scenario under which *B* has a non-merit desert basis that is just so powerful that it overcomes *A*'s merit. Suppose *B* is a biologist who has discovered a cure for a worldwide pandemic, saving millions of lives. In this case, perhaps *B*, despite being a tiny bit less meritorious than *A*—*qua* college master—deserves the job. I'll concede that (§4.2). But even in these absurd cases matters cannot be pushed far: If *B* would be a *significantly worse* college master than *A*, then nothing *B* had done, no matter how noble, could render him deserving of the job.

There is, however, one good reason why we should not be too quick to dismiss non-merit desert bases. This is the possibility that, for some jobs, gradations in excellence do not exist. For some jobs, many applicants may be equally meritorious.[11] When that is so, we *should* appeal to a non-merit desert basis to decide who ought to get the job.

Suppose, by way of illustration, that we work for the postal service and must hire a new mailman. Candidate *A* is a high school graduate who spent the summer volunteering in a soup kitchen. Candidate *B* graduated alongside *A*, but spent his summer lounging on the beach. When it comes to the job, they are equally meritorious (each can sort mail with equal efficiency, each can deliver it at the same pace, etc.) We are simply unable to discriminate between them on the basis of merit. Therefore, we turn to a non-merit desert basis as a tie-breaker, and hire *A* because of his charity work. He deserves the job more than *B* does.

Finally, although I have put things in terms of "hiring" to this point, the principle applies more broadly—to, for example, graduate school admissions. It is morally wrong to choose applicant *A* over better-qualified applicant *B* because *A* is white and *B* is black. It is morally wrong to choose *C*, who is transgender, over better-qualified *D* in the name of diversity. And so on.

College admissions is the trickiest case, as evidenced by the hot public debate and litigation over affirmative action. It is interesting that even as we are divided over this issue, most of us both (1) support special consideration for and extra resources to black high schoolers, and (2) oppose any affirmative action at the graduate school level. Why the asymmetry?

Meritocratic theory explains things. High school is plainly part of an equal opportunity framework, and graduate school is plainly not. Because the mean black child is disadvantaged relative to the mean white child, providing extra consideration to black children levels the playing field. That is required by justice (§4.3). And because we are talking about children and not adults, Formal EO is inapplicable.

In contrast, when it comes to graduate school, we are talking about adults in competition for a resource (*viz.* graduate education) which is plainly not part of equal opportunity. And so violations of meritocratic "hiring" here disturb our sense of justice and violate it theoretically.

College admissions is difficult because it lies at the middle ground. Are 20-year-olds children or adults? Is a college education necessary for a citizen to be able to develop a plan-of-life for herself and then embark upon it, or not? That is, is it part of equal opportunity?

These are contingent questions, and so what justice demands of us in practice in this respect depends on facts about how our economy is operating. The more having a college degree is a *de facto* requirement for being competitive in the labor market—as increasingly seems to be the case—the more we may be able to support violations of Formal EO in college admissions. I'll discuss affirmative action more in §9.2, but my own view is that, if this positive analysis is correct, the government should simply treat college education like it should treat high school education: with robust public investment providing quality schooling to all, regardless of family circumstances.

5.5   Meritocracy Is a Fair Social Framework

I have not talked about "fairness" to avoid complicating things. As best I can tell, justice and fairness are one and the same thing conceptually.

But I do wish, here, to put a few things in terms of fairness, by which I shall mean the *sentiment* expressed by a people toward the distributive system it lives under. It is important that we *feel* that the process by which jobs and other social goods get assigned is right/just/fair—however you want to put it—if only, as I have said (§2.3), because this indicates that our distributive choices were wise.

We begin with the premise that jobs are central to people's plans-of-life. While not universally true, it is very nearly so—especially now, in the aftermath of women's liberation. One's career, and the various jobs which comprise it, are central to one's identity.

The problem is, of course, that jobs are scarce—and so one person's ability to fulfill his plan-of-life comes at the cost of another's. This is recognized all-around, and is a source of sadness in the world. Although we may never be able to give all people all the jobs that they want, we can, now, provide a fair competitive framework. This is what meritocracy does.

Citizens in a meritocracy consider which jobs are necessary to pursue meaning in the world as they see it. They assess the costs, risks, and trade-offs involved. They come to an understanding of what they must do to achieve the things that they want. And they develop their plans-of-life accordingly, as *they* desire. And then they achieve these plans-of-life, or they do not, on the basis of their merit.

This fair structure does not exist in other competitive frameworks. When Rose, the most meritorious applicant for an academic job (in philosophy, say), loses out to Billy because of cronyism, racial discrimination, pedigree, or another factor irrelevant from the point-of-view of merit, this is bad. It is bad because it is unjust. It is bad because the university is getting an inferior academic (§5.8). But it is also bad because the costs that Rose incurred and the trade-offs that she made earlier in her career, which contributed to her merit now, went for naught.

In making herself a meritorious philosopher, Rose gave up many things: rewarding experiences, to include, perhaps, romantic relationships; travel; hobbies; and more. She gave these things up willingly, because what was important to her was becoming the best philosopher that she could be. And she *has* become the best philosopher, but yet now finds her plan-of-life frustrated by a person—Billy—who did not have to make these sacrifices. Billy thus "double dips" socially, enjoying the benefits of (1) the job and (2) the experiences that should have been sacrificed for (1) (and which Rose did sacrifice).

Of course, there are no guarantees: Rose might have inaccurately reckoned what it would take to achieve her goal. She might have worked too little or invested too much. But at least in those cases the responsibility falls on Rose alone. Any society that takes personal responsibility seriously, which meritocracy does (§6.9), must have this as a feature of the competitive framework. When distributive decisions are made strictly on the basis of merit, a person's ability to receive these distributions is limited only by her willingness and her ability to make herself meritorious in the appropriate way. And when a person has confidence that distributive decisions will in fact be made meritocratically, she can accurately assess the risks and trade-offs involved, and plan her life accordingly.

This is important because, as Sher puts it, "choosing among options in light of their consequences is just what living a life *is*" (2017: 90).[12] Autonomy requires that those consequences in fact obtain. If the competitive framework functions as it currently does—with nepotism, race, physical appearance, and countless other non-merit factors playing a role in hiring, depending on owners' tastes—then autonomy is undermined by the protean nature of distributive decisions. In a meritocracy, there is no ambiguity: Merit, and only merit, is what counts.

Compare meritocracy with egalitarian and libertarian approaches. Egalitarians are happy to violate any stable norm of hiring in order to, for example, produce a workforce with a particular gender or racial makeup. Under such a system, fairness and personal responsibility are violated in two ways. First, a person can control her destiny only to the extent to which doing so does not interfere with the moment's social planning. Rose may form a plan-of-life that includes holding some job, and she may make the investments and sacrifices necessary to excel in that job; but she may not get it if, at the moment of distribution, Rose does not possess the characteristics, irrelevant from the point-of-view of merit, that the social planner deems important. Second, an unmeritorious applicant, who has failed to responsibly prepare himself to discharge the duties of the job, may nonetheless get it—if that serves demographic goals.

Libertarianism also violates personal responsibility, as I will argue at length in §6.9. Our contemporary economy is replete with examples: intelligent and industrious young people unable to find jobs because they lack family influence; our cultural emphasis on pedigree and networking; and the exorbitant salaries paid to "supermanagers", whose compensation vastly exceeds their performance.

Now, it is true that non-meritocratic societies can provide a framework within which citizens can rationally develop and pursue plans-of-life. In a society ruled by cronyism, for example, a citizen who wants some job knows how he can pursue it: flatter the right people and make the right connections. This cronyistic framework might be "fair" in the limited sense that everyone is judged along a single measure (*viz.* the ability to curry favor), which is known to all. But note an important difference between these systems and meritocracy: Only in a meritocracy is a person's ability to fulfill his plan-of-life *in his own hands*. If Tony lives in Cronyville, he can set a goal for himself and then pursue it in the prevailing, cronyistic way. But at the end of the day, *other people* are going to make the decision about whether Tony reaches his goal or not. In a meritocracy, Tony makes that decision for himself, by doing what is necessary to get the things that he wants.

Later on (§6.5) I shall address this issue at length, but I'll just note here that a meritocracy would not put most jobs off-limits to most people, or segregate society into classes based on IQ, or produce any other dystopian results. To be sure, some people are born smarter than others; some people have a natural diligence while others must consciously apply themselves; some are charming, others shy. We all have our strengths and our weaknesses. But if we begin our adult lives having enjoyed Fair EO, then nearly all of us can, with sufficient effort, obtain most jobs.

It is true, of course, that for any given citizen there are jobs that, even in a meritocracy, are unavailable to him. I could not have been a basketball player, or a fashion model, or a jockey—no matter how hard I had tried. Maybe most people cannot be university professors. So what? That is not grounds for moral worry; a society in which citizens have a reasonable range of jobs available to them suffices. As Sher puts it, "it is merely perverse for someone to remain deeply upset over his inability to become a professional athlete when he is perfectly capable of making a successful career in education or business" (1987: 32).

Indeed, an economy in which every citizen had a substantive shot to serve in every job would be nightmarish: People who lacked hand-eye coordination could fly passenger jets; those who suffered from palsy could become neurosurgeons; and so on. Put aside the huge efficiency losses associated with such an economy—it institutionalizes a nasty form of individualism, where the needs of the community are totally subordinated to the egos of citizens. Better to have a society in which each citizen makes an honest reckoning of her strengths and weaknesses, eliminates some potential professions accordingly, finds a job for which she is well-suited, and enjoys a satisfying career while making a contribution to our collective economic life.

There is nothing desirable about a framework that provides jobs to people who are unsuited to them. Such a framework unjustly harms the plan-of-life of another (*viz.* the most meritorious applicant), and is absurd from an efficiency standpoint. And I think we all know this to be true. We do not think it unjust that our distributive system bars those with Down syndrome from becoming commercial airline pilots.

Moreover, we do not treat the severely disabled with dignity when we push them into roles which they cannot satisfy given their more limited merits. Dignity is not a result of obtaining the "best" job that one can; it comes from having a job to do and doing it well. When we see someone with Down syndrome bagging groceries, we do not say: "What a horrible injustice, that he must bag groceries." My response, at least, is just the opposite. I think it is laudable. We have a man who is making a contribution to our collective economic life. That is more than can be said for many able-bodied men. He is making some money on his own and enjoying a degree of independence. He is finding real meaning in the face of extraordinary challenge. To denigrate the economic structure that enables such a life is to denigrate the life itself.

5.6 Meritocracy Minimizes Resentment

So long as there is scarcity there will be sadness. By definition, some people's desires will go unfulfilled. And there may be other lamentable emotions, too: envy of those who have more and pity for those with less. But there need not be resentment—and in a meritocracy there will not be.

Resentment is morally-laden anger. It arises "in response to a certain *kind* of threat: that is, an unjustified, intentional injury, harm, or insult to oneself, or those with whom one identifies closely" (MacLachlan 2010: 425). In this way, while resentment is an unpleasant emotion, it is also an eminently *reasonable* one.

Some philosophers, like Jeffrie Murphy, even exalt resentment on the grounds that it provides the motivation for combatting injustice:

> What are the values defended by resentment . . . ? I would suggest three: self-respect, self-defense, and respect for the moral order. . . . Just as indignation or guilt over the mistreatment of others stands as emotional testimony that we care about them and their rights, so does resentment stand as emotional testimony that we care about ourselves and our rights.
>
> (2003: 19)

I think that is basically correct, and it suggests that while we should not try to eliminate resentment, exactly, we should welcome a social order that does that as a side-effect. That would be evidence that an important moral sensor—our capacity to feel resentment—is picking up on less and less injustice in the world.

Meritocratic hiring minimizes resentment. When we lose out on a job to another on meritocratic grounds, our capacity to sympathize with the successful candidate is undiminished; we bear her no ill-will. We put ourselves in her shoes, understand that we competed on equal terms for the position, and accept that she is simply better equipped to do the job than we are. We recognize that she is the more deserving applicant and that the communities to which the office has a fiduciary duty (§5.8) benefit more from her selection.

Meritocracy fosters social cohesion through competitive processes that do not generate resentment. Indeed, there can be dignity in loss—so long as it comes after a competition, on a level playing field, against a more meritorious peer. How many Olympic silver medalists have felt resentment towards the winners? I would wager very few.

Other hiring norms *do* generate resentment. If Smith is on the academic job market, and he knows that he is the most meritorious applicant for a job, but he does not get it owing to his race, or his gender, or the advantage of an insider candidate, or his lack of pedigree, etc., then Smith does feel resentful—as he should.

Anti-meritocratic hiring also generates resentment among *winners*. The knowledge that one has obtained a benefit despite not deserving it on the basis of merit undermines one's ability to enjoy the thing. One cannot take pride in an "achievement" that reflects no credit to oneself, and that came at the cost of another.

Indeed, this is precisely what happens with affirmative action programs that violate meritocratic standards (§9.2): They reduce self-confidence and increase anxiety among those who *benefit* from them. These are generally blacks or women, but the same result holds when the beneficiaries are a socially dominant group, like white men (e.g. if they enjoy preference for nursing jobs). (See, e.g. Leslie, Mayer, and Kravitz 2014.)

Resentment undermines social cohesion and, if widespread enough, threatens the distributive system itself. Each one of us participates in shared economic life in order to enjoy a level of welfare unattainable on our own, in the state of nature. Even when we advance incompatible interests we are bound by this common tie. And as reasonable beings we can accept that distributive decisions may not work out in our favor every time; we recognize these shortcomings as inevitable parts of a system which is, in the large, in our interest.

A resentful person does not feel this way. He regards the system as illegitimate. He no longer views himself as working cooperatively with good-willed peers; his peers are now his enemies, and the system is their tool of violence again him.

Every distributive system has winners and losers, and each of us will be both of these from time to time. But a distributive system need not have resentful losers (nor resentful winners, for that matter). If we are to work together, sharing in the benefits and the burdens of economic life, we need a distributive system whose decisions we can respect even when they don't go our way. Meritocracy provides this.

5.7 On the Importance of Second Chances

A person's plan-of-life may be disrupted as easily from within as from without. All of us make mistakes, and some of these do us professional injury. Some errors in judgment put our very careers in jeopardy—as is the case when a person commits a serious crime.

I think that we should like to live under a distributive system that recognizes this plain fact: that any of us might, at any time, err, and that even the most upright among us avoids this fate only by dint of fortune, at least in part. A just distributive system will, therefore, allow people to recover from their missteps. Meritocracy provides this to the maximum (non-ideal) extent possible.

This is for two reasons. First, meritocracy minimizes the use of proxies when determining merit (§5.9). A person's criminal history is relevant in hiring only to the extent to which it is a useful proxy for merit, which is far less than its actual use suggests.

Second, the meritocratic hiring principle prevents hiring committees from denying jobs to best-qualified applicants on grounds of taste. Consider a case in which a job applicant has a criminal history which, it is agreed all around, is of no relevance to the desired position. Example: A man who committed a victimless crime—drug possession or solicitation of a prostitute, say—applies for a job as a salesman.

Suppose, despite being the most meritorious applicant for the job, the hiring committee rejects him owing to his criminal past. According to the meritocrat, this denial is unjust, to be proscribed by law.

This call to hire the best-qualified former criminal is not obvious. To be sure, some justifications for rejecting the call are implausible on their face: "People who commit crimes are inherently evil, and should be shunned." But an employer may have a sensible, taste-based objection: "Whether it's reasonable or not, our other workers will be made uncomfortable by having a criminal in their midst; if we employ this man, their productivity will suffer."

To the meritocrat, neither of these justifications holds water. Whether this hire will cause owners, workers, or customers discomfort is irrelevant. The effect of the hire on the firm's bottom line is irrelevant.

One might object by claiming that past criminality *always* serves an informational function—since an important feature of any job is compliance with the law. Past criminality suggests that this element of merit is lacking.

But this objection should not sway us. One reason is pragmatic; as I noted in §5.3, we should be cautious about accepting tortuous justifications like these. Almost always they are used as cover for anti-meritocratic bias.

Additionally, plausible arguments might be given *in favor* of criminal history: A willingness to commit a (non-violent) crime suggests confidence, maybe; or an ability to connect with customers whom law-abiders cannot reach; or a certain worldly wisdom. The possible arguments here are endless. And I think they are all ultimately bad ones, just like the argument for using criminal history as a demerit. If you are involved in hiring, rely only on those features of a candidate that are plainly relevant from the point-of-view of merit. If you do that, then you will have done what justice requires.

This is not to say that there is no professional cost to criminality. There is the loss of human capital which one suffers (generally as a result of prison time), and meritocracy poses no objection to that loss. (A meritocrat might, of course, object to unreasonable sentences on grounds independent of economic justice.)

What is unjust on the meritocratic approach are the so-called "collateral consequences" of conviction that impinge on the distributive sphere.

Jones committed a crime, suffered criminal and civil sanctions as a result, and thereby society and his victims were made whole. While incarcerated, he was unable to invest in his plan-of-life: He was unable to pursue education, develop skills, gain work experience, and so on. It is not unjust that his plan-of-life was stunted in this way. But since, *ex hypothesi*, criminal justice was meted out, there is no residual of injustice which the distributive system must address. Therefore, it is an injustice to deny Jones a job now if he is the best-qualified applicant.

5.8 Fulfilling Fiduciary Duties

One interesting feature of hiring is that those making hiring decisions often have moral duties to third parties. HR departments are the agents of company directors, and they must hire with stockholders' interests in mind. University search committees must choose new professors with an eye towards their students, who have a reasonable expectation of competent teaching. And so on. I'll call these *fiduciary duties of hiring*, although I do not mean this in the strong sense of "fiduciary": Search committees do not act entirely on the behalf of students, but they are accountable, to a degree, to them.

The major lesson of this chapter is that we act unjustly when we discriminate on grounds irrelevant from the point-of-view of merit. The injustice is done primarily to the meritorious applicant who deserved the job, although we also treat the less meritorious applicant, who got the job, unjustly—and perhaps ourselves as well. Here I point out that violations of meritocratic hiring often do an injustice to another party: namely, the community that would have benefited from the selection of the more meritorious applicant.

Shareholders of the widget factory will receive the greatest return if their HR department hires the best widget maker; not the most attractive one, nor the whitest, nor the person with whom it has a personal connection. In the academic context, insofar as teaching is a component of the job (i.e. insofar as there *is* a fiduciary duty to students which must be discharged in this particular hire), students will learn the most from a meritorious teacher. And so on. This is all obvious (although complicated, marginally, by the problem of taste discrimination—§5.9).

Michael Walzer has commented on this idea, in fact arguing *against* desert-based hiring on grounds of fiduciary duties (note that Walzer's concern is "offices", which are a subset of jobs as I construe them). Walzer says that

> an office . . . cannot be deserved because it belongs to the people who are served by it, and they or their agents are free (within limits . . .) to make any choice they please. Search committees are unlike juries in that their members look forward as well as back: they make

predictions about the candidate's future performances, and they also express preferences about how the office should be filled.

(1983: 136)

A few things to say about this. First, there is an ambiguity present. Saying that an office "belongs" to those whom it serves suggests a libertarian ownership relation. But in most hiring contexts, that is too strong. Consider a teaching college that has a new tenure-track line: This office serves students at the college, but it does not "belong" to them in any strong sense of ownership. The correct relationship is the weaker fiduciary one I described.

Second, the meritocrat agrees with Walzer that search committees have latitude in determining how merit will be defined (§5.3). This is especially true for senior positions, in which hiring is less about filling an operational need and more about shaping policy. It is perfectly legitimate for the fellows of a college to decide that they want their new master to focus on fundraising rather than research, and thus to consider fundraising skill as an element of merit.

The meritocrat's point is that committees do not have *carte blanche* here. Their discretion is less than Walzer suggests. Committees must comport themselves in accordance with the meritocratic hiring principle. The owners of a bank may not rely on facts about applicants' "racial purity"; voters may not incorporate race into their candidate selections; a medical practice hiring a new doctor may not take into account her bra size. And so on.

In addition, Walzer's concern about the need to "look forward" in hiring does not imperil desert-based theories grounded in merit (see also Miller 1992). Merit both looks backwards to determine who deserves the job, and forwards—by putting superior performers into positions of responsibility, so that their performance can redound to the benefit of the community.

5.9 Just and Unjust Discrimination

I consider three complications to meritocratic hiring. I begin with the problem of *taste discrimination*, first explored by Gary Becker (1957). Becker observed that a rational firm will pay less to equally qualified black employees (e.g.), and perhaps not hire them at all, if there is some disamenity value to their employment. While the people actually doing the hiring may not be racists, there is racial animus *somewhere* which results in discrimination against blacks.

For example, if some of the firm's employees are racist, then the firm's managers may rationally prefer a less-qualified white applicant to a more-qualified black applicant: Having blacks in the firm induces a productivity loss in the racist employees. Or, if customers are racist, then they may patronize the firm less when it hires blacks, decreasing revenue. Accordingly, these prejudices get reflected in the labor market, in hiring and wages.

The meritocratic response to this form of discrimination is clear. Considerations of taste cannot justify race-based discrimination. The firm's bottom line must be subordinated to the demands of justice, which include hiring the better-qualified black applicant (and paying him commensurate with his skill). This is especially unproblematic when one remembers that those who will suffer from the "inefficiency" of hiring blacks are precisely those who act unjustly in the first place: customers (who must contend with the higher prices their racism produces) and firm employees (whose jobs are put at risk because their firm is less profitable).

It is true that some non-racists may be harmed as well (e.g. the firm's non-racist employees). This is an unfortunate side-effect, but it is not sufficiently important to impugn the meritocratic hiring principle. An analogy would be a firm that knowingly sells a harmful product, gets caught, and goes out of business as a result. Not all the firm's employees were complicit, and it is unfortunate that those employees must suffer, but that doesn't change things: The firm should be eliminated.

Now, taste discrimination is unsustainable in competitive markets (non-racist firms hire labor at lower cost and push the racist firms out of the market). More serious is the problem of *statistical discrimination*.[13] This is the use of facts about the distribution of ability within a group, like a racial group, to assess the ability of a particular applicant who belongs to that group.[14]

A rational firm hires the applicant with the highest expected productivity. Applicants send signals of their productivity (in the form of CVs, interviews, letters of reference, etc.) to firms. But these signals are noisy. When there is noise, knowledge of the distribution of ability within the group (both the mean and the variance) will be used by a rational firm to judge the applicant's expected productivity.

The critical point about statistical discrimination is that there is no racial animus, anywhere: The firm is doing its level best to determine who the best-qualified applicant is. Moreover, statistical discrimination is *unavoidable* in real-world hiring contexts. Every feature of an applicant's CV is really just a proxy for what the firm actually cares about, which is productivity in one form or another. Past performance is hugely correlated with future success but is no guarantee; prizes are suggestive of merit, but only suggestive; letters of reference are useful but imperfect. To ask a firm to not rely on proxies is to ask that it give up the goal of merit-based hiring—which it cannot justly do.

What should our rules be for using proxies? First, in those cases in which they are unnecessary, we should not use them. Suppose that we are judging a bodybuilding competition. We all agree that Serge is aesthetically superior to Lou. We then see that Serge trains at Elite Gym and that

Lou trains at Superelite Gym. We also all agree that bodybuilders from Superelite Gym are, on average, aesthetically superior to bodybuilders from Elite Gym. It is obvious that that fact ought to play no role in our decision about who should get the trophy. And this irrelevance has nothing to do with the value of the proxy: The proxy is accurate, telling us something meaningful—that Lou belongs to a class which is, on average, more meritorious than the class to which Serge belongs. But in this case there is simply no need to resort to a proxy; it would be unjust to do so.

When it comes to more common hiring contexts, in which proxies cannot be avoided, we must take care to (1) prefer more accurate proxies to less accurate proxies, and (2) weight our proxies appropriately. This might seem obvious, but in fact these rules are violated all the time in the real world. Academic hiring provides a perfect example: Not only is pedigree granted more weight than is warranted by its proxy value, it is often used as a litmus test to categorically exclude applicants who do not possess it. As Val Burris puts it,

> the evidence on academic hiring . . . shows that the most prestigious departments hire almost exclusively from the graduates of similarly prestigious departments to an extent that exceeds anything that can be explained by the meritocratic application of universalistic standards regarding past or potential scholarly productivity.
>
> (2004: 244)

This is because

> there is little evidence of any independent effect of the prestige of one's PhD-granting department upon productivity, either at the predoctoral stage or later in the academic career. The strongest predictors of postdoctoral productivity are predoctoral productivity (publications and/or citations) and how quickly candidates complete the doctorate.
>
> (p. 241)[15]

It is unclear, the extent to which reliance on pedigree is a form of cronyism (which Burris suspects), rather than a good-faith misuse of a proxy. I imagine it is a bit of both. But we have a responsibility to combat it either way: a responsibility to meritorious and unpedigreed applicants, who are not given what they deserve; to the communities to whom we have fiduciary responsibilities, which are being subjected to inferior research and teaching; and to our own intellectual culture—which is being degraded by an elitism unconnected to merit.

Next, there is the question of whether family-owned business may violate the meritocratic hiring principle on grounds of familial loyalty. They might do this either by explicitly choosing a less-qualified family member out of the pool of applicants, or by failing to advertise the job, thus making the family member the most meritorious by default.

To answer this question, we must first distinguish between family-owned businesses like Walmart (51 percent of which is owned by the Walton family), and family-owned businesses like the little hardware store on the corner. The case for an exception to the meritocratic hiring principle is stronger for businesses of the latter type. This is because they have more in common with hobbies than economic enterprises; they are less obviously part of our collective economic life. The all-important profit motive is sometimes missing; families may even maintain unprofitable businesses if they have the external means to do so. Family-owned businesses regard their customers, whom they may know personally, as more than merely sources of revenue. And family-owned businesses often operate informally, without standard practices or business plans.

Imagine a man who to decides to open a music store, Guitararama, in his retirement. He wants to play music with his friends, support local musicians, and, perhaps, make a little money on the side. He needs an employee, and so he hires his brother. Has he acted unjustly?

It seems to me that he has not. His store is best regarded as a hobby. The man is not making employment decisions with an eye toward profits. He cares little for market supply, demand, or pricing. He has few customers. He provides little tax revenue. None of these considerations is dispositive, but they are suggestive.

Suppose Guitararama grows. New locations open, hundreds of employees are hired, there are lawyers and accountants, and the chain becomes an important part of the local economy. Now the meritocratic hiring principle applies. If the man hires a less-qualified family member, then he acts unjustly.

Of course it will be asked: Where is the precise cut-off? The answer is that there is no precise cut-off. Like so many concepts (how much hair must a man lose before he is *bald*?), this one is vague. We tend to know these things when we see them.

Note also that as firms get bigger and bigger, fiduciary duties (§5.8) become stronger and stronger. When Guitararama is a single store, deviations from merit-based hiring have little effect on stakeholders; when it is a large chain this is no longer true.

It is important to note that just because a person acts unjustly in hiring, by showing preference to a family member or a friend, that does not mean that he is deeply morally blameworthy. A comparison may be useful. Imagine you have a brother, whom you love, and who you know has committed a serious crime. He comes to you to ask your help in concealing his crime from the police. You do this; you do not turn him in, you help him dispose of evidence.

The intuition is that you have not done anything too morally blameworthy. I think this is correct. Indeed, your loyalty may even be admirable. But we would not say that what you are doing is *just*. No: Your brother committed a crime, he hurt another person, and he deserves to be punished. Your actions, however noble they be, come at the expense of justice.

The same is true when it comes to hiring. Loyalty to family and friends is to be expected. This means, positively, that perhaps we cannot completely eradicate nepotism in hiring. But we can diminish it, and we should. And it means, normatively, that we will never be too hard on people when they fail to be purely disinterested employers, and show some preference toward a spouse, sibling, or friend.

But our concern is what justice demands of us—so that we can arrange our institutions accordingly. And justice demands that we not deviate from merit-based hiring (except, as discussed, when it comes to small family firms).

One can get a sense of the badness of nepotism by trying to sympathize with the perspective of the person who will lose out because of it. One can easily say, "I know my spouse, I know how hard she'll work, what a good job she'll do." But another applicant's spouse can tell the exact same story. And another applicant is in deep need. Another has overcome adversity. Still another is heartbroken, and could use a bit of good news. The potential arguments here are innumerable. The only way to resolve them, doing justice to all, is to focus on merit.

5.10 The Curious Case of Political Competence

Political offices involve distinct moral complications. Chief among these is the idea, endorsed by many (although not by me—see Mulligan Manuscript), that it is important that our politicians reflect the preferences of those who elect them. If so, then merit alone cannot be the only thing relevant to just political selection. It would be unjust to select any politician, no matter how competent he be, if his policy preferences were different from those that prevailed in the electorate.

I do not wish to wade into that issue, but instead to say a few words about the political lessons which can be drawn from the argument I have given.[16]

To begin with, the key difference between (1) the 99 percent of jobs which we have concerned ourselves with and (2) political offices has to do with the potential collision between justice and efficiency that meritocratic hiring may produce. Justice is the most important moral concern, but because its satisfaction may come at the cost of consequences that we deem morally important, it is possible that we might be morally obligated to act unjustly.

Recall the thought experiment of §5.2: We could obtain an excellent consequence—namely, saving many lives—by hanging an innocent man. If the number of potential lives saved gets big enough, the action becomes morally permissible, maybe obligatory. But the intuition about justice remains unchanged: It is *always* unjust to hang an innocent man, no matter the consequences.

This divergence is rare in actual practice for two reasons. Reason one: Since justice is a matter of giving people what they deserve on the basis of their merit, doing justice to applicants normally produces the best consequences. Reason two: In the cases in which justice leads to suboptimal consequences (e.g. in cases of taste discrimination), the suboptimality is small. We are not justified in overriding the meritocratic hiring principle.

But when it comes to political jobs, reason two no longer holds. Political jobs are especially sensitive to the justice/efficiency distinction, owing to the power they have and the number of people they affect. For example, suppose candidate *A* is plainly more meritorious than candidate *B*. But *A* is hated by a foreign despot; if he is elected, war is likely to result. In this case, justice requires that *A* be elected, in accordance with the meritocratic hiring principle; however, justice gets trumped by the moral importance of avoiding war.

Nevertheless, the heuristic remains a good one: Select political leaders purely on the basis of their merit. That is just, and it fulfills our fiduciary duties to our fellow citizens. Indeed, compliance with this rule is probably more important now than it has ever been, in light of the politics of 2016.

Question: Do American voters obey the meritocratic hiring principle? Answer: No. Whole classes of people are excluded from public office on grounds irrelevant from the point-of-view of merit. If you are an atheist, a Muslim, or a homosexual, high-level political positions are *de facto* unattainable to you, regardless of your merits. About half of Americans would not vote for an atheist presidential candidate; 42 percent would not vote for a Muslim; and 32 percent would not vote for a homosexual. Given that the popular vote margin has not exceeded 9 percent in the last 32 years, these prejudices are fatal to the political hopes of members of these classes (or at least those who are unwilling to lie about their character).[17]

The United States is hardly worse than other countries in this regard and better than most, but it is neither just nor to the advantage of the political community to exclude a candidate based on her reasonable religious views or sexual preference. Odd that political philosophy remains silent about this injustice, shrugging its shoulders when the democratic polis exercises its discriminatory will. The meritocrat objects. Reasonable religious views, sexual preference, race, gender—what have you—are all irrelevant from the point-of-view of merit and must be ignored. This is true whether we are talking about a widget maker or a president.

Some might say that this is question-begging. After all, aren't the American people asserting that homosexuality, the Islamic faith, and atheism are in fact demerits? That is, can't we view the contemporary political process as a way to determine who is, in fact, the most meritorious candidate? We cannot. While we might regard our democratic politics as epistemically valuable (see, e.g. Landemore 2012), or as uniquely just

(Estlund 2008), it is not a method for identifying merit. There is nothing like a reasonable consensus that atheism, Islam, and homosexuality are demerits (if anything, there is reasonable consensus that they are *not*), and so they must be ignored. Thus, the many Americans who, during the 2008 and 2012 election cycles, regarded Obama's race as a demerit or even a dispositive reason to vote against him, acted unjustly.[18]

Just as some people are systematically and irrationally excluded from politics, others are provided with advantages which unjustly help them attain these offices. The result is inferior political and economic outcomes. Research has shown, for example, that real-world electoral results are more closely correlated with voter evaluations of candidates' beauty than their evaluations of intelligence, competence, likability, or trustworthiness.[19] Even if it were true that beauty is correlated with something relevant, like competence, that's not what's going on: "Voters favor good-looking candidates either because they enjoy watching them, or because good-looking politicians are more successful in social interaction" (Berggren, Jordahl, and Poutvaara 2010: 15). (This bias is related to the ubiquitous "beauty premium", to be discussed in §6.4.)

No surprise, then, that voters lament the low quality of their politicians: They do not select them with an eye toward merit.

If we want better people in government, we must change the incentives facing aspiring politicians. There is a reason that meritorious people do not seek public office. They know that any flaw, mistake, salacious detail, etc. in their past will be investigated, uncovered, and then gleefully ridiculed by a hypocritical public, egged on by talk radio and television networks which are simultaneously the least accurate and most popular ways for people to "inform" themselves about politics. As Gibbon says, "the most worthless of mankind are not afraid to condemn in others the same disorders which they allow in themselves; and can readily discover some nice difference in age, character, or station, to justify the partial distinction" (1776: 180).

It is *because* a person deserves to lead us that she suffers from these "flaws": Any life full enough to qualify a person for high office will include features that the public wrongly regards as defects. How often have we bemoaned some politician's past impropriety, and thought that, if only she had not done this thing, she would be perfect? That is not how life works: Excellence is achieved only by dint of failure and stupidity along the way. These are the causes of merit, not its competitors. Perhaps we feel this deep down, as evidenced by our greater willingness to forgive a person of high merit than one of low merit for the very same infraction.

I am reminded of a photo taken at the funeral of former French President François Mitterand. Standing in front of his coffin is his wife of 51 years, his mistress, and his illegitimate daughter. Between the women there is a sense of, not approval exactly, but understanding and respect: for a meritorious man, who, like all men and of course all women, was flawed. This is the proper sentiment to be shown toward our leaders. It is not to approve of the conduct. It is to acknowledge that something discomfiting is to be found in the life of *every* politician.

And if politicians' infidelities should not concern us, and I think that they should not, then surely those features of a person which have no moral baggage whatsoever ought to be excluded from consideration as well. Religious views, sexual orientation, and the like simply have no place in our political discussions or at the ballot box.

5.11 The Justice/Efficiency "Trade-Off", Part 2

Unlike the economic gains that equal opportunity (§4.8) produces, which are not obvious, the common sense idea that meritocratic hiring is efficient is indeed what theory and evidence tell us. The one exception has to do with taste discrimination, but, as I have argued, that should not detain us.

The many ways in which our actual economy violates meritocratic norms, and the damaging economic effects thereof, will be discussed at length in the next chapter. As just one example of the gains we might expect by conforming to the meritocratic hiring principle, Hsieh et al. (2013) estimate that 15–20 percent of the growth in per capita output since 1960 is attributable to the reduction of anti-meritocratic discrimination against blacks and women.

The market, driven by the profit motive, is a powerful force for eliminating racism, sexism, and other forms of anti-meritocratic bias. But history tells us that it is insufficient. The government has a role in regulating labor market conduct. For example, unlike taste discrimination, statistical discrimination cannot be competed out of the marketplace, and it may be inefficient. Perfectly rational statistical discrimination against blacks may lead blacks to underinvest in their education, and the social cost of that may exceed the benefits to firms (Lundberg and Startz 1983).[20] If the government can address this negative externality without impinging on the meritocratic hiring principle, it ought to do so.

Finally, note that the considerations adduced in this chapter suggest that there is something to Rawls's (1971) claim that natural talents are a common asset. But it is not exactly that these talents are a common asset; taken literally, that is clearly false. Instead, when these talents are put to economic use, they redound to the benefit of the entire economic community. When you hire on the basis of merit, you do justice to applicants, maximize your own profits, and create value for others in the marketplace. In a meritocracy, our talents, natural or otherwise, are harnessed towards the common good by putting the right people in the right jobs.[21]

Notes

1 See, e.g. Narveson (1993) and Nozick (1974).
2 See Steinpreis, Anders, and Ritzke (1999).

3 On women's advantage on the academic job market, see, e.g. Dicey Jennings et al. (2015) and Williams and Ceci (2015).

4 The research on the anti-meritocratic role of pedigree in academic hiring is extensive; see, e.g. Burris (2004); Clauset, Arbesman, and Larremore (2015); Jacobs (1999, 2004); and McGinnis and Long (1997).

5 Pew Research Center. 2014. Public strongly backs affirmative action programs on campus. URL = <www.pewresearch.org/fact-tank/2014/04/22/public-strongly-backs-affirmative-action-programs-on-campus/>, retrieved 7 August 2017.

6 Gallup. 2013. In U.S., most reject considering race in college admissions. URL = <www.gallup.com/poll/163655/reject-considering-race-college-admissions. aspx>, retrieved 7 August 2017. See also Longoria (2009).

7 Olsaretti rightly argues that if desert is to serve as a principle of distributive justice, it cannot "be parasitic on an independently formulated conception of justice" (2004: 18).

8 See also Feinberg (1963); Miller (1976); Pojman (1999); Scheffler (1992); and Sidgwick (1874).

9 Feldman (2016: 53–7) offers other reasons for rejecting the appraising attitudes account.

10 I agree with Feinberg when he says, "I am not sure how, if at all, these judgments of moral appropriateness are to be verified; but I suspect that they resemble certain aesthetic judgments—for example, that crimson and orange are clashing colors" (1963: 92).

11 This possibility is raised by Daniels (1978) and Walzer (1983).

12 Sher also says, correctly, that "because actions do foreclose options, it follows that any agent who exerts a sustained effort is making an important sequence of allocative decisions. In diligently pursuing his goal, he is investing a major portion of his scarce time and energy in his goal's achievement. . . . Since our lives are constituted by our actions, our time and energy are thus the very stuff of which we fashion our lives. Hence, any agent who devotes a major portion of his time and energy to achieving a goal is quite literally making that goal a part of himself" (1987: 61).

13 See especially Aigner and Cain (1977); Arrow (1973); and Phelps (1972).

14 I discuss statistical discrimination in detail in my 2017.

15 See also Baldi (1995); Clauset, Arbesman, and Larremore (2015); Keith and Babchuk (1998); Jacobs (1999, 2004); McGinnis and Long (1997); and Oprisko, Dobbs, and DiGrazia (2013).

16 I discuss matters related to merit in politics in my 2015 and Forthcoming.

17 Gallup. 2012. Atheists, Muslims see most bias as presidential candidates. URL = <www.gallup.com/poll/155285/atheists-muslims-bias-presidential-candidates.aspx>, retrieved 9 August 2017. These data are a few years old. I suspect the situation has improved. Further improvement is needed.

18 "Anti-African-American racism appears to have been an important component of the 2008 election, perhaps considerably reducing Obama's share of the vote" (Pasek et al. 2009: 982). See also Piston (2010).

19 See Banducci et al. (2008) and Berggren, Jordahl, and Poutvaara (2010).

20 See also Lundberg and Startz (2000) and Schwab (1986).

21 *Cf.* Goldman (1977).

5.12 References

Aigner, D. J. and Cain, G. C. 1977. Statistical theories of discrimination in labor markets. *Industrial and Labor Relations Review* 30: 175–87.

Arneson, R. J. 1999. Against Rawlsian equality of opportunity. *Philosophical Studies* 93: 77–112.

Arrow, K. J. 1973. The theory of discrimination. In *Discrimination in Labor Markets*, eds. O. Ashenfelter and A. Rees, 3–33. Princeton: Princeton University Press.

Baldi, S. 1995. Prestige determinants of first academic job for new sociology Ph.D.s 1985–1992. *Sociological Quarterly* 36: 777–89.

Banducci, S. A., Karp, J. A., Thrasher, M., and Rallings, C. 2008. Ballot photographs as cues in low-information elections. *Political Psychology* 29: 903–17.

Becker, G. S. 1957. *The Economics of Discrimination*. Chicago: University of Chicago Press.

Berggren, N., Jordahl, H., and Poutvaara, P. 2010. The looks of a winner: Beauty and electoral success. *Journal of Public Economics* 94: 8–15.

Burris, V. 2004. The academic caste system: Prestige hierarchies in PhD exchange networks. *American Sociological Review* 69: 239–64.

Clauset, A., Arbesman, S., and Larremore, D. B. 2015. Systematic inequality and hierarchy in faculty hiring networks. *Science Advances* 1: 1–6.

Daniels, N. 1978. Merit and meritocracy. *Philosophy & Public Affairs* 7: 206–23.

Dicey Jennings, C., Kyrilov, A., Cobb, P., Vlasits, J., Vinson, D. W., Montes, E., and Franco, C. 2015. Academic placement data and analysis: 2015 final report. URL = <www.dropbox.com/s/b9p0dx817qkcb3e/APDAFinalReport2015.pdf?dl=0>, retrieved 9 August 2017.

Estlund, D. M. 2008. *Democratic Authority: A Philosophical Framework*. Princeton: Princeton University Press.

Feinberg, J. 1963. Justice and personal desert. In *NOMOS VI: Justice*, eds. C. J. Friedrich and J. W. Chapman, 69–97. New York: Atherton.

Feldman, F. 2016. *Distributive Justice: Getting What We Deserve from Our Country*. New York: Oxford University Press.

Gibbon, E. 1776. *The History of the Decline and Fall of the Roman Empire*, Volume 1. London: Strahan and Cadell.

Goldman, A. H. 1977. Justice and hiring by competence. *American Philosophical Quarterly* 14: 17–28.

Hsieh, C.-T., Hurst, E., Jones, C. I., and Klenow, P. J. 2013. The allocation of talent and U.S. economic growth. *National Bureau of Economic Research*, working paper 18693.

Jacobs, D. 1999. Ascription or productivity? The determinants of departmental success in the NRC quality rankings. *Social Science Research* 28: 228–39.

———. 2004. Ascription and departmental rankings revisited: A correction and a reanalysis. *Social Science Research* 33: 183–6.

Keith, B. and Babchuk, N. 1998. The quest for institutional recognition: A longitudinal analysis of scholarly productivity and academic prestige among sociology departments. *Social Forces* 76: 1495–533.

Lamont, J. 1994. The concept of desert in distributive justice. *Philosophical Quarterly* 44: 45–64.

Landemore, H. 2012. *Democratic Reason: Politics, Collective Intelligence, and the Rule of the Many*. Princeton: Princeton University Press.

Leslie, L. M., Mayer, D. M., and Kravitz, D. A. 2014. The stigma of affirmative action: A stereotyping-based theory and meta-analytic test of the consequences for performance. *Academy of Management Journal* 57: 964–89.

Longoria, R. T. 2009. *Meritocracy and Americans' Views on Distributive Justice.* Lanham, MD: Lexington Books.

Lundberg, S. J. and Startz, R. 1983. Private discrimination and social intervention in competitive labor markets. *American Economic Review* 73: 340–7.

———. 2000. Inequality and race: Models and policies. In *Meritocracy and Economic Inequality*, eds. K. Arrow, S. Bowles, and S. Durlauf, 269–95. Princeton: Princeton University Press.

MacLachlan, A. 2010. Unreasonable resentments. *Journal of Social Philosophy* 41: 422–41.

McCloskey, H. J. 1957. An examination of restricted utilitarianism. *Philosophical Review* 66: 466–85.

McGinnis, R. and Long, J. S. 1997. Entry into academia: Effects of stratification, geography and ecology. In *The Academic Profession: The Professorate in Crisis*, eds. P. G. Altbach and M. J. Finkelstein, 342–66. New York: Routledge.

Miller, D. 1976. *Social Justice.* Oxford: Clarendon Press.

———. 1992. Deserving jobs. *Philosophical Quarterly* 42: 161–81.

Mulligan, T. Forthcoming. Plural voting for the twenty-first century. *Philosophical Quarterly.*

———. 2017. Uncertainty in hiring does not justify affirmative action. *Philosophia* 45: 1299–311.

2015. On the compatibility of epistocracy and public reason. *Social Theory and Practice* 41: 458–76.

———. Manuscript. Social choice or collective decision-making: What is politics all about?

Murphy, J. G. 2003. *Getting Even: Forgiveness and Its Limits.* New York: Oxford University Press.

Narveson, J. 1993. *Moral Matters.* Peterborough, Canada: Broadview Press.

Nozick, R. 1974. *Anarchy, State, and Utopia.* New York: Basic Books.

Olsaretti, S. 2004. *Liberty, Desert and the Market: A Philosophical Study.* Cambridge: Cambridge University Press.

Oprisko, R. L., Dobbs, K. L., and DiGrazia, J. 2013. Honor, prestige, and the academy: A portrait of political science tenured and tenure-track faculty in Ph.D.-granting institutions (2012–2013). Paper presented at the 2013 annual meeting of the American Political Science Association, Chicago.

Pasek, J., Tahk, A., Lelkes, Y., Krosnick, J. A., Payne, B. K., Akhtar, O., and Tompson, T. 2009. Determinants of turnout and candidate choice in the 2008 U.S. presidential election: Illuminating the impact of racial prejudice and other considerations. *Public Opinion Quarterly* 73: 943–94.

Phelps, E. S. 1972. The statistical theory of racism and sexism. *American Economic Review* 62: 659–61.

Piston, S. 2010. How explicit racial prejudice hurt Obama in the 2008 election. *Political Behavior* 32: 431–51.

Pojman, L. 1999. Merit: Why do we value it? *Journal of Social Philosophy* 30: 83–102.

Rawls, J. 1971. *A Theory of Justice.* Cambridge: Belknap Press.

Sandel, M. J. 2009. *Justice: What's the Right Thing to Do?* New York: Farrar, Straus and Giroux.

Scheffler, S. 1992. Responsibility, reactive attitudes, and liberalism and philosophy and politics. *Philosophy & Public Affairs* 21: 299–323.

Schwab, S. 1986. Is statistical discrimination efficient? *American Economic Review* 76: 228–34.

Sher, G. 1987. *Desert*. Princeton: Princeton University Press.

———. 2017. Doing justice to desert. In *Oxford Studies in Political Philosophy*, Volume 3, eds. D. Sobel, P. Vallentyne, and S. Wall, 84–97. New York: Oxford University Press.

Sidgwick, H. 1874. *The Methods of Ethics*. London: Macmillan and Co.

Smith, A. 1759. *The Theory of Moral Sentiments*. London: Millar, Kincaid, and Bell.

Steinpreis, R. E., Anders, K. A., and Ritzke, D. 1999. The impact of gender on the review of the curricula vitae of job applicants and tenure candidates: A national empirical study. *Sex Roles* 41: 509–28.

Walzer, M. 1983. *Spheres of Justice: A Defense of Pluralism and Equality*. New York: Basic Books.

Williams, W. M. and Ceci, S. J. 2015. National hiring experiments reveal 2:1 faculty preference for women on STEM tenure track. *Proceedings of the National Academy of Sciences* 112: 5360–5.

6   On the Distribution of Income

6.1 Money in a Meritocracy

How should money be distributed? Any theory of economic justice must answer this question.

We shall concentrate on the distribution of income and largely ignore wealth. This is possible because the intergenerational transfer of wealth is proscribed, or at least severely limited, in a meritocracy (§8.4). Therefore, one's wealth is merely the stock of one's accrued income (minus what is spent on consumables). There is an outstanding question—whether the income received through an investment of deserved income is itself deserved—but I delay analysis of that until §8.5. (It is deserved.)

We shall also use "income" capaciously, to mean more than wage income. These days, benefits are an important part of remuneration, and they must be included in any discussion of just distribution.

I hope that the reader already has the sense that, in a meritocracy, income would be distributed very differently from how it actually is, and how it would be under other distributive approaches. Clearly, any desert-based distributive system is inegalitarian. Neither a strict egalitarian distribution (where each citizen gets the same income) nor an economy structured around Rawls's difference principle (where unequal incomes are permitted insofar as that maximally benefits the least-advantaged class) respond to desert. Strict egalitarianism would only respond appropriately to desert if we were all equally deserving, which we are not, and Rawls's theory would permit a hugely undeserving person to receive a large share of income if that happened to benefit the poorest citizens. The meritocrat regards both principles as unjust.

Less obvious but equally important is the observation that unrestrained markets also fail to give economic agents what they deserve. There is no shortage of contemporary examples: exorbitant compensation packages given to mediocre executives; talented young people unable to find jobs because they lack family connections; and the increasing reliance on certifications and pedigree when more accurate proxies for merit are available.

These features of our contemporary economy are also worrying from the point-of-view of efficiency. We all have reason to prefer an economy that is responsive to merit, but that connection, always imperfect, is now badly frayed. Undeserving citizens are extracting enormous economic rents, capturing a larger and larger share of national income. This income has no effect on their welfare since they are so rich already. And since their income exceeds their merit, they are unable to invest it efficiently.

Things would be different in a meritocracy. Workers would concentrate on improving their human capital because this would be the factor relevant to compensation—not pedigree or personal relationships. The distribution of income would reflect the deserts of workers—which are unequal, to be sure, but not as unequal as our markets suggest. And through its regulatory authority, a meritocratic government intervenes, where necessary and when it can do so effectively, to maintain the meritocratic pattern. These matters will be discussed in due course.

I shall not defend the private ownership of real capital. Implicit in this book is the idea that people can spend their deserved income by investing in firms. That is, I shall assume that the meritocratic ideal is better realized under capitalism than socialism. A meritocratic argument to prefer socialism might be given, but I shall not undertake that task.

As for the choice of an economic system, I shall assume that we are using markets, and not central planning, to arrange economic activity. This *is* important, for the non-ideal reasons discussed in §2.4: A theory of justice must be feasible, and central planning seems incapable of sustaining prosperity.

That said, unlike libertarianism, which is conceptually wedded to markets, it is possible that a just, merit-responsive economy could be realized by central planning—if one day faster computers and more sophisticated economic models permit economic decisions to be more effectively made that way. But this is not the case now, for the reasons that Hayek (1945) gives, and as evidenced by central planning's history of failure.

6.2 Determining the Desert Basis

Clearly, the just distribution of income must have something to do with merit. However, it cannot be that one deserves income on the basis of merit *simpliciter*. Merit is contextual, and so claims like "Wilbur deserves an income of $50,000 on the basis of his intelligence" are at least underdescribed. Wilbur's intelligence cannot ground his economic deserts if it is not engaged economically.

If Wilbur is a pediatrician by day and at night plays virtuoso banjo in a purely private capacity, then figuring out how much Wilbur deserves is a matter of looking at his merits *qua* doctor. Even if Wilbur is the finest banjo player in the world, if he is not putting those merits to use in competition for scarce income, then they are irrelevant to distributive justice. (Just as the world's best widget maker deserves the job at the widget factory only if he has actually applied for it.) When Wilbur change professions, sending a demo tape to a record studio, is when his just economic reward begins to turn on his musical merits.

Desert-based distribution has been unpopular, but some work has been done and three possible desert bases have emerged in the literature. First, some philosophers say that income is deserved on the basis of the *costs* that one has incurred.[1] For example, if some profession requires expensive education, then workers in that profession deserve to be paid more; if working conditions are unpleasant, then those doing that work deserve a premium; and so on.

Whether this is in fact a desertist distributive principle is unclear. It's perhaps better understood as a form of egalitarianism—and a necessary one at that, as even strict egalitarians will want to incorporate these considerations. Indeed, if the currency of justice is welfare rather than resources this follows directly. And actual economies respond to these conditions in precisely this way, providing *compensating differentials* to workers who bear unusual costs (and paying less to workers who enjoy unusual benefits).

As one example of why this putative desert basis is problematic, consider a racist who accepts a job where he must work alongside blacks. He suffers psychic harm as a result. We do not think that he deserves extra income for this.

The second possible basis for deserved income, which I also reject, is effort.[2] I do not dispute that deserved income closely tracks effort; but this is because effort is an element of merit in almost every context. Indeed, it is almost always the most important element of merit.

It matters, though, that our economic efforts create value in the marketplace. Efforts to produce products that no one wants, no matter how intense these be, do not make a person deserving of economic reward (as some effort-inclined theorists, like Sadurski (1985), recognize).

More seriously, much of our expenditure of effort is aimed at reducing future efforts. We work hard now to accomplish a task, but also to develop our human capital so that similar tasks may be accomplished in the future with less effort. This is ubiquitous. Yet if we simply recognized effort, then the person who had invested in his human capital in this way would earn less for the same activity as someone who did not make the investment. But as we have seen, giving a person what he deserves means respecting his choices to develop his life as he sees fit—and it is wrong to punish a person who chose to invest and pay the concomitant opportunity costs.

It might be possible to develop an effort-based theory that could sum up past efforts along with the proximate effort to determine the ground for economic reward. But, in any case, that will not work for the meritocrat, who holds that human capital derived from genetic advantage is a legitimate ground for desert.

This brings us to the third proposed basis: economic contribution.[3] Among desert theorists, this has been considered the most plausible, and has been analyzed in a small but lively debate in the philosophical literature.[4]

Why does making an economic contribution render one deserving? Some say that there is value in satisfying others' preferences, and desert-claims derive their force, instrumentally, in that way:

> Contemporary desert-principles all share the value of raising the standard of living—collectively, "the social product". Under each principle, only activity directed at raising the social product will serve as a basis for deserving income. The concept of desert itself does not yield this value of raising the social product; it is a value societies hold independently. Hence, desert-principles identifying desert-bases tied to socially productive activity (productivity, compensation, and effort all being examples of such bases) do not do so because the concept of desert requires this.
>
> (Lamont and Favor 2016)

This is too quick. Consider, for example, teleological arguments for desert, *a la* Aristotle (§1.2): Why does the best flute player deserve the best flute? Because that is what flutes are for: to be played well. A similar argument might be made here: The point of economic life is to enrich ourselves collectively—and so those riches should be distributed to the economic agents who best fulfill this end. There is a natural fit between economic contribution and economic reward. That is an analysis under which the concept of desert itself yields economic contribution as the basis.

Whatever one thinks about that, the lesson of the empirical literature surveyed in Chapter 3 is that contribution is what drives our pre-theoretical judgments about distributive justice. Recall that this is the core idea of equity theory: What we get out of an enterprise should be commensurate with what we put into it.

Miller has things close to right when he says that

> people deserve the rewards of economic activity for their achievement, for the contribution they make to the welfare of others by providing goods and services that others want. Effort matters here only because it counts, along with talent and choice, as a factor in determining what a person achieves.
>
> (1999: 184)

But there is a missing element to this account of the desert basis: merit. Consider the following two cases:

(1) The CEO of company *A* is a highly meritorious woman. She always makes the rational decision when it comes to the management of her company. She is a brilliant businesswoman and a tireless worker. Due to unforeseeable events, *A* fails.

(2) The CEO of company *B* is terrible: She is stupid, a menace to her employees, and thoughtless when it comes to corporate decision-making. Nevertheless, by sheer dumb luck, and despite her mismanagement, *B* thrives.

Who deserves a higher salary, the CEO of *A* or the CEO of *B*? It's the former. She did everything we want a CEO to do; if we were to hire one of the two, we'd choose her; and none of her company's problems was attributable to her leadership.

Yet if brute contribution were all we cared about, regardless of its connection to merit, we would say that the CEO of *B* is the deserving one. After all, her company was successful while *A* folded. That is wrong, since, *ex hypothesi*, the CEO of *A* has all the laudable character traits—and the possession and application of those traits is the essence of desert. Moreover, rewarding *B* would incentivize the wrong type of behavior. An efficient economy responds to merit.

So the meritocratic desert basis, for the purpose of income, appears to be *meritorious contributions to the economy*. To reinforce the point, let us consider a case in which merits are equal but contributions differ. Imagine that Mary and Rachel are equally meritorious, and they set up lemonade stands of equal quality on two different streets. Mary sells a lot of lemonade and Rachel very little. We might be inclined to think that Mary deserves a greater income than Rachel even though their merits are, *ex hypothesi*, equal.

What we are responding to in this case, though, is an intuition that Mary has done something right that Rachel has not: Mary has exercised foresight in selecting a location for her business. And this foresight is precisely what makes for a good businesswoman; foresight is an element of merit which Mary has in greater measure than Rachel.

If Mary's and Rachel's merits were *truly* equal, and if we knew this—if we knew, from a god's eye view, that the only reason that Mary's lemonade stand thrived while Rachel's foundered was pure luck—then we would say, it seems to me, that Mary and Rachel deserve the same income.

What about a case in which a person, Tiffany, makes a contribution for reasons *unconnected* to her merit? Is there anything wrong with her being rewarded with some extra income *i*?

Maybe, maybe not. I am asserting only that Tiffany does not deserve *i*; that is, she has no claim of justice on *i*. This is not the same thing as saying that it is *unjust* that Tiffany has *i*. And it is possible that we could have good reason to reward Tiffany (perhaps to send a signal to other producers).

These assignments are only viable, however, if they do not tread on another's just deserts. We should protect Tiffany's undeserved possession of i if it is socially useful to do so—but not at the cost of Zelda, who *is* deserving.

6.3 What Is the Deserved Income?

Consider a community garden which must be tended throughout the growing season. When the vegetables are harvested, they are distributed to those who did the tending, in proportion to their tending. The fact that Tyler worked the hardest of everyone, insofar as that work was unproductive, is irrelevant; Tyler does not deserve more vegetables for tirelessly weeding an unplanted plot. (Again, for gardens as for economies, contribution and effort are highly correlated.)

It is tempting to think that there is a similarly obvious sense of "contribution" when it comes to economic life. Indeed, one might think that markets naturally remunerate people for their contributions. Consider a simple economy, competitive and closed. Goods and services are produced in order to satisfy people's wants. People contribute to production with their labor. Total output is equal to total compensation, and each person's income is equal to the additional output that he provides. This is his *marginal value product* (MVP).

That *ideal* markets are naturally just in this way—that marginal value product is a good measure of economic contribution—is a view that has been defended over the years, most famously by John Bates Clark (1899) and recently by Mankiw (2013). And I think that it is basically correct: *If* the market one is participating in is appropriately ideal (e.g. perfectly competitive), *and* one's income is equal to one's MVP, then one is getting one's just deserts.

The big problem for this view is that our economy is not "appropriately ideal", which raises the question of how far marginal productivity theory can take us normatively. The literature has gotten tangled up on this point: One often finds arguments "against" the justness of MVP that are in fact arguments that individuals are not being paid their MVP owing to market failure.

When thinking about how to measure contribution, the right strategy is not to try to give a precise definition of "contribution". Similar to the strategy of Chapter 5, it is more effective to say what contribution is *not*. We shall see that we can get quite far in the direction of justice through this negative strategy.

In the next section, I shall talk about aspects of contemporary compensation which are clearly undeserved—that is, which clearly do not reflect *bona fide* meritorious contributions. But I do want to comment here on some broad worries about using MVP to measure contribution.

First, there is the possibility of non-constant returns to scale. If returns to scale are decreasing, then there is a residual of national income left over after everyone is paid his MVP. And it certainly seems like there are just and unjust ways this residual might be distributed. In the case of increasing returns to scale, national income is insufficient to pay everyone his MVP.

This does not seem to be a serious barrier to income-based-on-contribution, since, if returns to scale are not constant, we could pay each citizen *in proportion* to his MVP. That seems like the straightforward solution, and Roemer and Silvestre (1993) have proven there is a general equilibrium solution for decreasing returns to scale—labor income in proportion to labor contribution and capital income in proportion to capital contribution. The resulting allocation is Pareto efficient.

A second question is whether it is fair to say that labor's marginal product reflects the contribution of labor, and labor alone. That may seem dubious: If labor has no tools to work with, it cannot produce anything at all. Don't owners of existing factors of production, like capital and land, contribute to the output produced by that final worker?

Some have considered this challenge a show-stopper:

> Neither J.B. Clark nor any subsequent supporter of [MVP-based distribution] has been able to show how the specific product of the marginal unit of labour can be distinguished from the specific products of the other factors that act in conjunction with the marginal unit of labour. Unless and until this distinction can be made, [marginal productivity theory] must remain devoid of any normative relevance within the context of a contributor theory.
>
> (Pullen 2010: 55)

But there is a way to disentangle contributions in situations like this one. This is by calculating each economic agent's *Shapley value* and paying him accordingly. Suppose, by way of illustration, that we have a capitalist, c, who provides the tools necessary for production. We also have two homogenous workers, w_1 and w_2. The tools can produce nothing on their own. The workers, without the tools, can produce nothing. But with the help of the capitalist, the first worker can produce $10 worth of product, and the second worker, $7 worth of product. So the three decide to work together, and thus produce $17 to allocate among them. Now how do we say who contributed what?

Lloyd Shapley (1953) suggests that we pay each his average marginal contribution, where the average is taken over all the possible ways in which this coalition of three may be built up. One way it can be built up is with c entering first, followed by w_1, followed by w_2. Here, c's marginal contribution is $0, as described, w_1's is $10, and w_2's is $7. Another possible order is w_1 followed by w_2 followed by c—and in that case, c's marginal product is the entire $17. There are six possibilities:

	MVP of c	*MVP of w_1*	*MVP of w_2*
c followed by w_1 followed by w_2:	0	10	7
c followed by w_2 followed by w_1:	0	7	10
w_1 followed by c followed by w_2:	10	0	7
w_1 followed by w_2 followed by c:	17	0	0
w_2 followed by w_1 followed by c:	17	0	0
w_2 followed by c followed by w_1:	10	7	0
Total:	$54	$24	$24
Average marginal contribution:	$9	$4	$4

The capitalist deserves $9, and each worker, $4.

Two things are interesting about Shapley value. First, it is the *only* way to solve these problems of entangled contributions such that three axioms are satisfied: (1) All of the output is distributed (i.e. the allocation is efficient); (2) identical individuals receive the same share of output; and (3) individuals who contribute nothing receive nothing. (There is one additional, technical axiom.) These are simple, uncontroversial, and alluring conditions.

Second, notice that the axioms don't make any reference to MVP at all! Rather, MVP arises naturally, as a normatively important quantity, out of the axioms. Perhaps this suggests that MVP is more than just a handy tool for disentangling questions about joint production.

The final complication is this: MVP is paid to factors of production, not to people. And so it is conceptually possible for an owner of a factor of production to be enriched while making no contribution himself.

But in a meritocracy, operating under equal opportunity, there is one way to own factors of production: namely, by investing one's deserved income in them. Therefore, the MVP of capital (e.g.) *does* reflect its owners' economic contributions—namely, those contributions that they made in the past, which provided them the income necessary to own the capital. In a society lacking equal opportunity, on the other hand, there need be no connection—a layabout who inherits wealth can invest it without ever making an economic contribution *himself*.

The meritocrat recognizes that "economic contribution" should include the contribution made by capital (see §8.5). And the meritocrat believes that *some* capital income is deserved. But just like not all labor income is deserved (e.g. one does not deserve the income one obtains through rent-seeking), not all capital income is deserved. One does not deserve the income generated by an inheritance, for example. (Indeed, one does not deserve the inheritance itself; and for this reason, and because it is incompatible with a meritocratic framework for society, inheritance should be confiscated—§8.4.)

We should not be swayed by those who believe that moralizing market outcomes is a fool's errand. They are unduly pessimistic. Arneson (2015), for example, says that there is no remotely sensible notion of individual desert that varies with the benefits that people gain from their economic production. This is not any defect of markets; there is no reason to expect them to somehow distribute benefits according to any common-sense norms of desert.

But contribution is a common sense norm of desert (indeed, from Chapter 3 we know that it is *the* common sense norm of desert), and it *does* vary, in ideal markets, with income. There are no *a priori* impediments to relying on a contribution norm.[5]

Now, *actual* markets do not distribute income in accordance with desert, but this is reason to intervene into markets in the name of establishing a more just pattern. It is not reason to give up on the dream of desert-based distribution. Indeed, the various forms of divergence between real-world market remuneration and desert are really forms of market failure.

Consider, for example, that in the real world, often workers who do the same task for a firm are regarded as interchangeable, despite differences in merit. They are all paid the same amount—namely, what the firm thinks the marginal worker among them can produce—but this has the effect of giving meritorious workers in the group less than they deserve, and unmeritorious workers more. This is understood intuitively by any working person with a sense of desert, who wonders why he is being paid the same as the lazy idiot down the hall.

The biggest problem, which we turn now to consider, is that our economy is sodden with *economic rents*—payments to individuals above and beyond their meritorious contributions. We encounter examples of this all the time: Dick Fuld, the former CEO of Lehman Brothers, was paid half a billion dollars to drive his storied firm into the ground and help crash the American economy. No merit, no contribution, but a large reward.

6.4 Economic Rents Are Undeserved

Classically, economic rents were regarded as "free gifts of nature": income that required no merit (effort, skill, etc.) to obtain. Unimproved land is the archetypical source of rent: Its owner may, purely by virtue of its scarcity, gain an income from it (hence the term, "rent"). As Smith says,

> as soon as the land of any country has all become private property, the landlords, like all other men, love to reap where they never sowed, and demand a rent even for its natural produce. The wood of the forest, the grass of the field, and all the natural fruits of the earth, which, when land was in common, cost the labourer only the trouble of gathering them, come, even to him, to have an additional price fixed upon them. He must then pay for the licence to gather them; and must give up to the landlord a portion of what his labour either

collects or produces. This portion, or, what comes to the same thing, the price of this portion, constitutes the rent of land.

(1784: 74–5)

Nowadays, economic rents are understood more broadly, typically defined as returns to factors of production in excess of what is necessary to maintain them in economic use (the land is just there, producing its bounty, whether you pay its owner or not).

In one way or another, economic rents arise out of a lack of competition. They are, thus, necessarily connected to imperfect markets. That this might have relevance for the meritocratic ideal has been pointed out by Franzini et al.: "Meritocracy requires competition. If competition is lacking, then, the concentration of earnings is not justifiable in meritocratic terms. As super-earnings are incompatible with competition, by the same token, they are incompatible with meritocracy" (2016: 64).

This is well-illustrated by the first kind of rent we will consider, which are the massive, undeserved incomes earned by so-called "superstars" (Rosen 1981). In some markets, small differences in merit can lead to huge differences in income, contrary to both justice and the market ideal.

Consider the legions of singers who are slightly less talented than Katy Perry (or who have slightly less sex appeal than she, or whatever). These singers don't have slightly fewer fans than Perry, they have *almost no* fans, and they make almost no money. Remuneration is not proportional to merit. The situation arises because (1) there are a lack of substitutes for Perry (if they existed, they would compete against each other and drive remuneration down until it matched merit), and (2) musicians like Perry can reach customers at low marginal cost.

Or compare major league baseball players (mean annual salary: $5 million) with players at the AAA level, many of whom earn less than a poverty-level wage. The difference is explained *via* the superstar effect. Obviously, the average major leaguer is not 100 times better than the average AAA player.

Is such a difference just? No, because the difference in remuneration does not reflect a difference in merit. Rents are not obtained on the basis of merit, but on the basis of facts about others—namely, the non-existence of competitors. Superstars are rich because they are monopolists. Rents cannot, conceptually, be deserved—they are not *about* the desert subject.

These examples illustrate why desert cannot be grounded in contribution *simpliciter*. Observe that superstars' incomes *do* reflect their contributions: Katy Perry satisfies consumers' preferences much more than non-superstar musicians do. Therefore, a pure contribution theorist must maintain that superstars' incomes are deserved in full. Not so for the meritocrat, who requires that contributions be tied to merit. The difference in merit between superstars and non-superstars is small, and so the just income difference is small as well.

How prevalent are rents in our economy? Dean Baker (2016) finds that four classes of rent (copyright/patent protection, the finance industry, corporate executive compensation, and anti-competitive practices in professional sectors), not exhaustive of all possible rents, comprise between 6.2 and 8.5 percent of GDP. According to Baker, these rents are the principal cause of the redistribution of income into the top 1 percent of earners which we have seen since 1980. Bell and Van Reenen (2014) obtain similar results, arguing that most of the recent income gains of the top 1 percent have gone to bankers, and that a large part of these are rents. Bivens and Mishel (2013) conclude the same.

So some economists have fretted over the increasing prevalence of rents in our economy, but they have been driven by concern about the inefficiencies associated with rents, or their contribution to inequality (Stiglitz 2012). The real reason they should concern us is that they are undeserved, and therefore unjust.

Economic rents arise when workers gain control over their own pay. Bebchuk and Fried (2004) find that CEOs are able to do this by exerting influence over their boards, a practice obviously incompatible with the competitive ideal of directors driving the hardest bargain they can on behalf of shareholders. As just one example of many that Bebchuk and Fried adduce, former Mattel CEO Jill Barad was simultaneously fired and paid a "golden goodbye" of $7.5 million plus early vesting of options. Payments like this are incompatible with profit-maximizing behavior, as the board had the ability to retain or fire Barad as it saw fit. The golden goodbye was a rent. Barad did not deserve that money.

Similarly, Bertrand and Mullainathan (2000, 2001) find that CEOs are rewarded equally for performance and for luck: For every 1 percent increase in accounting return, CEO pay increases by 2 percent—regardless whether that return was due to talent or to luck. Any CEO remuneration that arises through luck is a rent.

Next, consider the "beauty premium", first investigated by Hamermesh and Biddle (1994), who found that ugly men make 9 percent less, and handsome men 5 percent more, for the same work. Unless one is a fashion model, appearance is not a productive characteristic. It is simply an advantage on the job market—and so beauty premiums are rents. Obviously, intuitively, if surgeon X is better looking than surgeon Y, but the two are equal in surgical skill, then X does not deserve to be paid more than Y.

Finally, there is the class of rents that are contingent on the existence of government. Firms sometimes find it profitable to spend money lobbying for a favorable regulatory environment rather than engaging in productive activity. Attempts to obtain advantages like these fall under the heading "rent-seeking" and are another source of undeserved income. While rent-seeking can be profitable, it does not add to society's stock of goods and services and so cannot ground desert.

Rent-seeking illustrates why merit alone cannot serve as the basis for deserved income: Effective rent-seeking requires hard work and skill. Deserved income must be grounded in the confluence of merit and contribution.

I conclude this discussion of rent with a lesson and a warning. The lesson is that here as elsewhere, meritocratic justice naturally gives rise to the proper economic incentives. All of the incomes just discussed may be confiscated without deadweight loss. We will be better off if our corporate officers focus their talents on producing goods and services rather than pursuing undeserved income.

Henry George is maybe the most famous enemy of rents, and his words are prescient:

> When all rent is taken by taxation for the needs of the community, then will the equality ordained by nature be achieved. No citizen will have an advantage over any other citizen save as is given by his industry, skill, and intelligence; and each will obtain what he fairly earns. Then, but not till then, will labour get its full reward, and capital its natural return.
>
> (1886: 299)

The warning is this: We have established that rents are not justly held and that they are prevalent. This does not, on its own, justify government intervention into our markets. There are reasonable cases to be made that (1) *in the long term*, the market will eliminate rents on its own and, (2) *in the short term*, the market will do a better job of eliminating rents than any regulator can.

These are, of course, positive claims. I am sympathetic to (1), but that provides little consolation to us and to coming generations, which must suffer under an unjust and inefficient economy. And the dynamism of the market will always produce novel opportunities for rent extraction. So we should like to encourage the market along, if we can. But can we do that? Or is (2) true?

My view is that there are sensible and empirically well-supported policy steps which can be taken. I detail these in Chapter 8.

6.5 What Would a Meritocratic Economy Look Like?

How unequal would a meritocracy be, in terms of income and wealth? Would desirable jobs be disproportionately held by a single race or gender? What is the distributional effect of establishing equal opportunity? These questions are especially relevant given that "meritocracy" connotes, for some, a highly stratified society dominated by an elite class. That connotation is wrong. It is worth explaining why.

To be sure, we must accept the positive results of accepting meritocracy's principles, no matter what those turn out to be. If it turns out that equal opportunity, merit-based hiring, and income-through-meritorious contribution lead to wealth and influence concentrated in the hands of white men, that is just. The same is true if the elite class is black women, or transgendered Asians, or anyone else. We must be blind to everything but merit. John Bunzel expressed this sentiment three decades ago, and it still holds true:

> We need to remind ourselves, especially at a time when some people seem intent on dividing us all into special groupings based on race or sex or ethnic background, that there is no such thing as black justice or brown justice or female justice. There is only Justice. Justice wears her blindfold that she may recognize no favorites, but she holds a scale in which merit is weighed.
>
> (1983: 184)

In any case, a meritocracy would be highly egalitarian by contemporary standards. As best I can tell, it would be more egalitarian than the most egalitarian countries today (e.g. the Scandinavian states).

I stress that there is nothing intrinsically objectionable about inequality. But it can be a *sign* that meritocratic values are being violated, as is the case in the United States today, where the bottom 50 percent of Americans receives the same share of national income as the top 0.1 percent. Of course, people *do* work more or less than each other, and they *are* different in merit—and they should be compensated, unequally, for these differences. But they are not so different as our economy would suggest.

Why would the distribution of income and wealth be flatter in a meritocracy? There are a few reasons. First, equal opportunity requires the total, or near-total, confiscation of wealth between generations. The only wealth inequalities in a meritocracy are those produced *within* a generation, through differences in deserved income, and perhaps small gifts (§8.4).

The distribution of income would also be egalitarian by our standards. This is primarily because (1) the extraction of economic rents is curbed, and rent extraction happens at the top of the income distribution; and (2) equal opportunity is by definition human capital-flattening—and in a meritocracy, human capital essentially determines income.

In a meritocracy, income inequalities exist to the extent to which (1) earnings-relevant traits are genetically determined, and (2) adults make different choices about work, leisure, and investment in their human capital. (There are other relevant choices, such as the choice whether or not to commit crimes.)

We must confront a touchy question: How much *do* genetics influence a person's earnings? We have data on this, and it shows that there is indeed an influence—but a small one. For example, in an attempt to explain the large correlation we find between individuals' wealth and their parents' wealth, Black et al. (2015) compared the wealth of adoptees to that of both their biological parents and their adoptive parents. They found that "even before any inheritance has occurred, wealth of adopted children is more closely related to the wealth of their adoptive parents than to that of their biological parents" (p. 4), and that "innate ability is only a small factor" (p. 22) in the intergenerational wealth correlation. Bowles, Gintis, and Groves (2005); Mazumder (2005); and Piketty (2000) reach similar conclusions.

The most plausible means by which one's genetics influence one's earnings is intelligence, since intelligence is partly genetically determined and almost universally useful. Yet IQ is weakly correlated with earnings; Tarmo Strenze (2007), in a meta-analysis, estimates the correlation between intelligence and income to be 0.2. Moreover, that figure does not distinguish between IQ genetically derived and IQ environmentally derived. Under equal opportunity, the correlation would be weaker still.

With each passing year, I am increasingly convinced that—*setting differences in opportunity aside*—the single biggest determinant of success across contexts is brute hard work. And this is precisely what research tells us is true. Björklund, Jäntti, and Roemer (2012) seek to identify the determinants of income in Sweden—a country that approximates the equal opportunity ideal fairly well. They find that the most important determinant, by far, is effort—explaining 76 percent of income inequality. The second most important determinant is IQ, back at 13 percent. And the third, parental income, accounts for 8 percent of the inequality. Parental education, family structure, number of siblings, and body mass index each explain less than 2 percent of inequality. (Note, however, that "effort" is used in the residual, Roemerian way (§4.4 n. 8), and thus could include some natural traits not controlled for in the study. Perhaps creativity, insofar as it is unconnected to IQ, is an example here.)

The American situation is worse—parental wealth controls here. The important point is that the egalitarian's worry about achievement being a slave to genetics is misplaced. *Given equal opportunity*, economic outcomes do *not* turn on genetic facts. Hufe et al. (Forthcoming) carry out the most careful analysis of the causes of American income inequality. They find that Roemerian circumstances, including natural traits, explain 43.5 percent of the inequality. When natural traits are excluded, as I think they should be, that figure drops to 40.7 percent. There is little difference.

Caution is always in order when it comes to empirical analyses like these, drawn as they are from imperfect (although surprisingly good) datasets. The normative structure of meritocracy is what it is, and in time we shall see what the real-world ramifications are.

Next, I wish to address a worry which I suspect is prevalent, but which is rarely aired. Some worry that even equal opportunity would not eliminate racial stratification. Whether they are aware of it or not, these people are committed to the view that racial differences in earnings-relevant traits, like IQ, must be genetically determined to a large degree.

All scholars agree that there are IQ differences between races (e.g. there is a 1-standard deviation difference in IQ between the mean white and the mean black). What is not known is the extent to which these differences are genetically determined. We simply have no good answer to this question yet, and intellectual honesty requires that we accept that it is possible that genetics plays a role, even a dominant one, in determining IQ. (See Rushton and Jensen 2005 for a summary of the research on racial IQ differences.)

But I do not think that this prospect should trouble anyone. First, as described, the influence of IQ on economic success appears to be modest. Second, the only reason we find such a possibility troubling is our contingent history of discrimination toward blacks, and the racism which persists to this day. Were that eliminated—and it would be in a meritocracy—we would not fret about any correlations between race and IQ. After all, there is a correlation between height and IQ, apparently genetically determined (Silventoinen et al. 2006), and it bothers no one. The reason it bothers no one is that there is no discrimination against short people. Short people are judged on their merits—they do not suffer unwarranted statistical discrimination; they face no animus in the workplace; etc. That is, any individual short person who "breaks the mold" is judged fairly—that is, he is judged on the basis of his merit.

It is also vital to keep in mind that the "heritability of IQ", which is typically what is discussed, is categorically different than the extent to which IQ is genetically determined. A trait may be ~100 percent heritable but ~0 percent genetically determined. Heritability is a measure of the variation within a group which is attributable to genetic difference—nothing more. Imagine a group of people who are raised in *identical* environments. For this group, IQ is ~100 percent heritable: Given that they are raised in identical environments, any differences in IQ must be due to genetics. It may still be the case that environment determines their IQ—if the environment is good, they have similar high IQs. If it is poor, they have similar low IQs. This is why the heritability of IQ can be low in children and high in adults, as it actually is.

So despite its ubiquity, heritability is simply not a useful datum when talking about equal opportunity, economic justice, the possibility of disparate racial results, and so on. It is a red herring, which, as Feldman et al. put it, is used

> to release us from any obligation to search for and supply those conditions that may enhance the lives of each member of our society. . . .
> Heritability has no bearing on socioeconomic inequality and what to do about it.
>
> (2000: 76)[6]

I note that meritocratic measures to combat wrongful discrimination (i.e. violations of Formal EO) will also benefit groups that are typically regarded as the victims of injustice, such as racial minorities. My view is that claims of discrimination are overblown, and that affirmative action, as it is currently practiced, is unjust (§9.2). But, in any case, a meritocracy actively combats implicit bias, explicit racism, and other forms of anti-meritocratic discrimination.

6.6 On Solidarity

Roemer has challenged me on my distributive rule, claiming that merito-cratic inequality would undermine economic solidarity. (This possibility has been raised in the literature—see, e.g. Cohen 2009.) He has provided a nice example of why solidarity is an important public good: Imagine that workers at some firm start doing precisely what is required of them by their contracts, no less and no more. They obey all regulations to the letter, they refuse all overtime, and so on. (I.e. they "work-to-rule".) The effect of this strict contractual compliance is that production grinds to a halt. This possibility cannot be eliminated by better contracts; it is impossible to write a contract that perfectly describes the requirements of any job. Thus, a productive economy *must* have social solidarity. Workers must be willing to go above and beyond their contracts.

I agree that solidarity is essential. But this objection to meritocracy is unsound for two reasons. First, even if it were true that inequality *per se* undermines solidarity, as I have explained, a meritocracy would not reach that standard of inequality.

Second, this objection mistakes the symptom of a loss of solidarity for its cause. When we see a loss of solidarity we may see major inequality, but this is because there is solidarity in a meritocracy, and a meritocracy happens to be not very unequal.

A lesson of Chapter 3 is that human beings have little affection for equal treatment; we find it distasteful. We do not want to participate in an egalitarian economy. Equity theory tells us that we want to participate in an economy in which our rewards are balanced against our contributions. Since we want to make unequal economic contributions, we want unequal economic rewards, too. We feel that we and our fellow workers are being treated fairly when our economy is meritocratic. It is the meritocratic ethos, not the egalitarian one, which unites people.

6.7 The Myth of Neutrality

Let us return to the issue of perfectionism, touched on in §2.5. In the neoclassical conception of the market, there is no notion of some preferences being superior to others. Preferences are taken as exogenous, and the market regarded as valuable for its ability to satisfy these preferences without waste. There is simply no way to talk about the quality of the preferences themselves; a market for Justin Bieber's music that produces $10 million in consumer surplus is just as good as a market for Beethoven that produces $10 million in surplus.

The major normative approaches find this unproblematic. Libertarians don't care what products are being bought and sold, so long as they are being bought and sold freely. Utilitarians point out that people are made happier by Bieber rather than Beethoven (and so in that instrumental sense, Bieber's music is better than Beethoven's). And egalitarians tend to be loath to impugn the tastes of some citizens as inferior. Indeed, for many, talk about the "quality" of preferences is worse than wrong—it is incoherent.

The purpose of this section is to explain why questions of value cannot be avoided, to show that they are relevant to justice, and to argue that meritocratic theory fruitfully addresses them. Note that while the considerations I raise are not incompatible with the neoclassical approach, they are also not currently accommodated within it. We consider three problems of value: those of *false beliefs*, *endogenous preferences*, and *depraved tastes*.

The problem of false beliefs may be illustrated simply. Suppose that a pharmaceutical company puts a drug on the market which it claims extends the human lifespan. But the drug does not do this; in fact it is toxic. Here the "value" of the drug is high, reflecting individuals' expressed preferences. But this is not the sort of value that we typically have in mind, and plausibly this company ought not to profit from its sales.

Put differently, there can be a divergence between (1) the degree to which consumers believe that some good satisfies their preferences and (2) the degree to which it actually does. This divergence can come as a result of brute bad luck (rational and competent consumers couldn't have known of the drug's dangers), or failure on the part of market participants (the drug company lied, or consumers desired something that they knew, or should have known, would hurt them).[7]

One question is whether the government could satisfy consumers' fully-informed preferences better than consumers can themselves. And here I agree with the libertarian: Such a thing is not possible given current technology. (Although note that "nudging"—subtle, unobtrusive behavioral modifications *via* the choice architecture—seeks to do precisely this.)

But suppose one day it becomes possible: Would we endorse intervention into markets then? Would we think it more just, if we could ensure that a company is richly rewarded for producing a vaccine that actually saves people's lives, rather than one that harms them owing to their false beliefs? It seems to me that we would endorse that intervention, and we would regard that remuneration as more just. Libertarianism cannot arrive at this conclusion.

Next is the problem of endogenous preferences. We say that markets are valuable because they efficiently satisfy consumers' preferences. However, there is a circularity in such a justification, since it is the market itself that creates these preferences, at least to a large degree. Affinity for Justin Bieber's music is not God-given; it is inculcated in consumers by the market. Indeed, it is the *raison d'être* of the advertising industry to shape preferences in this way.

Efforts have been made to incorporate preference formation into economic theory,[8] but economists continue to treat preferences as unproblematically exogenous. This will not do, and not only because it undermines the moral justification for markets.

More seriously, the endogenous preference problem exacerbates false beliefs. Suppose a few people hold false beliefs about preference satisfaction and make bad market decisions as a result. Upon seeing this, other people conclude, wrongly, that they may satisfy their similar preferences in the same way. So they enter the market, and the problem snowballs. Demand creates its own demand.

As an example, consider the "gluten-free" industry, which is a multibillion-dollar one. We all want to be healthy, but some believe that various ailments, from depression to constipation to autism, are caused by what the author of the New York Times best seller, *Wheat Belly*, calls the "chronic, perfect poison" of gluten. Celebrities have jumped on the gluten-free bandwagon, friends have commended the "benefits" of going gluten-free to each other, and so on. It is all untrue—like homeopathy and GMO scaremongering—but it is natural, perhaps even rational, for individuals to form beliefs about the efficacy of these products by looking at the market demand for them.

This is a problem. Sick people are buying products which will not heal them. R&D money is being wasted on projects which any meritorious observer already knows to be fruitless. Respect for truth, expert opinion, and the scientific method are being undermined.

The important point here is that it is *impossible* for government to remain indifferent about the preferences of its citizens. That is the myth of neutrality. Every decision—to regulate or not to regulate, to tax or refrain from taxing—shapes preferences. Even the most liberal governments, whether they admit it or not, must make some decision about which preferences are good and which are bad.

The libertarian response here is that preferences created through active government intervention are different from those the market would produce, were it left alone. That is true, but it is a bad reply. First, it is an instance of the naturalistic fallacy. Because something is natural does not make it good. Second, it violates a fundamental principle of rational choice: Not doing *A* and thereby letting *B* happen is no different than actively choosing *B* rather than *A*.

The third problem of value is that of depraved tastes. Imagine a society in which there is some hated minority race. The hatred is irrational; people are simply racists. Sammy, a television producer, develops a program in which members of the minority are publicly ridiculed.

Given prevailing, racist opinion, the program is wildly successful, making Sammy a rich man.

Isn't there something unjust about Sammy's wealth? Isn't he selling a product that is simply inferior? I think so, but it is hard to explain that injustice with current conceptual tools. Attempts to accommodate the intuition by appealing to meta-preferences, or fully-informed preferences (maybe if people really knew the harm done by the program, they would not enjoy watching it) will not work, since the question may simply be pushed: Suppose fully-informed people really do prefer, all the way down, to watch this program. What then?

I don't think that the diagnosis of injustice changes even if we imagine that the minorities have become so inured to their suffering that they now enjoy the abuse that they receive. Suppose Sammy's product makes *everybody* happy—what would we say about the economy then? I would insist that this economy is unjust. It is producing products of intrinsically low value.

If we wish to stay within the neoclassical framework—and I think that we should—we must address depraved tastes and questions of preference formation through a subjective approach to value.

This is possible. But we must attack the problem obliquely. The possibility of directly inculcating good preferences and identifying good products is a fool's errand. This is not just because of a lack of information. Questions about what we should and should not desire, what things are good and what things are bad, are the deepest of the human experience. We will not solve them soon.

Meritocracy suggests a second strategy. Rather than try to enumerate the correct preferences, we pursue them indirectly, through a focus on merit. In a meritocracy, the resources which stimulate demand and which determine production are put in the hands of meritorious people. This is the optimal way to ensure that consumers have good preferences, and that our products are high quality ones.

Every decision about consumption and investment affects preference formation. If all the world's wealth were held by people of low moral and intellectual quality, they would invest it poorly (in, e.g. racist media companies or producers of homeopathic drugs), and they would consume bad products (e.g. Sammy's program). In time, other economic agents would follow suit, and our economy would be an unhappy one.

On the other extreme, a radical egalitarian distribution of wealth would essentially turn preference formation into a popularity contest. Each individual would have an equal say about which firms would prosper, and which products bought and sold.

In this way, income and preferences are tightly bound up. Economists have long known that income gets determined by people's preferences (decisions about leisure, work, and consumption determine which allocations are Pareto efficient). What is interesting, and novel, is that things go in the other direction, too: Preferences are determined, in part, by income.

Why would a meritocratic distribution be ideal? I'll give an argument by analogy. Think of investment and consumption in terms of voting. When a person spends $1 on a homeopathic drug, it is a vote for an economy in which people desire these drugs and they get bought and sold. When a person spends $2, this is two votes for such an economy. And so on. The distribution of wealth determines the number of votes an economic agent has, and, thereby, his influence.

The question to ask, then, is: What distribution of votes maximizes the probability that the right preferences and products, *whatever they be*, obtain? Is it an elitist distribution, in which a handful of people have all the wealth and, therefore, all the votes? Or is it a democratic distribution, in which wealth is shared equally so that each citizen has the same influence?

The answer to both questions is "no". An optimal voting system distributes votes to people *in proportion to their merit*. We know this formally: A group seeking to maximize the probability that a correct outcome obtains will weight each member's vote in proportion to (the log-odds of) his competence.[9] It is reasonable to suppose that something similar is at work within the market structure.

To reiterate: Preferences are formed by market decisions. The number of these market decisions a person may make is determined by his wealth. When a person's income exceeds his merit, the process by which value is pursued is not optimal; he exerts too much influence over this process. When a person's income is less than his merit, he exerts too little influence. When income reflects merit, he contributes to the search for value in the optimal way.

We cannot say what the right preferences and the good products are. What we can say is what sort of economy is likely to form and produce these. This is a meritocratic economy. In a meritocracy, we are led to the correct preferences—whatever they be—even as the government refrains from making particular judgments about the wisdom of market decisions.

Teun Dekker has suggested something similar: "Even if one believes that there are objective answers to questions of value, one might still believe a democratic procedure to be preferable because it is more likely to arrive at correct judgements than using expert judges." (2010: 319). That is the right idea, although, as we have seen, a "democratic procedure", under which each individual, regardless of his merit, exerts the same influence, is not optimal.

6.8 Problems With Libertarian Economic Theory

Unlike the egalitarian's objection to desert—which is focused and Rawlsian (and to be addressed in Chapter 7)—the libertarian's reasons for opposing meritocracy, and desert-based justice generally, are diffuse. Although libertarianism and meritocracy have some things in common, like an affection for markets, there are a number of incompatibilities between the two theories.[10]

Meritocracy, like all desert-based theories, is *patterned* and *historical*, to use Nozick's terminology. It is "patterned" because it "specifies that a distribution is to vary along with some natural dimension" (Nozick 1974: 156). It is historical because we must have knowledge of the past in order to judge the justness of the distribution now (i.e. we must know what meritorious contributions a person has made).

It is important that our distributive theories be historical. Most people would not find plausible any theory of justice that does not appeal to historical information about the persons to whom we are distributing. Eric Mack (2014) gives an example: Imagine that we are choosing from a number of potential distributions, and some of the people to whom we are distributing were involved in "slavery-like exploitation". This information would doubtless influence our judgments about justice, yet it plays no role in non-historical (i.e. "end state") theories. (Mack correctly notes that desert-based theories do not suffer from this flaw.)

I say five things against libertarianism in this section. First, I respond to Nozick's famous "Wilt Chamberlain" thought experiment, in which we are challenged to explain how injustice could possibly result from an initially just distribution of resources followed by seemingly unproblematic free choices. Second, I explain the limits of government interference in the name of protecting the desert-based pattern of distribution. Third, against Hayek, I explain why recognizing desert need not come at the expense of creating value. Fourth, I argue, also against Hayek, that a meritocratic economy is practical. And fifth, I respond to the idea that a meritocracy is undesirable because it leaves the poorly-off without good excuses for their socioeconomic position.

Nozick invites us to imagine a world in which our favorite patterned theory of justice is realized (1974: 160–4). The distribution of wealth in this world, D_1, is *ex hypothesi* just. We now suppose that basketball fans develop an interest in watching Wilt Chamberlain play. Each fan voluntarily pays a quarter more in ticket price to watch Wilt. These quarters are given to Wilt, who, at the end of the season, ends up with a much larger share of wealth than anyone else. We now have a final distribution D_2 which has deviated from the putatively just pattern—but only as a result of the free choices of everyone involved. Nozick asks: "Is this new distribution D_2, unjust? If so, why?" (p. 161).

For the desert theorist, D_2 is not necessarily unjust. We cannot answer the question of whether D_2 is just or not without further information. We need to know if the market activity led to Wilt having the relevant desert bases in appropriately larger measure. D_2, is just if and only if that is the case—and not because it flowed from D_1 through free exchanges.

So the justness of the scenario will turn on the desert basis chosen. For the meritocrat, D_2 is indeed unjust, because Wilt's contribution (i.e. the value he created for his fans, in the form of entertainment), did not come with an increase in merit. If, on the other hand, Wilt responded to the fans' support by becoming a better basketball player, then his additional remuneration is deserved.

There is nothing outlandish about this case: Athletes are prime examples of the "superstar" phenomenon discussed in §6.4. The real-life Wilt was handsomely paid, because of his merit as an athlete, to be sure, but also because of his monopoly power. Nozick suggests as much in his example: Wilt would have played basketball for his D_1 salary—and so the extra money he made at D_2 was a rent. The meritocratic argument for confiscating rents applies.

As Barbara Fried has pointed out, Nozick sneakily conflates two senses of free exchange in his example; "transfer by gift and by exchange, which Nozick casually treats as posing identical problems in entitlement theory, raise completely different problems" (1995: 240). In the former case, which provides Nozick with the intuition he wants to harness, the moral consideration is whether a person who owns something fully may give it away however he desires. But in the latter case, which is the one relevant to economic distribution, the question is whether we come to own, in the first place, the economic rents which we may extract. The meritocrat denies this: Ownership comes only to the extent to which meritorious contributions were made. The fans can gift their deserved income to Wilt if they like.

The meritocrat wants to enforce a pattern of distribution. But it is a limited one, confined to the *intra*generational distribution of income. If an adult wishes to give away some of his deserved income, there is no barrier to his doing so. These gifts would not disrupt any pattern, since there is no call to enforce a pattern of wealth within a generation.

I note that most people don't agree with Nozick about the justness of Wilt's wealth at D_2; Konow tests the case (using Michael Jordan as the example), and finds that 76 percent of people view Wilt's earnings at D_2 as unfair, "cast[ing] doubt on broad support for Nozick's minimal role for wealth redistribution" (Konow 2003: 1207).

Consider the following variant on Nozick's thought experiment: Again we start with an initially just distribution D_1. This time, though, the fans ignore Wilt and develop an interest in the team's wacky waterboy, Bonzo. The fans find Bonzo's sideline antics amusing; his lack of coordination endearing; and his ribald comments hilarious. The fans freely decide that what is important to them when they attend games is not to see high quality basketball being played but to be entertained by Bonzo. Management calls Wilt into a meeting. "Wilt, we appreciate your excellent performance on our team. You have done much for this franchise and the sport of basketball. We now offer you a free choice. As you know, there is huge market interest in Bonzo. As a result, he will be replacing you at center and will be paid accordingly. Although you will not be playing basketball for us anymore, you will be responsible for discharging the duties of waterboy, at $10,000 a year. Accept these terms or be released."

In this case, we have an initially just distribution of wealth and a final distribution that resulted from Nozickian principles of free exchange; no one was coerced to make the exchanges that they did, no one was defrauded, no one was stolen from. People made Nozickian-legitimate choices in the free market. Therefore, according to Nozick's theory, the final distribution D_2 is just. It seems to me that that cannot be right. Wilt has a legitimate cause for moral complaint. He is right to be upset that his path-of-life, his financial security, and his happiness have been frustrated by the inanity of the masses, as expressed through the free market.

Note, too, the damage done to Wilt's *liberty* in this case. Wilt decided to take advantage of his natural talents and devote himself, through years of hard work, to excellence in basketball. His plan-of-life centered on this devotion, and he had a reasonable expectation that it would not be frustrated by the whims of the basketball-watching public. But now Wilt, who has done nothing wrong and everything right, finds his professional and financial futures frustrated.

Mack says that "to enjoy liberty . . . is to be free of disruptions caused by other persons in the ongoing activities which constitute one's life" (1978: 184). That seems right to me, and it also seems right to say that Wilt suffers just such a disruption. Now, it is true that a meritocracy would frustrate the liberty of the public to watch Bonzo at center. But given that *somebody's* liberty must be frustrated, we ought to prefer frustrating the liberty of the public, which has badly erred, rather than the liberty of Wilt, who is excellent.

There is a common sense distinction between conforming one's plan-of-life to the reasonable preferences of others, as expressed through the market—which we all must do to some degree and which is in no way objectionable—and being forced to subjugate yourself to the tastes of others, no matter how depraved, to secure a livelihood.

For this reason, there is something disharmonious—downright collectivist—about libertarian affection for unrestrained markets. Ayn Rand laments that "the man at the bottom . . . contributes nothing to those above him, but receives the bonus of all of their brains" (1961: 186), but in fact just the opposite is true: Those men at the bottom determine demand and thereby wield control over the economic futures of meritorious people. In a meritocracy, rewards reflect merit, and the excellent do not have to degrade themselves in the pursuit of their well-being.

In a meritocracy, economic benefits reflect merit, but under *laissez-faire*, they are received in proportion to *popularity*. Meritorious people who produce high quality goods and services receive the economic rewards that they deserve only when the marketplace recognizes the value of their products. But when that does not happen—when merit and popularity come apart— then economic reward falls not on the meritorious but on the popular.

The libertarian cannot have things both ways: We can reward excellence, whether or not that excellence is recognized by the market; or we can allow unfettered economic exchanges, in which case popularity will wholly determine whose lives go well and whose go poorly.

The libertarian might say that desert-based justice leads us down a dangerous path. If the state has a role in ensuring that income is distributed in accordance with desert, why not extend this to other goods, like romantic relationships? If that were to follow then any desert-based theory would fail by *reductio*; none of us wants the government meddling in private affairs in that way. This is a typical libertarian worry: The idea of bureaucrats telling us whom to love, venerate, and associate with is terrifying.

But this objection should not sway us. To begin with, the state already does affect access to these private goods. Relationships, esteem, and popularity depend in large and lamentable part on one's wealth. Sometimes these goods can be bought outright, but often the connections are subtle: Wealth is considered attractive in a mate, people associate with those who can provide expensive experiences, and so on. The state cannot remain neutral, though it can pretend to be.

It is interesting that throughout *Anarchy, State, and Utopia*, Nozick uses *highly meritorious* characters to elicit the intuitions he desires. He chose Wilt Chamberlain, after all—arguably the greatest basketball player of all time—and not Bonzo the waterboy, thus avoiding the potential intuition change that comes when free exchanges redound to the undeserving. Or consider this objection, made by Nozick against equal opportunity: "If the woman who later became my wife rejected another suitor (whom she otherwise would have married) for me, partially because (I leave aside my lovable nature) of my keen intelligence and good looks, neither of which did I earn, would the rejected less intelligent and less handsome suitor have a legitimate complaint about unfairness?" (p. 237).

That is right as far as it goes, but it is again an example of a Nozickian thought experiment that avoids conflict with desert. A better question to ask is this: What if Barbara rejected Nozick in favor of a *less deserving* suitor? Imagine that Nozick, with his famous good looks and obvious brilliance, fell in love with Barbara at the same time that a man of lesser merit did. Owing to unequal opportunity to pursue her, Barbara decided on the less deserving man instead (suppose Nozick had to work full-time while the other man took her on fancy dates enabled by his trust fund). My intuition is that Nozick has a legitimate complaint about injustice. And it's not that Barbara did something unjust, or that she isn't morally allowed to choose whomever she desires when it comes to marriage. What is unjust is that for some people, the good things in life are closed off to them for reasons irrelevant from the point-of-view of merit. And when I say that the man is "less deserving" than Nozick, I don't mean less deserving as determined by a bureaucrat—I mean less deserving *by Barbara's own lights*. Under equal opportunity, she would have chosen Nozick instead.

In short, this objection parodies meritocracy. Any plausible distributive system includes liberal protections against government overreach. Any moral ideal becomes risible if taken to the extreme. Meritocracy is fully compatible with robust freedom for its citizens; indeed, as I shall argue in the next section, if freedom is construed in its positive sense, meritocracy provides more of it than libertarianism does.

The third libertarian objection is associated with Hayek (1960, 1976). Hayek observes, correctly, that markets can fail to track merit or desert,[11] and he claims that this is a good thing. According to Hayek, "we do not wish people to earn a maximum of merit but to achieve a *maximum of usefulness* at a minimum of pain and sacrifice and therefore a minimum of merit" (1960: 96). In this way, Hayek suggests, giving a person what she deserved would come at the cost of her ability to create value for others in the marketplace.

In reply, I note that even if our normative goal were the maximization of the surplus, as Hayek suggests, meritocratic regulation is justified on those grounds: Economic rents are inefficient, as are negative externalities like pollution (§8.3).

Hayek is right that remuneration based on market demand serves an important purpose, signaling firms to move from one line of production to another in a socially useful way. But that is not true universally; it is true only insofar as none of the considerations raised in §6.7 hold. It is a bad thing when firms invest our scarce resources in the development, production, and distribution of homeopathic "remedies".[12]

Moreover, we cannot only concern ourselves with sending useful economic signals. We must also incentivize the sort of character that positively impacts an economy. Hayek argues that producers of demand products should be rewarded because that's good for productivity. But demand is only good for productivity when it's demand for a quality product, and high quality products are produced by high quality people. One important feature of markets is the way that they reward innovation, efficiency, and effort. But when markets work poorly, individuals' talents go unrecognized and reward redounds not to the meritorious but rather to those with the right family or social connections. These are market failures, to be dealt with through regulation.

The next libertarian objection is a wholly positive one: that no feasible institutional structure could effectively promote desert within an economy, at least while avoiding unacceptable harms to efficiency.

If *that* is the libertarian's reason for opposing meritocracy, then he has already conceded a great deal to me. If the libertarian believes that in an ideal world people are rewarded because they deserve to be, then he accepts my principal conclusion. Of course, libertarians who are attracted to Nozickian entitlement theory cannot accept this.

In any event, there is nothing infeasible about the institutional structures for which meritocracy calls. Quite the opposite, one of the strengths of this approach to justice, I have argued, is that it is attainable from present circumstances. Meritocracy is largely compatible with free markets, and where it is not, the required regulation is straightforward. Many meritocratic policies, such as Pigovian taxes (§8.3), have been developed in detail and endorsed by experts right, left, and center.

Hayek and other libertarians parody the meritocratic ideal by suggesting that there would have to be some kind of centralized and omniscient "merit czar", who knows exactly what each citizen deserves and distributes income accordingly. No one thinks that we should have such a czar, and no such czar is necessary. Meritocrats believe that limits should be put on executive compensation, especially when executive performance is poor; that people who destroy social value, not create it (e.g. producers of negative externalities) should not benefit from that destruction; that anti-discrimination laws are justified; and that the state should spend money to promote the education and health of children born to poor or inattentive parents. None of these policies is infeasible, none requires central planning, none is oppressive.[13]

The final objection to meritocracy I consider here was also lodged, as best I can tell, by Hayek. The objection is this: In a meritocracy, disadvantaged citizens have no good excuse for their inferior socioeconomic position. If people truly got what they deserved, then those on the bottom rungs could not in good conscience blame their hardship on the vagaries of the market or bad luck. They would have no choice but to confront the hard fact that they failed. Hayek regards the market's inattention to desert as a sort of psychological salve. For him and for others inclined to this objection, desert's demand that each person make an honest reckoning of the reasons for his place in society is far from a strength. As Schaar puts it, a meritocracy "leaves the losers with no external justification for their failures, and no amount of trying can erase the large element of cruelty from any social doctrine which does that" (1967: 234).

This objection has no force, and indeed strikes me as an especially cynical way of looking at things. That a political order lends itself to self-delusion is a weakness, not a strength. It is neither unreasonable nor cruel to expect each adult citizen to take responsibility for his past actions and inactions, his merits and demerits, and his successes and failures. If we are to take personal responsibility seriously (§6.9), then we cannot fret over the unreasonable reactions of those who have suffered at their own hands. All plausible political arrangements have winners and losers. That is an unfortunate fact of scarcity. And maybe it is inevitable that the losers will be upset about their place in society. But surely it is preferable to have an economic arrangement in which those at the bottom are there by their own making. If Alice and Billy are both "losers", but Alice's status is due to her being lazy and evil, and Billy's is due to racial prejudice, surely we ought to be more concerned with correcting Billy's undeserved disadvantage, no matter how upset Alice is. Given that we do not live in a world of plenty, and that no matter what political order we endorse, *somebody* is going to be upset, we ought to prefer a system in which the bottom rung is populated with Alices rather than Billys.

Think of it this way: If the Yankees, after losing the World Series to the Mets after seven fair-and-square games managed by honest and competent umpires, were to complain about the unfairness of the result and the injustice of their runner-up status, we would have little sympathy. We would tell them to suck it up and try harder next time. That the Yankees might, as a matter of brute fact, be angry about their loss is not particularly interesting, and of no moral importance. That anger would be unreasonable. It is the role of psychologists, not philosophers, to say how to placate sore losers.

6.9 Positive Liberty and Personal Responsibility

It is widely assumed that libertarianism best promotes the value of liberty. This is correct if liberty is interpreted in its negative sense, as the absence of interference. If you dismantle the government, you maximize negative liberty (setting aside that private interference would increase as public interference decreases).

But liberty may be interpreted in a positive way, too—as the ability to shape one's life as one sees fit. Positive liberty is closely connected to the concept of autonomy, and endorsed by thinkers as diverse as Kant, Marx, and J. S. Mill.

South Sudan is a paragon of negative liberty: The nascent government has put few constraints on its citizens and even these it lacks the power to enforce. A South Sudanese can in theory do anything he wants; his government will not trouble him. But, of course, he can do nothing at all with his life, in part because his government is so impotent. He cannot travel; there is no infrastructure. He cannot pursue a profession; there is no economy. He has only one path-of-life available to him: fending off famine, disease, and war. He lacks positive liberty.

The idea that we should like to live in a maximally free society is appealing, but imprecise. It is imprecise, one, because it does not make clear whether the freedom at issue is negative or positive. And these may be at odds. (I'll use "liberty" and "freedom" interchangeably.)

Two, the connection between individual freedom and social freedom is ambiguous. Suppose there are 10 people in world A. One of them has 92 paths-of-life open to him; the other nine have a single path-of-life open. In world B, there are also 10 people, each of whom has 10 paths-of-life available. Is A "freer" than B? (Since there are a total of 101 paths-of-life open in A, compared to 100 in world B?) It seems to me not, but the answer is not obvious. We have to make a judgment about how social freedom turns on individual freedoms.

For these reasons, we should not be too quick to concede the banner of liberty to the libertarian. I believe that a meritocracy would provide more positive liberty to its citizens than a libertarian state would. The most important reason is that, in a meritocracy, no citizen has paths-of-life walled off because of birth into disadvantage. This follows from equal opportunity. The only paths-of-life that an individual citizen cannot pursue are those for which he is disqualified by virtue of genetics or free choice. And surely it is not a violation of liberty when a path-of-life is walled off owing to free choice.

It should be plain that many people today, even in prosperous countries like the United States, lack positive liberty. If you are born black in inner city America, into a broken home and amidst a culture of violence, you are hugely limited in your prospects—no matter your natural merits. The same is true for the children of the white rural poor, who face under-funded schools and broken local economies.

Now it is true that establishing equal opportunity might decrease the positive liberties of some citizens—most notably, the rich, who are, *prima facie*, on the losing end of the relevant redistributive policies (but see the efficiency benefits of these policies—§4.8). But this does not seem like a problem, especially if a flatter distribution of individual freedoms is better from the point-of-view of freedom writ large.

Of course, unlimited positive liberty is impossible; as Isaiah Berlin reminds us, "that we cannot have everything is a necessary, not a contingent, truth" (1969: 170). All we can do is try to provide as much of it in our society as is possible. And when liberties are constrained because of scarcity, all we can do is try to live with that without resentment.

In this way, meritocracy is freer than either Nozick's nighwatchman state or a *laissez-faire* economy. I conjecture that a society that (1) takes initial human capital endowments as given, (2) provides equal opportunity to all, and then (3) distributes scarce social goods on the basis of merit alone maximizes social freedom. Proving that requires some consensus about what we mean by "social freedom", so I leave it as a conjecture for now.

All that said, libertarians are correct that, no matter how we construe liberty, history has shown it to be best-promoted by market economies. It is almost incomprehensible, how much more positive liberty we have now than we did 200 years ago. This is true of the poorest and the richest among us. But it is a logical error to think that this implies that positive liberty is maximized in an unregulated economy without redistribution. We are so much freer now than we used to be because we are so much richer now. Freedom turns importantly on economic output, but it is not tantamount to output. And, in any case, meritocratic redistribution should increase output. Thus, to the extent to which freedom is a result of economic growth, libertarians ought to support this redistribution. And they do not (see, e.g. Hayek's (1976) and Nozick's (1974) opposition to equal opportunity).

Next: It has often been thought that desert is closely connected to the concept of responsibility (see, e.g. Sadurski 1985), and a meritocratic economy cultivates an ethos of personal responsibility.

Equal opportunity ensures that no one has a poor life forced upon him for reasons outside of his control. Individuals gets jobs only if they have prepared themselves responsibly (i.e. developed the relevant merits). And when people do get rich in a meritocracy, it is because they developed and applied those merits. People are held to account for the uncompensated costs that they impose on others (§8.3). And so on.

It is no surprise that as the meritocratic framework of our country has been dismantled since 1980, we have seen a decline in personal responsibility. Conservatives attack liberals for irresponsibility: for using abortion as a form of birth control; for funneling money to "welfare queens"; for buying homes that they could not afford and then demanding bailouts. Now, some of this is silly—but there is truth here too.

On the other hand, liberals attack conservatives: for failing to take care of the climate; for launching stupid wars and having others fight them; and for funding their own consumption on the backs of future generations (because about half the national debt is held by foreigners, young Americans will be saddled with the debt payments but they will not inherit the bonds).

Again we have normative agreement—personal responsibility is morally important—which gets masked by discord over positive matters.

I have concentrated on the ways in which our economy promotes irresponsible conduct. To egalitarians, this will already be obvious. My hope here is that I can convince some libertarians that their attraction to free markets is motivated more by considerations of desert, efficiency, and personal responsibility than distinctly libertarian values. In the face of other economic arrangements that have been tried, free markets seem to best recognize personal responsibility, drawing distinctions of merit which other systems do not. It is natural but false to suppose that if taken to extreme *laissez-faire*, markets will best promote personal responsibility. They will not.

Joshua Preiss discusses the clash between libertarian theory and personal responsibility at length in an excellent recent article, noting that

> in the political and economic status quo, preferred libertarian policies . . . undermine the ethic of personal responsibility that Americans from across the ideological spectrum value and many conservatives and libertarians celebrate. In the present American context, those who value personal responsibility (libertarian or otherwise) must reserve a central place for policies that mitigate opportunity and distributive inequalities.

(2017: 622)[14]

This is correct.

It seems to me that something like the following has happened within the distributive justice debate: (1) People pre-theoretically like the "meritocratic ideal"—unequal outcomes; achievement-based-on-merit; an emphasis on personal responsibility. (2) They seek a principled justification for this sentiment. (3) They believe that libertarianism provides it, in part because they judge, correctly, that egalitarianism is hopelessly at odds with the ideal. And so (4) they endorse libertarian public policies—even as these are precisely the wrong ones for pursuing the ideal they found compelling in the first place.

6.10 On the Possibility of a Social Safety Net

As best we can tell (§3.2), when people think about the morality of an economy, they have three ideals in mind: justice, efficiency, and need (by which they mean keeping citizens above a distributive floor). In theory, these three ideals might come into conflict. We know that justice is the most important of the three, followed by need, followed by efficiency— but that does not mean that justice simply trumps need and efficiency, and need simply trumps efficiency. It means that the three will receive different weights when the possibility of trading them off against each other arises.

In this section, I consider the possibility of maintaining a social safety net in a meritocracy. Unlike efficiency, which is promoted by meritocratic justice in a somewhat obvious way, the question of trade-offs between justice and need must be addressed, and the extent of the meritocratic social safety net made clear.[15]

To begin with, it should be clear that, in a meritocracy, all children (i.e. everyone younger than the age of moral agency, whatever we decide that to be), is caught by a robust safety net. This is not an additional conceptual idea, nor would it require public policies beyond those demanded by justice. This is simply part and parcel of equal opportunity. Ensuring that all children have their basic needs met—food, education, health, etc.—is necessary, but not sufficient, for equal opportunity.

So considerations of need proper are restricted to adults. Who might be in need in a meritocracy? Two classes of people. The first class contains those citizens who are *unable* to provide themselves with a minimal level of welfare. This includes citizens who were seriously disabled from birth, those who were in accidents, those who were injured in war, etc.

The second class contains those citizens who *choose* not to provide themselves with a minimal level of welfare. While in theory this includes citizens who literally choose not to work and would starve without public aid, this class is really composed of citizens who made past choices such that now they cannot provide for themselves. For example, the choice to use narcotics imprudently may, in time, render one addicted and unable to provide for oneself. We might call the first class the "deserving poor" and the second class the "undeserving poor".

I stress that we are assuming, as I think that we should, that the common intuition is correct: It is morally good for a state to provide a social safety net to its citizens. I would keep even deeply undeserving people out of the gutter—if that could be done at no cost. But of course there is a cost. So the real question confronting us is whom we *actually* have an obligation to help *in light of opportunity costs.*

Let us address the undeserving poor first. Suppose that Gary, a career criminal, is unemployed owing to drug addiction. He has hurt innocent people over the course of his life. He has been put through rehab before, on the public dime. And now he will die without X dollars of public aid.

We must remember that when we decide to give Gary those X dollars, we decide not to improve the welfare of terminally ill children; we decide not to fight climate change, or fund a cure for cancer; we decide not to support equal opportunity. Public aid for Gary runs afoul of the Singer Test (§2.3). That is, a theory that requires that we choose Gary over those terminally ill children is likely wrong. In contrast, a theory that requires that we help Tyler, a good man badly injured in a car accident, does not have that visceral implausibility. (I stress that this is a metatheoretical point. It might well be that morality requires that we help the children rather than Tyler. But we would not recoil at a theory that instructed us to choose Tyler over them.)

We are under no moral obligation to help Gary. Indeed, if providing aid to him comes at the cost of one of the worthy causes just described, we are morally required *not* to help him. Morality requires that we let him die. Until we enter a post-scarcity era, a person who has enjoyed genuine equal opportunity and squandered that opportunity has no moral entitlement to resources that could go to unambiguously noble causes. If this seems harsh, it is only because we so often fail to keep opportunity costs in mind.

Now, when we think of *actual* Garys—that is, people like Gary, whom we know—the intuition is not so strong. This is because equal opportunity is badly lacking in the actual world. It is rare that we can say with any confidence that an actual person, in dire straits, is really there by his own making.

Arneson (1997) argues for a wide-scope safety net in part on these grounds: that claims about citizens' irresponsibility get undermined by the possibility of unfortunate contingencies in their past. That I don't dispute. But what we are trying to get at is how a just, meritocratic society ought to treat Gary. In such a society, he would have enjoyed equal opportunity and been judged on his merits.

The real-world justifiability of a strong safety net, protecting people like Gary, will therefore turn on the degree to which a society is just. A just society, still grappling with scarcity, must not extend aid to Gary. In an unjust society, in which equal opportunity and meritocratic discrimination are lacking, the case for aiding Gary is stronger. Of course, even here that aid would have to be balanced against the other good these resources could do (like the establishment of justice).

One might think that this example, which involves criminality, skirts a tougher question: What about the virtuous but non-contributing? Suppose Dave does not have a nasty bone in his body, but he also has zero desire to work. He collects welfare, spends his days at the park, and survives on public support.

This changes nothing. As far as the social safety net goes, Gary and Dave should be treated the same. The only reason that a safety net is available in the first place is because so many of us are willing to sacrifice our leisure and work instead. This is why we do not live in a Hobbesian nightmare. Dave's unwillingness to make the sacrifices that make all this possible excludes him from public aid.

Let us turn to the other class of adult citizens, the deserving poor. I note that the intuition here is very different. Suppose Tyler, an everyday member of the American workforce, gets in an accident that renders him unable to work. We are contemplating providing him with a public income. We bring the Singer Test to mind and ask: Is that acceptable in light of the opportunity costs? To my mind, the answer is "yes": Helping Tyler is not beyond the pale.

To summarize: All children in a meritocracy are protected by a social safety net. Not only does this not conflict with justice, it is *required by justice*. In addition, children cannot have done anything to make themselves undeserving—since they are not yet moral agents. Conceptually, there can be no conflict between justice and need for this part of society.

The safety net also extends to the deserving poor. When we help an individual who, because of disability, unemployment, etc. is unable to achieve a basic level of welfare on his own merits, that does not conflict with justice. Justice is about desert, and in particular it is about matching citizens' income with their meritorious contributions to the economy. The disabled and unemployed (etc.) stand outside of this structure.

The safety net does *not* extend to the undeserving poor. When a person is capable of making an economic contribution but refuses to do so, that does create a deviation from the just pattern of distribution. This person deserves nothing (because he made no contribution but could have), yet the safety net provides him with income (either cash or an in-kind benefit).

It is also important to limit the social safety net for communitarian reasons. We want to cultivate an ethos of personal responsibility, and that is obviously undermined when irresponsibility gets rewarded. We also want to cultivate solidarity and a sense of shared sacrifice, and when able-bodied people do not work those values are undermined.

Finally, while we will always be faced with the question of what to do with the undeserving poor, the problem will be far less acute in a meritocracy than it actually is. The efficiency gains and positive externalities associated with equal opportunity will redound to those in danger of falling into this class. More human capital means less chance of struggling to find employment and a better ability to deal with life's travails. In a meritocracy, citizens do not get stuck in a cycle of criminality, because there are no "collateral consequences" of conviction (§5.7). When a person commits a crime and pays his debt to society the matter is put to rest—from that moment on, he will be judged on his merits. And if merit percolates into politics, more sensible public policies will result. It is becoming clear that much of the want in America has been caused or perpetuated by the drug war. Meritorious people across the political spectrum have been warning us of this for years.

6.11 The Justice/Efficiency "Trade-Off", Part 3

An economy structured around the principles outlined in this chapter will approach maximal productivity for the following reasons.

First, whenever remuneration and contribution come apart, there exists an incentive to engage in activity that does not create value in the marketplace. This is precisely what is happening in America today: Labor is being diverted into industries in which unproductive enterprise and rent-seeking are most prevalent—consulting, finance, and law. These fields are especially attractive to the most skilled and highly-educated among us, a natural consequence of the fact that rent extraction is easiest and most common at the top of the income distribution.

I do not mean to suggest that the aforementioned industries are unimportant. They are vital to a well-functioning economy, and meritorious firms and people in them should be handsomely rewarded. In recent years, however, these industries have seen a mammoth divergence between remuneration and value-added. Consider, for example, the extraordinary incomes of hedge fund managers, most of whom run what are essentially professional gambling outfits. Most hedge funds fail, and those that survive deliver truly mediocre performance to their clients: Their "dollar-weighted returns are reliably lower than the return on the Standard & Poor's (S&P) 500 index" (Dichev and Yu 2011: 248). The hedge funds that do enjoy success—in the sense of generating good returns for their investors—do it by exploiting technical inefficiencies in markets. They extract rents.

Second, whenever remuneration and merit come apart, there is a disincentive for people to acquire human capital. As anyone in the labor market these days knows, personal connections are critical to finding a job. We go to conferences to network; websites like LinkedIn facilitate connections; and professional certifications (many of which have been introduced, unprompted, by the private sector) flourish. It is in an individual's interest to spend his time and money networking, getting certified, etc.—but these activities provide *no* human capital growth. They just give people an interpersonal advantage in the labor market. Resources spent in this way are wasted; they could be put toward productive enterprise, but they are not.

Similarly, if you are CEO, and your salary depends on good relations with the compensation committee and not merit, you will rationally develop that relationship rather than become a more competent executive. There is economic waste on the part of the firm (which pays more to the rent-extracting CEO than it needs to keep her employed), and on the part of the executive (she doesn't develop her merits, because that is not in her interest). This is why we know that if "today's executives . . . were paid less there would be no loss of productivity or output" (Mishel and Davis 2015: 9). Productivity and output would increase if we attacked these anti-meritocratic features of our economy.

Nevertheless, government can only do so much. More important is a cultural change: Greater concern for merit; greater attention to actual performance; and less interest in race, pedigree, and rough proxies for merit.

Third, as discussed in §§6.7–6.8, in a meritocracy capital accrues to those who are best able to make wise decisions about its investment—meritorious people. Capital is not distributed among citizens equally. That would give some citizens more capital than they could make efficient use of, and some less (as it gives some citizens more than they deserve, and some less).

Similarly, unrestricted capital transfers, permitted under *laissez-faire*, are undesirable. Some transfers that the libertarian finds unproblematic—for example, inheritance—put capital in the hands of those with the right family or friends, rather than in the hands of those who can invest it wisely. Whatever we might want to say about how justly egalitarianism or libertarianism treats individual citizens, both theories protect economic inefficiencies.

Fourth, there are a variety of technical reasons to prefer a meritocratic income distribution. I'll just mention one recent result here: In the setting of a public goods game,[16] Nax et al. make the "astonishing finding" that meritocracy eliminates sentiments of unfairness among players *and* produces the efficient outcome:

> The results of our study show that meritocracy can dissolve the fundamental tradeoff between efficiency and equality. Creating a public good does not necessarily generate inefficiencies, nor . . . requires the intervention of a central coercive power for their suppression. Fairness preferences and suitable institutional settings, such as well-working merit-based matching mechanisms, can align agents' incentives, and shift the system towards more cooperative and near-efficient Nash equilibria.
>
> (2015: 15)

Notes

1 See Ake (1975); Dick (1975); and Lamont (1997).
2 See Milne (1986) and Sadurski (1985).
3 See Miller (1976, 1989, 1999) and Riley (1989).
4 See Dekker (2010); Hsieh (2000); Miller (1989); and Sheffrin (2013).
5 There is arguably a technical complication involving the possibility of multiple economic equilibria. In equilibrium theory at its most general, uniqueness is not guaranteed. However, it is not clear to me that this is of any normative interest. First, technical conditions may hold such that our economic equilibrium is in fact unique. In which case, this consideration is moot. Second, the process by which the actual equilibrium is reached may trigger desert. For example, under a Walrasian *tâtonnement* process, individuals and firms choose how much of a commodity they wish to buy and sell at various prices. In that way, they exercise control over which equilibrium they arrive at. Third, we might simply average over equilibria. And fourth, this is a hyper-abstraction. An eminently reasonable response is: "Yeah, maybe there are multiple equilibria 'out there', in some sense, but we're in this equilibrium, and so we ought to be paid for our contributions here!"
6 For useful discussions of heritability, genetic and environmental contributions to merit, etc., see Fishkin (2014).
7 The distinction is sometimes put in terms of "*ex ante* preferences"—those formed under imperfect information—and "*ex post* preferences", which are those a person would have, were he better-informed. For discussion, see Cowen (1993); Hausman and McPherson (1994); and Sen (1977).
8 See, e.g. Bowles (1998); George (2004); Gintis (1972); and McPherson (1982).
9 See Grofman, Owen, and Feld (1983) and Nitzan and Paroush (1982).
10 These issues discussed in this section are also addressed in my 2017.
11 Sidgwick (1874) noted this, too.
12 Hayek's objection runs against a long tradition in classical liberal thought, beginning with Smith, which holds that markets are valuable because of their ability to promote excellent products and remunerate excellent producers—in short, because they cultivate merit. "For Smith it is almost a metaphysical requirement that markets reward virtuous behavior" (Herzog 2013: 88).
13 *Cf.* Schmidtz (2016): "[Hayek] thinks a merit czar would be intolerable. However, the nightmarish aspect of this vision has everything to do with the idea of central planning and nothing to do with the idea of merit. Anyone who takes merit seriously agrees with Hayek that it is imperative to decentralize evaluation. If Hayek is right that there is no place for a merit czar in a good society, then, contra Hayek, the implication is not that merit does not matter but precisely that merit does matter".
14 Roemer (1995) makes a similar point.
15 I attend to the trade-off between justice and need in this section. But what is the relationship between efficiency and need? There is no simple answer to this question, but it is worth pointing out that some programs aimed at satisfying citizens' basic needs are efficiency-enhancing. People who are in desperate need do desperate things, and the cost of dissuading them from doing these things may be less than costs they would inflict. And there are other reasons, too, to think that need and efficiency are not terribly at odds; e.g. Acemoglu and Shimer (1999) show that unemployment insurance is (productively) efficient, increasing workers' willingness to take on risky employment and nudging firms toward optimal capital investment.

16 In these games, players secretly decide how much of their private wealth to donate to a central pot; this gets multiplied and then redistributed back to the players. The game-theoretic solution is to donate nothing at all, mimicking the classic public goods collective action problem.

6.12 References

Acemoglu, D. and Shimer, R. 1999. Efficient unemployment insurance. *Journal of Political Economy* 107: 893–928.

Ake, C. 1975. Justice as equality. *Philosophy & Public Affairs* 5: 69–89.

Arneson, R. J. 1997. Egalitarianism and the undeserving poor. *Journal of Political Philosophy* 5: 327–50.

———. 2015. Equality of opportunity. In *The Stanford Encyclopedia of Philosophy (Summer 2015 Edition)*, ed. E. N. Zalta. URL = <https://plato.stanford.edu/archives/sum2015/entries/equal-opportunity/>, retrieved 25 August 2017.

Baker, D. 2016. The upward redistribution of income: Are rents the story? *Review of Radical Political Economics* 48: 529–43.

Bebchuk, L. and Fried, J. 2004. *Pay without Performance: The Unfulfilled Promise of Executive Compensation*. Cambridge: Harvard University Press.

Bell, B. and Van Reenen, J. 2014. Bankers and their bonuses. *Economic Journal* 124: F1–F21.

Berlin, I. 1969. Two concepts of liberty. In *Four Essays on Liberty*, ed. I. Berlin, 118–72. Oxford: Oxford University Press.

Bertrand, M. and Mullainathan, S. 2000. Agents with and without principals. *American Economic Review* 90: 203–8.

———. 2001. Are CEOs rewarded for luck? The ones without principals are. *Quarterly Journal of Economics* 116: 901–32.

Bivens, J. and Mishel, L. 2013. The pay of corporate executives and financial professionals as evidence of rents in top 1 percent incomes. *Journal of Economic Perspectives* 27: 57–78.

Björklund, A., Jäntti, M., and Roemer, J. E. 2012. Equality of opportunity and the distribution of long-run income in Sweden. *Social Choice and Welfare* 39: 675–96.

Black, S. E., Devereux, P. J., Lundborg, P., and Majlesi, K. 2015. Poor little rich kids? The determinants of the intergenerational transmission of wealth. *National Bureau of Economic Research*, working paper 21409.

Bowles, S. 1998. Endogenous preferences: The cultural consequences of markets and other economic institutions. *Journal of Economic Literature* 36: 75–111.

Bowles, S., Gintis, H., and Groves, M. O. 2005. Introduction. In *Unequal Chances: Family Background and Economic Success*, eds. S. Bowles, H. Gintis, and M. O. Groves, 1–22. Princeton: Princeton University Press.

Bunzel, J. 1983. Rescuing equality. In *Sidney Hook: Philosopher of Democracy and Humanism*, ed. Paul Kurtz, 171–87. Buffalo, NY: Prometheus Books.

Clark, J. B. 1899. *The Distribution of Wealth: A Theory of Wages, Interest and Profits*. New York: Macmillan Company.

Cohen, G. A. 2009. *Why Not Socialism?* Princeton: Princeton University Press.

Cowen, T. 1993. The scope and limits of preference sovereignty. *Economics and Philosophy* 9: 253–69.

Dekker, T. J. 2010. Desert, democracy, and consumer surplus. *Politics, Philosophy & Economics* 9: 315–38.

Dichev, I. D. and Yu, G. 2011. Higher risk, lower returns: What hedge fund investors really earn. *Journal of Financial Economics* 100: 248–63.

Dick, J. C. 1975. How to justify a distribution of earnings. *Philosophy & Public Affairs* 4: 248–72.

Feldman, M. W., Otto, S. P., and Christiansen, F. B. 2000. Genes, culture, and inequality. In *Meritocracy and Economic Inequality*, eds. K. Arrow, S. Bowles, and S. Durlauf, 61–85. Princeton: Princeton University Press.

Fishkin, J. 2014. *Bottlenecks: A New Theory of Equal Opportunity*. New York: Oxford University Press.

Franzini, M., Granaglia, E., and Raitano, M. 2016. *Extreme Inequalities in Contemporary Capitalism: Should We Be Concerned about the Rich?* Cham, Switzerland: Springer.

Fried, B. 1995. Wilt Chamberlain revisited: Nozick's "justice in transfer" and the problem of market-based distribution. *Philosophy & Public Affairs* 24: 226–45.

George, D. 2004. *Preference Pollution: How Markets Create the Desires We Dislike*. Ann Arbor: University of Michigan Press.

George, H. 1886. *Progress and Poverty: An Inquiry into the Cause of Industrial Depressions, and of Increase in Want with Increase of Wealth—the Remedy*. London: Kegan Paul, Trench & Co.

Gintis, H. 1972. A radical analysis of welfare economics and individual development. *Quarterly Journal of Economics* 86: 572–99.

Grofman, B., Owen, G., and Feld, S. L. 1983. Thirteen theorems in search of the truth. *Theory and Decision* 15: 261–78.

Hamermesh, D. S. and Biddle, J. E. 1994. Beauty and the labor market. *American Economic Review* 84: 1174–94.

Hausman, D. and McPherson, M. 1994. Preference, belief, and welfare. *American Economic Review* 84: 396–400.

Hayek, F. A. 1945. The use of knowledge in society. *American Economic Review* 35: 519–30.

———. 1960. *The Constitution of Liberty*. Chicago: University of Chicago Press.

———. 1976. *Law, Legislation and Liberty*, Volume 2. London: Routledge & Kegan Paul.

Herzog, L. 2013. *Inventing the Market: Smith, Hegel, & Political Theory*. Oxford: Oxford University Press.

Hsieh, N.-H. 2000. Moral desert, fairness and legitimate expectations in the market. *Journal of Political Philosophy* 8: 91–114.

Hufe, P., Peichl, A., Roemer, J., and Ungerer, M. Forthcoming. Inequality of income acquisition: The role of childhood circumstances. *Social Choice and Welfare*.

Lamont, J. 1997. Incentive income, deserved income and economic rents. *Journal of Political Philosophy* 5: 26–46.

Lamont, J. and Favor, C. 2016. Distributive justice. In *The Stanford Encyclopedia of Philosophy (Winter 2016 Edition)*, ed. E. N. Zalta. URL = <https://plato.stanford.edu/archives/win2016/entries/justice-distributive/>, retrieved 25 August 2017.

Mack, E. 1978. Liberty and justice. In *Justice and Economic Distribution*, eds. J. Arthur and W. Shaw, 183–93. Englewood Cliffs, NJ: Prentice-Hall.

———. 2014. Robert Nozick's political philosophy. In *The Stanford Encyclopedia of Philosophy (Winter 2014 Edition)*, ed. E. N. Zalta. URL = <http://plato.stanford.edu/archives/win2014/entries/nozick-political/>, retrieved 25 August 2017.

Mankiw, N. G. 2013. Defending the one percent. *Journal of Economic Perspectives* 27: 21–34.

Mazumder, B. 2005. The apple falls even closer to the tree than we thought: New and revised estimates of the intergenerational inheritance of earnings. In *Unequal Chances: Family Background and Economic Success*, eds. S. Bowles, H. Gintis, and M. O. Groves, 80–99. Princeton: Princeton University Press.

McPherson, M. S. 1982. Mill's moral theory and the problem of preference change. *Ethics* 92: 252–73.

Miller, D. 1976. *Social Justice*. Oxford: Clarendon Press.

———. 1989. *Market, State, and Community: Theoretical Foundations of Market Socialism*. Oxford: Clarendon Press.

———. 1999. *Principles of Social Justice*. Cambridge: Harvard University Press.

Milne, H. 1986. Desert, effort and equality. *Journal of Applied Philosophy* 3: 235–43.

Mishel, L. and Davis, A. 2015. Top CEOs make 300 times more than typical workers: Pay growth surpasses stock gains and wage growth of top 0.1 percent. *Economic Policy Institute*, issue brief 399.

Mulligan, T. 2017. What's wrong with libertarianism: a meritocratic diagnosis. In *The Routledge Handbook of Libertarianism*, eds. J. Brennan, D. Schmidtz, and B. van der Vossen, 77–91. New York: Routledge.

Nax, H. N., Balietti, S., Murphy, R. O., and Helbing, D. 2015. Meritocratic matching can dissolve the efficiency-equality tradeoff: The case of voluntary contributions games. *LSE Research*, working paper.

Nitzan, S. and Paroush, J. 1982. Optimal decision rules in uncertain dichotomous choice situations. *International Economic Review* 23: 289–97.

Nozick, R. 1974. *Anarchy, State, and Utopia*. New York: Basic Books.

Piketty, T. 2000. Theories of persistent inequality and intergenerational mobility. In *Handbook of Income Distribution*, Volume 1, eds. A. B. Atkinson and F. Bourguignon, 429–76. Amsterdam: Elsevier.

Preiss, J. 2017. Libertarian personal responsibility: On the ethics, practice, and American politics of personal responsibility. *Philosophy and Social Criticism* 43: 621–45.

Pullen, J. 2010. *The Marginal Productivity Theory of Distribution: A Critical History*. New York: Routledge.

Rand, A. 1961. *For the New Intellectual: The Philosophy of Ayn Rand*. New York: Signet.

Riley, J. 1989. Justice under capitalism. In *NOMOS XXXI: Markets and Justice*, eds. J. W. Chapman and J. R. Pennock, 122–62. New York: New York University Press.

Roemer, J. E. 1995. Equality and responsibility. *Boston Review* April/May: 3–7.

Roemer, J. E. and Silvestre, J. 1993. The proportional solution for economies with both private and public ownership. *Journal of Economic Theory* 59: 426–44.

Rosen, S. 1981. The economics of superstars. *American Economic Review* 71: 845–58.

Rushton, J. P. and Jensen, A. R. 2005. Thirty years of research on race differences in cognitive ability. *Psychology, Public Policy, and Law* 11: 235–94.

Sadurski, W. 1985. *Giving Desert Its Due: Social Justice and Legal Theory*. Dordrecht: D. Reidel.

Schaar, J. H. 1967. Equality of opportunity, and beyond. In *NOMOS IX: Equality*, eds. J. R. Pennock and J. W. Chapman, 228–49. New York: Atherton Press.

Schmidtz, D. 2016. Friedrich Hayek. In *The Stanford Encyclopedia of Philosophy (Winter 2016 Edition)*, ed. E. N. Zalta. URL = <https://plato.stanford.edu/archives/win2016/entries/friedrich-hayek/>, retrieved 25 August 2017.

Sen, A. K. 1977. Rational fools: A critique of the behavioral foundations of economic theory. *Philosophy & Public Affairs* 6: 317–44.

Shapley, L. S. 1953. A value for *n*-person games. In *Contributions to the Theory of Games*, Volume 2, eds. H. W. Kuhn and A. W. Tucker, 307–17. Princeton: Princeton University Press.

Sheffrin, S. M. 2013. *Tax Fairness and Folk Justice*. New York: Cambridge University Press.

Sidgwick, H. 1874. *The Methods of Ethics*. London: Macmillan and Co.

Silventoinen, K., Posthuma, D., van Beijsterveldt, T., Bartels, M., and Boomsma, D. I. 2006. Genetic contributions to the association between height and intelligence: Evidence from Dutch twin data from childhood to middle age. *Genes, Brain and Behavior* 5: 585–95.

Smith, A. 1784. *An Inquiry into the Nature and Causes of the Wealth of Nations*. London: Strahan and Cadell.

Stiglitz, J. E. 2012. *The Price of Inequality: How Today's Divided Society Endangers Our Future*. New York: W. W. Norton.

Strenze, T. 2007. Intelligence and socioeconomic success: A meta-analytic review of longitudinal research. *Intelligence* 35: 401–26.

7 Defending Desert From John Rawls

7.1 Rawls's Influence on the Desert Debate

In Chapter 3, we saw just how entrenched desert is in people's pre-theoretical reasoning about justice. Philosophers have long been aware of this, and the danger that it poses to other approaches to justice. This is, perhaps, why Rawls engages in his wholesale, quasi-metaphysical rejection of desert: Unless can he show the concept to be uninstantiated, even incoherent, it will play a prominent role in the process of reflective equilibrium and affect our theories accordingly.

It is hard to overstate the influence that Rawls has had here. Many contemporary scholars believe that he pretty well killed off the concept of desert. That's wrong, and my purpose in this chapter is to explain why.

Some philosophers have already replied directly to Rawls. And some of these replies, like those given by Sher and Alan Zaitchik (§7.3), I regard as sound.

Still other philosophers have tried to bypass the Rawlsian objection to desert. For example, Schmidtz says, "we are born into our natural and positional advantages by mere luck, and that which comes to us by mere luck cannot be deserved. This further aspect is what I reject" (2002: 778).

I shall end up disagreeing with Schmidtz in both respects. *Pace* Schmidtz, luck does indeed undermine desert. But, *pace* both Rawls and Schmidtz, we are not born into our natural advantages by mere luck.

Perhaps Rawls's influence is related to the peculiarly American tendency to abnegate responsibility for the course of one's life and ascribe it to facts about one's birth. As we have seen, this is justifiable in part: Because the power of hereditary wealth and influence is now so strong (and getting stronger—see Piketty 2014), the meritocratic ideal of equal opportunity and achievement based on merit lies in tatters. Still, our culture, and philosophers especially, push things too far. Other cultures find it odd; in Japan, for example,

> the secret to success is considered to be hard work. Why does one student get straight A's in math, science, geometry, and language, while her best friend gets all C's? In the United States, almost everybody

answers that question by saying that the all-A student is smarter. In Japan, almost nobody would answer that way. The reason some kids do well in school and others don't is almost universally considered to be effort. If you work hard, you'll get A's; if you didn't get A's, you didn't work hard enough. I've visited hundreds of Japanese classrooms over the years, and virtually every one has the word *doryoku* framed on the wall. The word means effort.

(Reid 2000: 135–6)

We have seen that, *given equal opportunity*, the Eastern sentiment is correct. Genetic differences do not control one's socioeconomic future; indeed, they appear to have but a small influence (§6.5).

Rawls's objection to desert is an interesting one, and we can see why it was lodged and why it has been so influential—namely, defects in equal opportunity. But, for reasons which I will now give, it ought to be rejected. I suspect, too, that were Rawls's objection considered by thoughtful people living under robust equal opportunity, it would not be regarded as plausible.

7.2 Two Other Rawlsian Objections to Desert

While the objection I mean to rebut in this chapter is widely regarded as Rawls's core critique of desert, Rawls's actual views on desert are harder to pin down. His remarks in *A Theory of Justice* are unclear, and philosophers have identified several lines of attack on desert in that work (see Scheffler 2000 for a survey of these). I wish to attend, briefly, to two of these alternative objections.

One objection which Rawls makes, but which will not work against meritocracy, is pragmatic. Rawls muses that even if people could deserve things, and even if a desert-based distributive scheme were immune to reasonable rejection, "moral worth would be utterly impracticable as a criterion when applied to questions of distributive justice. We might say: Only God could make those judgments." (Rawls 2001: 73). Or simply:

(R-1) The idea of rewarding desert is impracticable.

(Rawls 1999: 274)

To the contrary, nothing is more practical than desert-based reward, *as meritocracy construes it*. Unlike Rawls's own theory—the implementation of which remains hazy—I have made clear the ways in which our economy does and does not accord with the meritocratic ideal. And I shall discuss, in the third part of this book, the specific public policies that meritocracy requires. Moreover, even if it were sound, R-1 would only tell against virtue-based distribution, which no contemporary theorist (save, I believe, one—Kristjánsson (2003)) endorses. Just distribution does not require deep knowledge and analysis of moral virtue; it simply requires that we evaluate individuals on their merit. What could be more practical than awarding the gold medal to the runner who, as best we can tell, was the fastest?

The second objection is the one that Rawls really may have had in mind, at least later in his life:

> Moral desert . . . cannot be incorporated into a political conception of justice in view of the fact of reasonable pluralism. Having conflicting conceptions of the good, citizens cannot agree on a comprehensive doctrine to specify an idea of moral desert for political purposes.
> (2001: 73)

Or:

(R-2)   (1) Our distributive system must be justified on grounds acceptable to all reasonable citizens.

        (2) All desert-based distributive schemes are justified under comprehensive moral doctrines which some reasonable citizens will reject.

THEREFORE, desert-based distributive schemes are unjustifiable.

Reply: Again setting aside the implausibility of distribution based on virtue, if any distributive system can surmount the hurdle of public justification, it's meritocracy.[1] Why? For one thing, if the original position is in fact the disinterested point-of-view which can command reasonable consensus, then that probably leads to meritocracy, in light of the evidence cited in Chapter 3.

Moreover, meritocracy asks us to endorse intuitions about justice that are widely held, across lines of gender, class, and culture. Meritocracy includes robust equal opportunity. It proscribes all forms of anti-meritocratic discrimination. It deals with the equity/efficiency trade-off. It reaches across ideological lines. It provides non-ideal guidance. If meritocracy is not publicly justifiable, what could be?

7.3 Rawls Against Desert

In any case, I am doing analysis, not history, here, and so I will not try to divine what Rawls really intended. The argument most commonly attributed to him, rightly or wrongly, and which has had such influence, is the one that the desert theorist must confront. It goes like this:

(R-3)   (1) A person P deserves x on the basis of y only if P deserves y.

        (2) If y originated in fortunate family or social circumstances then it is not the case that P deserves y.

        (3) All putative desert bases originated in fortunate family or social circumstances.

THEREFORE, P does not deserve x.

Although R-3 is sometimes interpreted as an argument about free will and moral responsibility, that is unfair to Rawls, for to show that some political principle loses its force under hard determinism is not to accomplish too much.[2] As political philosophers, we begin from a presumption of free will (§1.3) when we ask, "How should we arrange our economy in order to do justice to economic agents?" The question itself implies that we have some choice in the matter. Political philosophers need not show that their principles operate under hard determinism, just as they need not show that their principles operate if we are brains-in-vats. That we have free will, and that we are not brains-in-vats, are pragmatic presuppositions of rational inquiry within the domain of political philosophy.

Moreover, if we think that there is something to the idea that our politics ought not be arranged on the basis of controversial philosophical doctrines—and Rawls (2005) certainly believed this—then any argument that relies on considerations of free will should not be regarded as a legitimate objection to desert. The free will problem is a hotly contested one, even among professional philosophers (see Bourget and Chalmers 2014).

No: Rawls's argument has the apparent power that it does because it seems that *even if* we have free will *and* there is a robust sense of moral responsibility, it's still the case that all those things which we naïvely think make us deserving are themselves undeserved—to such a degree, in fact, that the concept of desert ends up uninstantiated.

Terence Tao may have deserved the Fields Medal on the basis of his work in number theory and analysis, and he may have deserved those accomplishments on the basis of his intelligence and his effort. But did Tao really deserve *those* things? Did he deserve to be a mathematical super-prodigy, with a mathematical ability at age seven greater than that of most adults?[3] Rawls would say "no":

> We do not deserve our place in the distribution of native endowments, any more than we deserve our initial starting place in society. That we deserve the superior character that enables us to make the effort to cultivate our abilities is also problematic; for such character depends in good part upon fortunate family and social circumstances in early life for which we can claim no credit.
>
> (1999: 89)

According to R-3, all of our desert-claims can be traced back to bases which are matters of fortune; anything that is a matter of fortune is undeserved; and therefore, since desert bases must themselves be deserved to make the desert-claim *bona fide*, no one deserves anything at all. If Rawls is right, then "the possibility of our being deserving ended with the Big Bang" (Schmidtz 2006: 35).

R-3 has been subjected to two principal criticisms. The first—given by Zaitchik (1977)—uses a Moorean strategy: While there may be a good argument out there that much of what we think we deserve we in fact do not, R-3 says that we deserve *nothing*—and, worse, no matter what we do, we can never deserve anything at all. And that just seems wrong. If I bake an apple pie, surely I deserve a slice. On this criticism, any anti-desert argument that rules out the possibility of anyone, anywhere, at any time, deserving anything, is unsound by *reductio*.

I take no stance on the soundness of such an approach here. Instead, I want to point out that it illuminates an important ambiguity in R-3. Consider the phrase "originated in", found in premises (2) and (3). It is not clear if Rawls meant for this phrase to be understood categorically, as "originated wholly in", or whether it is a more limited claim, akin to "originated partially in".

If the former, then R-3 is unsound because premise (3) is false—you deserve a slice of pie, in part, because you decided to bake the thing—and that basis has nothing to do with "fortunate family and social circumstances". If that were the right interpretation of R-3, then many—maybe all—of our desert-claims would be vindicated.

However, if "originated in" is understood in the latter, partial sense, then premise (2) is implausibly strong, equivalent to saying that any desert-claim that rests, *even slightly*, on "fortunate family and social circumstances" is *totally* neutralized. It may be a matter of fortunate social circumstances that I have an apple-picking friend and, thus, the ingredients for a pie. But to say that that contingency completely neutralizes my claim to deserve a slice of pie is absurd. It just means, perhaps, that he deserves one too.

The correct interpretation of R-3—the only interpretation that preserves Rawls's point—is that desert-claims lack moral force just to the extent to which their underlying desert bases are matters of fortune. The greater the role that fortune plays in these, the weaker the desert-claims are. And since, according to Rawls, either the proximate desert bases are wholly matters of fortune or are themselves grounded in bases that are wholly matters of fortune, desert-claims lack *any* moral force. This will be important later.

The second criticism leveled against R-3 is that premise (1) is false. This is the approach taken by Sher (1979, 1987). (Zaitchik suggests something similar.) Sher denies that desert bases must themselves be deserved, and the bases of those bases deserved, and so on, *ad infinitum*. Instead, the regress stops with certain bases—like effort—which are not so unequally distributed as to preclude the less-endowed from achieving on the basis of them. That suffices to recover desert.[4]

Still, many are not convinced—for even if one formulation of Rawls's argument is unsuccessful, the intuition persists: It is unjust for one person to profit over another on the basis of things which—leave aside whether they are deserved or not—are really just matters of luck. Rawls raises this worry throughout *A Theory of Justice*: Our desert-claims eventually end up resting on "*fortunate* family and social circumstances in early life" (1999: 89, my emphasis); or result from "historical and social *fortune*" (1999: 64, my emphasis) and "*luck* in the natural lottery" (1999: 65, my emphasis); or are "*arbitrary* from a moral point of view" (1999: 63, my emphasis).

But this is false. Before explaining why, one preliminary is necessary. Note that a person may become meritorious, and thus putatively deserving, in one of three ways: (1) free choices, (2) social circumstances, and (3) genetics.

Factor (1), on its own, gives us no heartache. Suppose two identical twins, raised under similar conditions, both apply for a job at the widget factory. If one is more meritorious than the other because she decided to major in widgetology in college while her brother studied philosophy, then she plainly deserves the job.

Factor (2) is indeed problematic, as I have argued throughout this book. Inequalities of opportunity undermine desert. But this is not an argument against desert; it is an argument for equal opportunity. In a meritocracy, which operates under equal opportunity, (2) will not arise.

Rawls might have conceded all of this (recall that Fair EO is part of his second principle of justice), but it would not have vindicated desert in his eyes. Why? Because even if equal opportunity prevails, and even if a person's choices to develop her merits are free ones, those merits—effort, intelligence, creativity, and so on—ultimate rest on getting "lucky" in the genetic lottery—factor (3).

This is Rawls's crucial error. Our merit, *insofar as it is genetically determined*, is not a matter of luck. It is not lucky that Tom, Jr. and Lorraine happen to be my parents, nor is it lucky that I have the genetic code that I do. Tom, Jr. and Lorraine are the only parents that I could have, and my genetics are essential to me. These properties of a person are, in fact, as far from lucky as one can get: They are metaphysically necessary.

7.4 The Essentiality of Origin

In *Naming and Necessity*, Kripke poses the question,

> could the Queen—could this woman herself—have been born of different parents from the parents from whom she actually came? . . . How could a person originating from different parents, from a totally different sperm and egg, be *this very woman*?
>
> (1972: 112–13, emphasis in the original)

Kripke then explains why such a thing is not possible: While the Queen might have had a very different path of life than she did—she might have abdicated the throne and joined the circus—she could not have come from different (biological) parents, nor from different gametes. Put differently, it is an *essential property* of the Queen that she has the biological origin that she actually does; in any possible world in which she exists, she has this origin.

And if a property is essential, then it is had not at all as a matter of luck. Bruce Springsteen actually has the property of not being an international trade agreement, and it is clear that this property is essential: There is no possible world in which Springsteen exists and is an international trade agreement. (To be sure, there are possible worlds in which there is an international trade agreement named "Bruce Springsteen", and there are possible worlds, including the actual one for all I know, in which Springsteen is interested in international trade agreements. But there is no possible world in which Springsteen himself is an international trade agreement.) We can say that this couldn't be otherwise, that the subjective probability that Springsteen is an international trade agreement is 0, and so on. In other words, however we want to define "luck", Springsteen's having this property is not a matter of it. Indeed, it seems that to ask "Is Bruce Springsteen lucky not to be an international trade agreement?" is to make something like a category mistake.

A number of properties have been proposed as essential, and biological origin is the most common of these. Kripke's argument is primarily (but not exclusively) intuitive, but a number of philosophers—including Graeme Forbes (1985); Colin McGinn (1976); Harold Noonan (1983); and Nathan Salmon (1981)—have made it precise. I will not contribute to the defense of the essentiality of origin here but rather explore its ramifications for desert. That a person has, as a matter of metaphysical necessity, her origin in her actual parents, zygote, and gametes is widely accepted but not totally uncontroversial. So I must to some extent take it as an assumption of my argument. However, just as the essentiality of origin provides grounds to believe in the viability of desert, the latter may give us reason to think that Kripke's idea is a sensible one.

7.5 What's Wrong With Rawls

We are now in a position to identify the flaw in Rawls's reasoning. Let us consider a concrete instance of R-3:

> (R-3*) (1*) A person P deserves x on the basis of y only if it is not the case that y originated in fortunate family and social circumstances.[5]
>
> (2) Kristen won the tiara on the basis of her beauty.
>
> (3) Kristen's beauty originated in her parents.
>
> (4) Kristen's beauty originated in fortunate family and social circumstances.
>
> THEREFORE, Kristen does not deserve the tiara.

R-3* is unsound because premise (4) is false; Kristen's beauty did not originate in fortunate circumstances but in metaphysically necessary ones: She is beautiful because she has the genetic code that she actually does, and it is an essential property of Kristen that she has this genetic code.

Accordingly, one cannot reduce Kristen's desert-claim to the tiara to the claim that she was luckier in the natural lottery than the other contestants in the pageant. Kristen deserves the tiara simply because she is more beautiful than they are. Rawls wants us to look at Kristen, trace her superior beauty back to her genetics, say that her having those genetics was a matter of luck, and then conclude that Kristen cannot deserve anything on the basis of her beauty. But that is to assert something that the essentiality of origin tells us is wrong. Kristen is not lucky to have had the parents that she did and to have received the genetic material to which her beauty is due; they are the only parents that she could have had, and the only genetic material which she could have received.

In contrast, consider the pageant contestant who is beautiful because of plastic surgery enabled by a bequest from a rich relative. In this case, there are some possible worlds in which that contestant receives the bequest and some in which she does not—and therefore it *is* a matter of luck that she is beautiful. That contestant may not deserve the tiara. But in R-3* we are talking about genetic beauty, and so it does not undermine Kristen's desert-claim.

In evaluating real-world desert-claims, we must weigh (1) the degree to which a putative desert basis is genetically determined against (2) the degree to which it is due to social advantage. The claim to deserve is strengthened in proportion to (1) and weakened in proportion to (2). It is metaphysically necessary that I have the parents that I do, but it is not metaphysically necessary (just actually true) that I was raised by caring parents—I could have been switched at birth and raised by deadbeats. The traits that ground my desert-claims are to some extent genetically determined, and to some extent the results of being raised in a good home, with quality education, health care, etc. Only the former are metaphysically necessary, and therefore only the former falsify premise (3) of R-3.

This does not help Rawls. As I explained in §7.1, it is not true that if a desert-claim is to any extent due to fortune then that claim is bunk in its entirety. After all, one might just as easily say that if a desert-claim rests, to any extent, on a trait unrelated to fortune then that claim is bona fide in its entirety. That's not plausible either. The correct answer is that our desert-claims are weakened just to the extent to which they rest on fortunate traits. Desert, as a concept, survives.

These considerations shed light on linguistic oddities related to desert-claims. Consider these sentences:

(1) What did Rory do to deserve the prize?
(2) Kirk doesn't deserve the job.
(3) Dean, like all working people, deserves to earn a living wage.

These sentences are perfectly intelligible. Even those who do not believe that working people deserve a living wage can understand what is being said. Now compare:

(4) Do you think that Luke deserves his character?
(5) Emily did nothing to deserve her efforts.
(6) Jess deserves to have different natural talents than he actually has.

In contrast to (1)-(3), these sentences are puzzling. Yet they or their kin are frequently used by Rawlsians when objecting to desert-claims. We should regard these objections as not just false but unintelligible for the reasons given: Effort, character, and the other traits that can ground desert aren't things that you *have*—they're things that you *are*.[6] While we can all understand the question "What did Rory do to deserve the prize?", "what did Rory do to deserve her effort?" is puzzling; it is hard to see, conceptually, what Rory could do to make herself deserving of the efforts that she makes. Effort is not a benefit that is visited upon a person; it is an act of the will that stands a category apart from the more contestable desert bases. The linguistic strangeness of sentences like (4)-(6) is a reflection of metaphysical confusion on the part of those who utter them. It is simply not sensical to wonder what I did to deserve my essential properties; these are the very things that constitute my identity.

Sandel anticipates an argument like mine when he writes that "a person's natural endowments are somehow . . . more deeply constitutive of his identity than his socially conditioned abilities" (1982: 74). But Sandel goes on to reject the notion: "Even if some distinction between essential and merely accidental characteristics of the person is valid, there seems no obvious reason why it must correspond to the distinction between natural and social assets." (p. 74). I have provided a straightforward, if not obvious, reason: The connection between essential characteristics of the person and natural "assets" is found in the essentiality of origin. Indeed, these should not properly be understood as an asset—as something one possesses—at all. Natural assets are essential properties and thus *constitute* that person.

Effort, perhaps the most commonly-cited desert basis, is the exercise of the will in the pursuit of some end. And this, the concentration of one's consciousness on the matter at hand, is something so personal, unique to the individual, ineluctable and indescribable, that it constitutes a person as essentially as anything could. Some days I exert effort and some days I do not; like everyone, some days I am sedulous and others I am lazy. But my capacity to exert effort is unique to me and is an essential part of my personal identity. It is hard to see how there could be any conceptual space between this capacity of mine and my identity, and if that is so then the Rawlsian cannot criticize my deserts as they result from my efforts. For it is not due to fortune that I have the capacity to exert effort that I do—it is metaphysically necessary; it is a trait which I have in every possible world in which I exist.

On the Rawlsian metaphysic, on the other hand, people have a robust identity totally independent of their traits. Rawls's theory suggests that we could tinker with these traits at will, adding, subtracting, and modifying them, without losing the person they constitute. We take a man, make him born to other parents, change his intellectual capacities, replace his will with that of another, and so on, but we do not change the man himself. That picture of personal identity seems wrong to me and it always has. My essential properties are constitutive of *me*—they cannot be modified at will, I have them in every world in which I exist. It is for this reason that we ought not to lament our natural flaws; a person is a holistic whole, and his natural flaws constitute his identity just as his natural gifts do.

Rawls's argument strips away so much of an individual's character that it is no longer coherent to talk about what that individual does or does not deserve. Of course, there are good arguments out there that start, "You don't deserve your X." They are good arguments because they limit the X (to, e.g. inheritance). But X *cannot* be unlimited, as R-3 claims. After the point at which all non-essential properties of a person have been added to X, adding anything else undermines the existence of the "You". The claim no longer makes sense.

Consider the important and obvious dividing line between (1) the establishment of equal opportunity through social policies like public education and anti-discrimination laws and (2) the establishment of equal opportunity through genetic modification. Why shouldn't we insist, a Rawlsian might say, that the establishment of equal opportunity stretch back beyond the crib and into the womb? Assuming that the technology will one day be available to us, why not ensure that everyone is born with the same physical and mental traits?

Our intuition is that that would be an outrageous route to equal opportunity, while social policies like increased spending on public education are quite sensible. These intuitions are accurate. When person A grows up in an environment of privilege and wealth and B in an environment of poverty and crime, if we want to equalize opportunity for A and B, we can do so through social spending. We can't do so through genetic modification—for if we do that then we haven't equalized opportunity for A and B, we've destroyed A and B. Tinkering with the genes of a zygote is changing the person that it will one day be.

Although I have focused my criticism on Rawls, the point I make in this chapter has broader ramifications for the distributive justice debate. Ronald Dworkin, for example, argues that wealth differences that are "traceable to genetic luck" (2000: 92) are unfair. But we see now that there are no such wealth differences (since there is no genetic luck). The metaphysical defense of desert I present here affects not just the Rawlsian but the luck egalitarian as well.

Nicholas Rescher makes a similar point to mine in a discussion of so-called "constitutive luck":

[A person's] dispositions and talents are part of what makes her the individual she is; it is not something that chance happens to bring along and superadd to a preexisting identity. . . . With people there is no antecedent, identity-bereft individual who draws the lot at issue with a particular endowment. One has to be there to be lucky.

(1995: 30–1)[7]

These metaphysical considerations have been ignored with the desert debate.

As an aside, libertarians who ground their theories in self-ownership seem to make a similar mistake. What it means for a person to own some property is perfectly clear. But it is mystifying, what it means for a person to own *himself*. The ownership relation is thought to require two distinct entities.[8] The City of New Orleans can own real estate and thereby gain some rights over it, but does the City of New Orleans own itself? What does that mean?

So self-ownership, too, suffers from a problem of degree. It can be said, perfectly coherently, that a person owns: real estate, personal property, perhaps even his body. But the idea cannot be carried to the ultimate conclusion that the libertarian needs—that a person owns himself entirely. In trying to do that, the libertarian undermines the existence of the subject of the ownership relation. Do you "own" your effort? Your intelligence? Your personality, fears, and desires? Do you own all those the things that make you, you? No: You *are* those things.

If we wish to talk about what people do or not do deserve, how to equalize opportunities among people, the liberties which we may possess, there must be an essential nugget of personhood upon which these notions operate. Otherwise, all this moral talk, *prima facie* meaningful, is in fact nonsense.

7.6 Some Conceptual Clarifications

My focus has been on showing that the Rawlsian rejection of desert *simpliciter*—that is, R-3—is a mistake. There are many metaphysical complexities that could be explored here, their ramifications for justice teased out. For example, it could be that personhood and essence are vague, in the sense that if P comes from a certain genetic code, then the greater the modifications made to that code, the more the resultant person is not P. That is, maybe there are gradations in personhood, tied to gradations in essence. That possibility would require thinking about whether we were grappling with a metaphysical or an epistemological issue; questions of thresholds; and all the other ground covered in the vagueness debate. (Even on that account, the argument I give would hold: There would just be another gradation to consider when determining deserts.)

Another conceptual issue: Suppose that Hubert and Julian are applying for a job in a meritocracy. Hubert is more meritorious because Julian has a genetic "defect" which causes him to get sick more, thereby developing less human capital. Would it follow that government intervention, aimed at correcting Julian's genetic disadvantage, is unjust?

It depends. To begin with, the right question to ask is not whether it would be unjust, but whether it's true that this intervention is not required by justice. To answer this, we must know whether Julian's condition is truly independent of environmental factors. If it is, then yes—justice does not require that the state offset it (again: this is not the same as saying that it would be *unjust* for the state to offset it).

But if Julian's condition is partly due to environmental factors—as most "genetic diseases" are—then an ideal equal opportunity regime would offset it. This is because these conditions are not genetically determined but are predispositions. Contingencies in the actual world still determine whether one gets the disease or not. So equal opportunity could be applied while respecting the underlying person.

But we are moving away from what is relevant to distributive justice. I am developing a feasible theory of justice in this book, and as far as I can see, no political system could possibly have sufficient insight, or the resources, to establish equal opportunity on such a fine-grained level. Only if it were the case that Julian's environmentally-derived condition were a common one, and could be offset through reasonable means (e.g. by adding some chemical to the water supply), would we actually have to worry about nullifying it. Similarly, an ideal equal opportunity regime would, I guess, offset any disadvantage arising when a child, say, stumbled across a copy of *Mein Kampf* in the library and developed some harmful racial attitudes. But if the establishment of justice—and not ideal speculation—is our goal, these details should not detain us.

I think, too, that there is something ugly about the idea that people who have a certain genetic profile (*viz.* a profile associated with economically disadvantageous phenotypes) need to "be repaired". As discussed in §4.2, what is good, and noble, and of ultimate value is not the possession of merit but rather its pursuit, application, and celebration. As far as justice is concerned, the state should to be indifferent to the natural traits of its citizens. It has no justice-related reason to prefer a set of citizens with a certain genetic profile over another, and this is true even if the former's traits are associated with economically advantageous phenotypes. Rawls himself puts the point well:

> The natural distribution is neither just nor unjust; nor is it unjust that persons are born into society at some particular position. These are simply natural facts. What is just and unjust is the way that institutions deal with these facts.

(1999: 87)

A just state does not seek to genetically "perfect" its people. As we have seen, that would come at the cost of eradicating some persons who would otherwise exist. A just government takes its citizens as they are, respects their identities, provides *them* with equal opportunity, and judges *them* on their merit alone.

Nothing I have said precludes the possibility of major genetic intervention to prevent people from being born with seriously disabling conditions. If we could, through genetic modification, prevent the birth of those with Down syndrome, it might be morally acceptable for the state to do that. But that is not a matter of economic justice. And make no mistake: Modifying some genetic code in this way does not ensure that a person is not born with Down syndrome—it is to prevent the existence of a person with Down syndrome, and to replace him with another.

7.7 Considering an Objection

One way to respond to the argument that I have given is to concede that R-3 is facially unsound but maintain that Rawls's rougher point still stands: It is as morally problematic to ground the distribution of social goods on bases that are metaphysically necessary as it to ground it on fortunate bases. On this objection, while I am right that features of a person, insofar as they are genetically derived, are not matters of fortune, they still not the sort of thing that can justify unequal distributive treatment.

Of course, such a response rests on a presumption of equal distributive treatment which might be contested. Set that aside. More important is that this objection, *when it is precisely put*, falls to the argument that I have given. This objection again tries to sneak bad metaphysics into distributive matters. Consider this argument, which might be given by the desert skeptic:

(R-4) (1) It is morally bad when some people are worse off than others through no fault of their own.

(2) It is not one's fault, that one has a certain genetic endowment. THEREFORE, it is morally bad when some people are worse off than others because of their genetic endowment.

This is a luck egalitarian argument in the Rawlsian spirit. And it is *prima facie* different than R-3. But upon inspection the difference is a linguistic, not a substantive one. Why? Because it again appeals to a bright-line distinction between identity and genetic endowment—and as we have seen, there is no such distinction. If you're going to talk about what people ought to have, morally, you must grant that these people are constituted by some features. And so if your talk about justice is going to be coherent, it cannot appeal to arguments that separate those features from the people who are supposed to "possess" them.

Any precisification of R-4 is going to be faulty. Is it morally bad when some people are worse off than others through *no choice of their own*? Maybe, but *P* neither chose nor did not choose his capacity to exert effort (e.g.); he *is* that capacity, in part. R-4-style arguments cannot completely undermine the justness of desert-based distribution, although they have immense force for real-world purposes, since most of our economic inequalities arise from contingent, social facts (§6.5).

Similar replies may be given if "choice of their own" is replaced by "unearned", "outside of their control", etc. At risk of belaboring the point, to ask whether your efforts are unearned is to make a category error: Efforts are simply not members of the class of things which you can earn. You can earn money or prizes, but you can't earn your efforts. And it's similarly confused to say "your efforts are outside of your control"; if there's anything in the world which you do have control over, it's your effort.

Maybe the Rawlsian objection is more persuasive if it is rephrased in this way: Fine, you can deserve things. Kristen deserves the tiara. But distributive justice is not like a beauty pageant. When it comes to pageants, it's true that the deserving contestant has a moral claim on the tiara on the basis of her deserts, but you can't generalize that moral judgment to broader economic life.

But why not? If we are so driven by desert considerations in all these particular cases—Kristen deserves the tiara, the murderer deserves prison, Jones deserves the job—why not think that a just economic system promotes its realization? The typical strategy has been to show, in the Rawlsian spirit, that all these individual judgments are confused because the notion of desert is bunk. But that argument is erroneous. And so the burden of proof shifts back to the opponent of desert to explain why it should be ignored in distributive justice.

There are other responses: People seem to prefer desert-based distribution, and that is an excellent reason to choose desert as the guiding principle for the system they must live under. You get a desert-responsive system out of reflective equilibrium. If Rawls is right about the justness of the original position, that may yield desert (§3.5). In short, once the egalitarian (or the libertarian) loses the conceptual battle and admits the possibility and coherence of a desert-based distributive system, Pandora's box is opened. There are plausible arguments in favor of desert-based systems. This book is one such argument, for one such system.

There is yet another line that the desertist might take. In many aspects of life, we don't require fault, or choice, or responsibility (etc.) to render a normative judgment. Julie lost the beauty pageant to Kristen because she is less beautiful. Let's put metaphysical issues aside and stipulate that Julie was not responsible for being less beautiful. How many people would say that, on those grounds, Kristen ought not to get the tiara? I would wager very few. Responsibility does not affect our normative judgment. Similarly, we sometimes hold people criminally and civilly liable even if they are not at fault—these are cases of strict liability—thinking that they ought to go to jail, or ought to pay compensation, despite being faultless.

Therefore, it is not clear why we must insist that one of these particular properties be fulfilled when deciding how we ought to distribute. To be sure, we want there to be a connection between individuals and their economic outcomes. Desert includes this connection through the aboutness principle (§4.1). Moreover, it seems like we might conjure up scenarios in which protecting distributive differences on the basis of choice conflicts with protecting differences on the basis of fault (which conflicts with responsibility, etc.) Single-mindedly insisting that a distributive scheme be completely responsive to one of them is not plausible.

7.8 One Final Note

The argument that I have given in this chapter shows that natural traits are essential, can ground desert-claims, and may therefore be appealed to in justifying economic inequalities. The argument does not show that *only* natural traits are essential.

There is a case to be made that there are a small number of non-genetic traits that also qualify as essential. That is, some non-genetic traits may be so closely linked to personal identity that they, too, can undergird our desert-claims, and need not be neutralized under equal opportunity.

Obviously, parental wealth is not one of these. Nor is one's hometown, nor one's *alma mater*, etc.: I am a Tulane graduate, but I might have gone to UConn, or to Yale, or wherever—and in the possible worlds where I did I am still myself. What about my being a philosopher? This, too, is clearly contingent—I might never have left the Central Intelligence Agency, like I did, to pursue a PhD. But what about my being *philosophical*? Is there a possible world in which I am me and yet not philosophically-minded? Of a philosophical bent? It seems to me that there is not. My being philosophical is an essential property and thus can serve as a desert basis (if that were appropriate in some context). It is not a matter of fortune that I am philosophical.

For the purposes of making the responsibility cut, meritocracy should really be seen as a "Genetics+" theory: Genetics can ground desert-claims, and so can a few less obvious traits (i.e. the "+"). Now, for the purposes of my argument here, nothing turns on this consideration's being correct: If it is, then it expands the class of desert bases to capture properties of a person which are essential yet unrelated to her biological origin.

I note that Brian Barry (1988) reaches a similar conclusion, but in a different way. He agrees with Rawls, erroneously, that "one's parentage and all the rest are radically contingent in the sense that there is no purely logical reason why they should not have been other than they were" (pp. 40–1). But he goes on to claim that (1) some social factors, despite being contingent, are not "morally arbitrary", and therefore (2) *a fortiori*, genetic factors are not morally arbitrary:

If I am right in suggesting that not all differences in attainment that cannot be traced to differences in natural endowment are morally arbitrary, then the final move, drawing natural endowments into the net as well, necessarily falls with it.

(p. 42)

So it seems that one might arrive at the metaphysical conception of the self that meritocracy and desert require *via* several routes: my metaphysical argument, Barry's argument in favor of morally relevant contingencies, perhaps an appeal to common sense.

Enumerating the "+" traits would be a difficult metaphysical project. I'll mention two things here. First, they might include some mild forms of family influence, thereby limiting the reach of equal opportunity into the family structure. But it is clear that the most salient and objectionable forms of family influence on a person—money, elite schooling, superior health care—are inessential.

Second, whatever the right definition of the "+" is, for practical purposes it can be ignored, as any real-world equal opportunity regime will be imperfect. We are nowhere near to the point at which subtleties like these could be relevant to policymaking. Let us commit ourselves to ending the intergenerational passage of wealth and influence, providing quality education and health care to all children, and ensuring that there is sufficient social support, outside of school, for the children of broken homes. Once that is done, we can then think about what further equal opportunity measures, if any, might be necessary in the name of justice.

A final comment about the Rawlsian metaphysics, within which a person may neither take credit nor be faulted for her economic outcomes. It is a good thing that it is incorrect, for it would be quite depressing if it were not. It would mean that when a person suffered a bad economic outcome, it would not be a result of bad choices or squandered opportunity, but a result of a flaw *inherent* to herself. There is no dignity or solace in that realization, and little possibility of achieving a different outcome the next time around. That is to say, there is no hope. Happily, we have seen that this is not the case (§6.5). So long as there is equal opportunity, our destinies are in our own hands.

Notes

1 Public reason is arguably a fatally flawed theory because it leaves open the possibility that *every* political arrangement may be ruled out by a failure to command reasonable consensus. See Mulligan (2015).
2 Some philosophers (e.g. Clarke (2003); Pereboom (2014); and Waller (2011)) believe that determinism rules out the possibility of moral desert. See also Vilhauer (2009) for a discussion of this issue.
3 See Clements (1984).

4 Lamont and Favor, in their article on "Distributive Justice" for the *Stanford Encyclopedia of Philosophy*, regard the "strong form" of Rawls's argument as "clearly refuted" by Sher and Zaitchik.
5 The revised premise (1*) is obtained by taking the contrapositive of R-3's premise (2) and joining it to premise (1) *via* hypothetical syllogism.
6 Gestures along these lines are made by both Nozick (1974: 228) and Schmidtz (2006: 60).
7 See also Hurley (2003) and Williams (1973).
8 Feser (2005) has concluded, in a similar spirit to my argument, that the metaphysics required by libertarian self-ownership has political implications which are unpalatable to the libertarian.

7.9 References

Barry, B. 1988. Equal opportunity and moral arbitrariness. In *Equal Opportunity*, ed. N. E. Bowie, 23–44. Boulder, CO: Westview Press.

Bourget, D. and Chalmers, D. J. 2014. What do philosophers believe? *Philosophical Studies* 170: 465–500.

Clarke, R. 2003. *Libertarian Accounts of Free Will*. New York: Oxford University Press.

Clements, M. A. 1984. Terence Tao. *Educational Studies in Mathematics* 15: 213–38.

Dworkin, R. 2000. *Sovereign Virtue: The Theory and Practice of Equality*. Cambridge: Harvard University Press.

Feser, E. 2005. Personal identity and self-ownership. *Social Philosophy and Policy* 22: 100–25.

Forbes, G. 1985. *The Metaphysics of Modality*. Oxford: Oxford University Press.

Hurley, S. L. 2003. *Justice, Luck, and Knowledge*. Cambridge: Harvard University Press.

Kripke, S. 1972. *Naming and Necessity*. Cambridge: Harvard University Press.

Kristjánsson, K. 2003. Justice, desert, and virtue revisited. *Social Theory and Practice* 29: 39–63.

Lamont, J. and Favor, C. 2016. Distributive justice. In *The Stanford Encyclopedia of Philosophy (Winter 2016 Edition)*, ed. E. N. Zalta. URL = <https://plato.stanford.edu/archives/win2016/entries/justice-distributive/>, retrieved 25 August 2017.

McGinn, C. 1976. On the necessity of origin. *Journal of Philosophy* 73: 127–35.

Mulligan, T. 2015. On the compatibility of epistocracy and public reason. *Social Theory and Practice* 41: 458–76.

Noonan, H. 1983. The necessity of origin. *Mind* 92: 1–20.

Nozick, R. 1974. *Anarchy, State, and Utopia*. New York: Basic Books.

Pereboom, D. 2014. *Free Will, Agency, and Meaning in Life*. New York: Oxford University Press.

Piketty, T. 2014. *Capital in the Twenty-First Century*, trans. A. Goldhammer. Cambridge: Belknap Press.

Rawls, J. 1999. *A Theory of Justice: Revised Edition*. Cambridge: Harvard University Press.

———. 2001. *Justice as Fairness: A Restatement*, ed. E. Kelly. Cambridge: Harvard University Press.

————. 2005. *Political Liberalism*. New York: Columbia University Press.

Reid, T. R. 2000. *Confucius Lives Next Door: What Living in the East Teaches Us about Living in the West*. New York: Vintage Books.

Rescher, N. 1995. *Luck: The Brilliant Randomness of Everyday Life*. Pittsburgh: University of Pittsburgh Press.

Salmon, N. U. 1981. *Reference and Essence*. Princeton: Princeton University Press.

Sandel, M. J. 1982. *Liberalism and the Limits of Justice*. Cambridge: Cambridge University Press.

Scheffler, S. 2000. Justice and desert in liberal theory. *California Law Review* 88: 965–90.

Schmidtz, D. 2002. How to deserve. *Political Theory* 30: 774–99.

————. 2006. *Elements of Justice*. New York: Cambridge University Press.

Sher, G. 1979. Effort, ability, and personal desert. *Philosophy & Public Affairs* 8: 361–76.

————. 1987. *Desert*. Princeton: Princeton University Press.

Vilhauer, B. 2009. Free will skepticism and personhood as a desert base. *Canadian Journal of Philosophy* 39: 489–11.

Waller, B. N. 2011. *Against Moral Responsibility*. Cambridge: MIT Press.

Williams, B. 1973. *Problems of the Self: Philosophical Papers 1956–1972*. Cambridge: Cambridge University Press.

Zaitchik, A. 1977. On deserving to deserve. *Philosophy & Public Affairs* 6: 370–88.

Part III
Meritocratic Public Policy

8 Meritocratic Taxation

8.1 How Have Scholars Thought About Taxation?

Philosophers interested in justice have not paid much attention to tax policy.[1] This inattention has persisted even though (1) taxation has obvious normative features, (2) philosophers are increasingly convinced that non-ideal considerations are relevant to the theoretical debate about justice (§2.4), and (3) taxation is one of the most hotly debated parts of our politics. Part of what I hope to do here is encourage collaboration between normative experts in political philosophy and positive experts in economics. The design of a just and efficient tax policy cannot happen any other way.

It is easy to infer the tax policies of some theories of justice. The libertarian answer to "who should be taxed?" is simple: nobody at all. If that is too quick, it is only slightly so; leading libertarians, like Nozick (1974) and Rothbard (1982), regard taxation as a form of *de facto* slavery on the grounds that one owns oneself and the product of one's labors. While it is true that some left-libertarians, like John Tomasi (2012), make theoretical space for limited taxation, these are internecine distinctions of degree, not kind. For libertarians, when it comes to taxation, the overriding moral concern is ensuring that putative property rights are not violated.

The utilitarian also has a simple answer to the tax question: Do whatever maximizes the general utility. Somewhat surprisingly—at least from the point-of-view of a philosopher, in the midst of the fiery debate about distributive justice—economists have almost wholesale accepted utilitarianism as their normative framework. Indeed, this is the foundational assumption of optimal tax theory, pioneered by Mirrlees (1971): Make some assumptions about citizens' utility functions and then treat taxation as a straightforward, positive problem of constrained optimization.

Why has utilitarianism had such outsized influence on tax policy? The answer, I think, is mundane: It is mathematically tractable. But the time has come to consider applying other normative approaches. After all, only 24 percent of philosophers are consequentialists of any stripe (Bourget and Chalmers 2014), and the average taxpayer is certainly not a utilitarian. Matthew Weinzierl (2014) finds little appetite for utilitarian (or Rawlsian) taxation among leftist, centrist, rightist, and libertarian citizens alike. In light of this, economists should keep in mind Peter Drucker's sensible warning: "There is surely nothing so useless as doing with great efficiency what should not be done at all" (1963: 54).

I am not the first person to have pointed this out. In an address to the Eastern Economic Association in 2010, Mankiw speculated that we might replace optimal tax theory with a "just deserts theory" that better reflected public preferences toward taxation.[2] Unfortunately, Mankiw mangled the normative theory in the typical way: He wrongly regarded merit, effort, and reward-for-contribution as libertarian values. But Mankiw's positive assessment turned out to be right: Steven Sheffrin (2013) recently surveyed citizens' beliefs about justice and taxation, and found that a desert-based approach may better accord with these.

A quick aside. As anti-meritocratic as things are now, they may get worse. Piketty (2014) argues that, owing to lower population and economic growth in the twenty-first century, inherited wealth will increasingly dominate the economy and thereby undermine entrepreneurship and meritocratic values. In short, one's success will turn even more on being born into wealth and even less on character or contributions. Piketty's remedy includes a global tax on wealth.

I mention this because I want the reader to notice something striking: Two economists who could not be less alike ideologically (Mankiw was a member of the George W. Bush administration; Piketty is the new hero of the left), both accede to a meritocratic normative background. That is, they both want a society where people get what they deserve; they just disagree about how to get there. Obviously, their disagreement is an important one within economics. But their agreement is more telling. For if we agree that a just society is a meritocracy, then although we may still disagree positively about how to approach it, we have discovered something of deep importance. Among other things, we have discovered that egalitarianism, libertarianism, and utilitarianism are wrong.

Over the course of this chapter I shall advance three meritocratic tax policies: taxes on rents, negative externalities, and inheritance. I have two preliminary remarks.

First, I want to note one significant exception to the prevailing focus on utility-maximizing taxation.[3] To wit, Marc Fleurbaey and François Maniquet have modeled income taxation under two normative assumptions: (1) We ought to eliminate income inequalities arising out of different abilities to earn a wage; and (2) we ought to preserve inequalities arising due to individual preferences regarding leisure and labor.[4] This is in the desertist spirit, although it differs from the meritocratic approach in many ways (e.g. for the meritocrat, inequalities arising out of different abilities to earn a wage, where those abilities are grounded in natural traits, are unproblematic).

Fleurbaey and Maniquet's main result is twofold. First, they show that, within their model, (1) and (2) are incompatible in the sense that we cannot promote both without losing potential Pareto-improvements along the way. Second, at the level of implementation, no matter whether you give precedence to (1) or to (2), you end up with the same income tax policy, which has as a salient feature a 0 percent marginal tax rate for the lowest income citizens (Fleurbaey and Maniquet cannot rule out a negative bottom marginal tax rate).

I also note a result of Roemer et al. (2003), who investigate the extent to which income tax policy in 11 countries fulfill the goal of Roemerian equal opportunity for income (§4.4). Nordic countries (Denmark, Norway, Sweden) all in fact taxed *above* the equal opportunity optimum, reflecting extant equal opportunity in these countries (or even a further striving for equal outcomes). In contrast—and unsurprisingly— the U.S. income tax rate would have had to more than double to reach the equal opportunity optimum. Roemer et al. calculate the efficiency cost of such a move to be 5 percent of national income. However, we can infer little from that figure, both because it is narrowly tailored to income taxation, and because some features unique to meritocracy, such as allowing natural traits to play a role in just outcomes, are efficiency-enhancing.[5]

The second and final point I wish to make in this section is this: It might be thought that meritocracy cannot be a guide to tax policy because I have failed to say (1) precisely how big the social safety net (§6.10) should be, and (2) precisely how we ought to weigh trade-offs between justice and efficiency (and justice and need, and efficiency and need).

All I do here is point out the low-hanging fruit. The policies I advance in this section tend to advance these goals simultaneously. Now, the inheritance tax proposal is more radical, and its efficiency impact less clear. This I will discuss in due course.

8.2 Taxing Economic Rents

We have seen (§6.4) that economic rents are undeserved. This has two important consequences for taxation. First, because the possessors of rents have no claim of justice to them, whether they should be confiscated by taxation and redistributed is a matter to be made on the basis of efficiency and need. Rent extraction happens at the top, and not the bottom, of the income distribution, so needs are not a concern. And rents are inefficient. So they should be confiscated.

Second, consider a simple economy, which has a just, meritocratic pattern of distribution. One day, J.D. is able to extract a rent. His total income now equals a deserved part plus the undeserved rent r. One consequence, discussed above, is that r is a ripe target for confiscation. It is not unjust if the government taxes it away. Another consequence is that someone else, Veronica, is receiving r fewer dollars than she deserves.[6] In this way, J.D.'s behavior produces two deviations from desert. J.D. gets more than he deserves, and—perhaps more worrying—Veronica gets less than she deserves.

In this case, there is a simple policy solution: Tax away r dollars from J.D. and transfer it to Veronica. Taxing rents creates no harmful disincentives; there is no deadweight loss; the full value of r may be transferred; and no third parties suffer deviations from desert as a result of this intervention.

Note that a claim of justice (i.e. a claim to deserve one's income) is a necessary, but not a sufficient, condition for it to be protected from taxation. If we lived in a world in which everyone received the value of her meritorious contributions, then everyone's income would be perfectly deserved. But that does not in turn imply that everyone's income would be immune from taxation. The point is simply that undeserved income ought to be exhausted before the government turns to deserved income for a source of revenue.

Many economists believe that we ought to tax rents before all else. Yet I can find no contemporary proposals for doing so, and the prospect is absent from the political debate about taxation. This is a result, I think, of the unique challenges associated with rent taxation. It can be hard to disentangle economic activity that makes a bona fide contribution from that which serves only to extract rents. Some forms of genuine contribution, like providing liquidity in markets, are subtle. Moreover, there is the potential for major economic distortion if we get things wrong. Many of us have the sense that CEOs are overpaid, but caution is called for before we regulate their compensation, given the influence that these men and women have over the labor and capital markets, the course of research and development, and the economy at large.

The lesson is that we should attack rents decisively—but through conservative means. I offer three suggestions. First, we can prohibit the "golden goodbyes" discussed in §6.4. Because—in the United States at least—boards of directors may hire or fire corporate executives at will, there is no justification for paying departing executives more than is required by their contracts. This is especially true when the executives are being dismissed for poor performance. These payments are inimical to the directors' duty to shareholders, and, as Bebchuk and Fried (2004) observe, send the wrong message to incoming hires—namely, that poor performance is no barrier to high reward. Golden goodbyes undermine merit.

Second, we can increase top marginal income tax rates. In 1982, the top marginal tax rate in the United States fell from 70 percent to 50 percent, and 5 years later it fell to 39 percent. This period was also the start of the accelerated income inequalities that confront us today. There are two explanations for this change. The first is the supply-side story: With lower taxes comes increased incentive to work, a larger productive contribution, and in turn a higher wage. The second explanation is that high top tax rates protect against rent extraction (why exert effort to get a rent when it will just be taxed away?), and, thus, lower top marginal rates lead to larger rents.

Piketty, Saez, and Stantcheva (2014) find that the latter is true: (1) There is no correlation between the lowering of top marginal tax rates and economic growth, and (2) most of the economic gains which have accrued to top earners are due to rent extraction, *via* Bertrand and Mullainathan's (2000, 2001) model. Piketty, Saez, and Stantcheva suggest a top marginal rate of 83 percent. Especially attractive now, I think, would be the addition of a new "supermanager" bracket—something like a 75 percent tax on all income over $5 million.

Third, we might consider an "inflatable wage ceiling" which would operate in the following way: Company owners or their agents would be limited by law to paying some maximum compensation to employees—say, $500,000 a year. So there would be a wage ceiling, but it would be an atypical one: Owners could exceed it so long as any excess payments were tied to performance in a reasonable way. For example, a board might contract with its CEO to pay her $500,000 annually plus $1 million for each percentage increase in profits she achieves.

Despite the connotation of "wage ceiling", this is in fact a weak constraint. In principle, there would be no limit on compensation, and directors would have broad latitude to define "performance" as they saw fit. For example, a CEO would not have to achieve profitability to exceed the ceiling; if the business environment were challenging, a board might reasonably decide that the CEO deserved $10 million if she could limit market share loss. But directors would not have *carte blanche* here—they would have to define "performance" in the best interests of the firm. Importantly, the incentives would be explicit, performance-based, and transparent—and the best defense against wasteful rents is shareholder scrutiny. An inflatable wage ceiling would help shareholders make their own, fully-informed judgments about two important questions: (1) "Are our directors acting as they should in compensation matters?" And (2) "have our workers, and especially our corporate officers, fulfilled their end of the compensation bargain?"

Some will charge that this constraint is so weak as to be toothless—the inflatable wage ceiling, they will say, is merely symbolic. That may be right. But to say something is "merely symbolic" is not to say that it is unimportant. Symbols have power. What holds for society at large—that there is value in celebrating excellence and ignoring irrelevancies, in part through symbols—holds for firms as well.

Finally, I imagine it is clear to the reader by now that I have a special distaste for current corporate compensation practices. Although this is not an unusual view—I think it is held by most economists—there are reasonable arguments on the other side. In fairness, I wish to register these here. Benjamin Hermalin (2005), for example, provides a model of CEO pay in which compensation rises with the diligence of his directors.

If board diligence has increased over the past three decades (owing to, e.g. regulation like Sarbanes-Oxley), then these CEO compensation packages may be deserved.

Although I do not find these arguments compelling in light of the countervailing evidence, nothing philosophically important turns on this. If corporate compensation reflects merit and not cronyism, then we have a labor market that is operating as it should, and we ought not meddle in it.

8.3 Pigovian Taxes and the Provision of Public Goods

So far as I know, Mankiw's address to the Eastern Economic Association was the first time that desert had been recommended as a normative ground for tax policy. Mankiw did not discuss policy in detail, except to suggest that a desert-based tax system might include (1) taxes on producers of negative externalities, and (2) progressive taxes in support of public goods, including transfer payments to the poor. In this section, I consider these two possibilities.

Mankiw has long been a proponent of Pigovian taxes (see, e.g. Mankiw 2009)—taxes on economic agents who impose costs on third parties, equal to the total social cost imposed. The typical justification for these taxes is that they are efficient. My argument is that they are required by justice as well.

For desert to yield Pigovian taxes, we must understand "economic contribution" to mean net, and not gross, contribution. Suppose Dean's market contribution is valued at $100,000. He is paid accordingly. Suppose, also, that through his economic activity he imposes social costs, external to the market, of $20,000. Then in order to say that Dean does not deserve $20,000 of his income, we must subtract the costs his economic activity creates when reckoning his economic deserts. (We must also consider the costs created by the marginal capital that Dean's labor employs.)

This would be a trivial point, if not for the fact that it illuminates a crucial difference between desert and libertarianism. Externality regulation—which seems to be required by justice, and which is widely endorsed by economists for efficiency reasons—sits uneasily within libertarian theory. On the one hand, if nothing that issues from free contracts is unjust, then it is not unjust to impose costs on third parties without their consent. But, on other hand, if we ought not to infringe on a person without his consent, then that seems to rule out *any* externality-generating activity whatsoever—and that is implausible and economically undesirable (see Railton 2003).

In contrast, desert nicely captures this desirable theoretical feature. The benefit that a person receives from our shared economic life (i.e. his income) is proportional to his net contribution to it. If economic justice is fundamentally about "align[ing] individual compensation with social contribution" (Mankiw 2010: 296), and not the dogged protection of economic liberties, as the libertarian believes, then the externality problem is dealt with cleanly.

Moreover, desert justifies subsidies for producers of positive externalities: If Jess's economic activity produces benefits that stretch beyond his customers—if, say, he sells environmentally-friendly technology that benefits the public health, then Jess deserves an income above and beyond that which he receives in the market. That could be provided in the form of a tax credit. Yet libertarians are even less inclined to intervene in markets in order to subsidize producers—and so economists who support these subsidies should look elsewhere for their moral justification. Desert provides it, with positive and negative externalities dealt with symmetrically.[7]

There are two other desert-based justifications for Pigovian taxes and subsidies. First, because it is a matter of conceptual necessity that whatever I do or do not deserve must turn on facts about *my* character (§4.1), I deserve to bear the burden of the costs associated with pollution, say, only if they are the result of my own decisions. But externalities are by definition imposed on me. I do not deserve the loss that results from another's economic activity, there is a moral drive to return me to my desert-mandated level, and the natural source for the resources needed to do this is the imposer of the loss in the first place.

Second, the core value of a desert-structured society is personal responsibility (§6.9). And in a responsible society, a person is held to account for the effects of his actions on others. If a person physically hurts another, he is brought before the court; if he imposes an economic harm on another, he is taxed.

Mankiw's second suggestion is that desert justifies progressivity in the tax code. Since higher-income citizens derive a greater benefit from public goods than lower-income citizens, they deserve to pay more (on average and at the margin). Note, first, that this suggestion, while certainly plausible, is categorically different from desert-based demands for taxes on rents or externalities. In those cases, we want to transfer wealth in the name of justice—away from the extractors of rents to those whose deserved income has been extracted; away from producers of negative externalities to those who have endured those costs. In considering public goods, we are asking a different question: Given some revenue target, who should pay?

According to the meritocrat, income and wealth that is connected to meritorious contribution is justly held; income and wealth that is unconnected to meritorious contribution is not. And before we consider confiscating justly held income—which we almost certainly must do—we should exhaust all sources of undeserved income and wealth. So here we are supposing that the government has done this and still needs more.

Mankiw's view harkens back to Smith's (1776), and it is fair to call it a desertist principle. But this benefit-based taxation is not the only contender.[8] A second possibility is taxation based upon a principle of equal sacrifice. This approach was first suggested by J.S. Mill (1848), and it is attractive for a few reasons. For one thing, public goods are heterogeneous (we all derive utility from some but not others), and it may be difficult to say with precision what a given person's benefit is. If this is so, then equal sacrifice may be sensible *a priori*. Perhaps, too, we ought to regard the provision of public goods as we sometimes regard military staffing. Just as we should not make exceptions to conscription on the basis of socioeconomic status—all able-bodied citizens ought to be subject to conscription, for equal terms—we should not vary the burden of taxation, either. This idea fits with the communitarian element of desert: Values like compassion (in the case of the safety net, a public good) and courage (in the case of the military, a public good) are best cultivated when every able-bodied citizen shoulders an equal burden.

I am going to leave this as an open question, whether meritocracy and desert call for benefit-based or equal sacrifice taxation. I lean toward the latter. Note that Weinzierl (2014, Forthcoming) has shown that the two approaches share a number of quantitative similarities, suggesting that the tax schedules they recommend may not be so different.[9]

To get a sense of what this tax approach would look like in practice, Young (1990) finds that American income tax schedules from 1957 to 1986 did a good job of placing an equal sacrifice on all taxpayers. An even better result could have been obtained with (1) more brackets for low-income taxpayers, (2) lower rates for low-income taxpayers, and (3) higher rates for high-income taxpayers. Young finds that equal sacrifice was abandoned with the 1986 Tax Reform Act.

8.4 A New Inheritance Tax

The single most important step we can take toward establishing a desert-based society is the implementation of a robust inheritance tax.

How does the current U.S. federal estate tax work? In short, it doesn't. It brings in almost no revenue (less than $20 billion annually), and this is because the law is weak. The top tax rate is only 40 percent; there is a $5 million exemption; and the law is filled with loopholes, the most serious of which is the stepped-up basis on assets that heirs enjoy. Not only does this render the tax toothless, it enables wealthy citizens to pay almost no tax whatsoever, even in their living years, by using what Edward McCaffery (2000) calls the "buy-borrow-die strategy": (1) Buy investment assets that produce little income, like real estate and growth stocks; (2) borrow to finance your lifestyle; and (3) when you die, pass these assets along to your heirs, who can immediately sell them tax-free owing to the stepped-up basis.

So estates represent a nearly untapped source of revenue. Havens and Schervish (2014) estimate that, conservatively, $66 trillion (in 2016 dollars) will be transferred from generation to generation during the first half of this century. At an optimal tax rate of 60 percent (Piketty and Saez 2013), the estate tax could serve as a major new source of government revenue.

The moral justification for the estate tax is twofold. The first justification, which is the more minor of the two, is simply that inheritances are undeserved. Heirs have no claim of justice on their inheritance because justice is a matter of deserts, and the goods that one deserves are determined by facts about one's character or one's contributions. The possibility that a person deserves an inheritance is ruled out conceptually.

There is a superficially plausible route toward justifying inheritance under desert, but it collapses under analysis. The idea would be that the person who earned the money—who does indeed deserve it—thereby deserves to pass it along to his heirs. That is, the argument is that taxing inheritance *does* violate desert—the deserts of benefactors, not heirs.

However, even if this were true—even if the person who deserves his money thereby deserves to give it to his heirs—it could only be an operative moral principle during the person's lifetime, for once a person dies, it is nonsensical to talk about what he deserves: He does not exist. Following that logic, gifts but not estates would be protected, and that is a non-trivial difference (e.g. the problematic stepped-up basis for estates does not apply to gifts).

In any case, it is not true that a person deserves to give away his deserved wealth however he pleases. Obviously, a person cannot justly spend his deserved wealth to support terrorism, and the government can and should prevent him from doing so. The same argument, attenuated, applies here. Just as the government can justly constrain wealth transfers in the name of the national security, it has a responsibility to ensure that the desert-based, meritocratic framework of society is maintained. This is the more important justification for the estate tax.

Recall the conceptual necessity of equal opportunity to desert (§4.3): Justice is about desert, and equal opportunity is a necessary precondition for giving people what they deserve. But inheritance violates equal opportunity in an obvious way. Therefore, a just government will eliminate, or at least severely curtail, the practice. Indeed, brute inheritance is the single largest driver of the awful intergenerational mobility which confronts us today (Mazumder 2005; Piketty 2000). So even if an estate tax were inefficient (because it discouraged some parents from working more), that is a distant concern in light of the injustice it perpetuates. In any case, a robust estate tax can replace parts of the tax code that are even more distortionary, such as the corporate tax.

Now there are a few things to note. First, the estate tax has nothing to do with envy. We are not motivated to implement the tax out of a sense of envy (for the goodies that scions have). Nor are we trying to minimize the occurrence of envy. We are simply trying to maintain the fair, meritocratic structure of society.

Second, as I have already mentioned, we are not trying to enforce a strict concordance between wealth and desert. Meritocracy calls for no such concordance, which is difficult to justify theoretically and implement in practice. The problem, from the meritocratic point-of-view, is that scions have underserved advantage over their peers. This is illustrated by the fact that, in the United States today, the wealthiest 1 percent of households inherit, on average, $3 million (Wolff and Gittleman 2014). There is simply no fair framework.

Question: Should inheritance and gifts be treated equivalently? The former is plainly a problem for the meritocrat, but is that true for the latter, as well?

I think that the answer is "no". We must scrutinize the extents to which these social practices undermine the meritocratic framework. And in this respect, when it comes to gifts between adults, the problem is very much less.

Suppose that Jimmy is rich as a result of his merit. He deserves his wealth. He then decides to give it all to his friend Robert. Does this violate the meritocratic framework of society? It is hard to see how. If Robert could subsequently pass it along to his children, it would; it would violate equal opportunity. But Robert cannot do this owing to the inheritance tax. Does it help Robert get a job that he otherwise could not? Not if Formal EO prevails; I cannot think of a job for which being rich is a *per se* merit. Does it disrupt meritocratic income distribution? For similar reasons, not when it comes to labor income.

It does disrupt the pattern of capital income—if Robert invests his new wealth, he will get an income stream which is undeserved. Yet this does not seem so worrisome when one remembers that Robert's undeserved income is coming only at the cost of Jimmy's income. And Jimmy has given his consent to this. This is wholly different from typical cases, in which a deserving person would have an income stream, which he wants, if not for a meritocratic violation.

There are complexities. One might object, for example, that some gifts may undermine meritocratic society in insidious ways. Suppose that Robert gets a fancy yacht from Jimmy (or he buys a yacht with the money Jimmy gives him), and Robert uses that yacht to wine and dine his clients at sea. His competitors, who do not have rich and generous friends, cannot do this. That would be anti-meritocratic, no?

It is hard to say; much will turn on the specifics. I suspect that most gifts—especially small gifts—do not disrupt the meritocratic framework. But if turned out, positively, that even small gifts violated the meritocratic framework, these, like inheritances, would have to be proscribed.

Third, the estate tax does not "level down" citizens. It merely ensures that no undeserved advantage accrues to some citizens—those lucky to have rich relatives. The estate tax helps ensure that these citizens' economic gains reflect their merits and not the merits of others.

We should also not dismiss the possibility, counterintuitive though it be, that it is not in a child's interest to receive an inheritance. There does seem to be something to Andrew Carnegie's warning that inheritance "deadens the talents and energies of the son, and tempts him to lead a less useful and less worthy life than he otherwise would" (1891: 371). We know that inheritance size is inversely proportional to labor force participation, and that, for those who are in the labor force, inheritance size is inversely proportional to earnings growth (Holtz-Eakin, Joulfaian, and Rosen 1993). And as a cultural matter, what we, the proponents of desert, wish to extol is pluck, innovation, talent, and good old-fashioned hard work. While a life of guaranteed luxury is not incompatible with these, they are not natural bedfellows.

Inheritances, therefore, have a number of morally problematic features: They are undeserved; they violate equal opportunity; they undermine the cultural value of merit; and they may not be in the best interests of their recipients. They are attractive targets for confiscation. In contemplating a particular tax rate, Piketty and Saez's 60 percent can only serve as a lower bound, since *any* inheritance may be incompatible with a desert-based society. At the same time, a 100 percent estate tax would be inefficient and a radical shock to our culture and our capital structure: Wealth has always been earned and then passed between generations, to be spent, invested, and, in the end, given to another.

I happen to think that these changes would be for the better, but even if this traditional feature of our capital structure were sacrosanct, modifications could still be made in the name of fairness. For example, if some capital C had to be passed between generations in the name of maintaining productivity, this could be done by lottery rather than by the heredity principles currently in use. When the owner of C died, under this lottocratic system, some random young person, rather than the owner's child, would receive C. Now, such a system is obviously absurd. But it is no more absurd than the windfalls that inheritance provides, and it is at least more fair. It's unjust to throw virgins into volcanoes, but if we are going to throw virgins into volcanoes then we should throw random virgins, rather than just the virgins of some minority race. Perhaps the most sensible approach would be to give C not to the son or the daughter of the person who earned it, as we currently do, but to the young man or woman who, we believe, is most likely to make productive use of it.

I have been using the terms "estate tax" and "inheritance tax" inter-changeably, but in fact they are not the same thing. An estate tax targets the stock of wealth built up by the decedent. An inheritance tax targets the flow of wealth from the decedent to her heirs. Accordingly, an estate tax is blind to heirs' ability to pay; if three siblings share in an estate equally, each one of them—janitor, lawyer, and CEO alike—receive the same amount of money, post-tax. An inheritance tax, on the other hand, may take into account differences in income and wealth. Indeed, the simplest way to tax inheritance is simply to treat it as (earned) income. A further surtax might be leveled against the inheritance; this is the approach favored by Lily Batchelder (2009), in her proposal for a comprehensive inheritance tax.

As Sheffrin (2013) notes, although the estate tax is unpopular, inheritance taxes might not be. The reason is desert: People think that because a person worked hard and became wealthy, he deserves to be able to do whatever he likes with that wealth (that is wrong, as we have seen). When the money is thought of in terms of inheritance, it is viewed as an undeserved windfall. The lack of connection between the money and merit is clearer. So even when the fiscal effect of an estate tax and an inheritance tax would be the same, the psychological impact could be quite different: "I would suggest that taxing inheritances does not trigger the same emotional chords as taxing estates. . . . Taxing those who inherit wealth removes the tax one level from those who earned the funds, creating more psychological distance" (Sheffrin 2013: 210).

I should say a word about why Americans are so opposed to the estate tax. It is, I believe, an artifact of the anti-meritocratic nature of our society. Parents love their children and want the best for them. And parents judge that their children will be deprived of the good things in life unless they, the parents, provide them. We have seen that this judgment is correct. In the United States today, one's socioeconomic status is determined to a commanding degree by one's parents.

Would we feel the same drive to protect intergenerational wealth transfers if we knew that our children would enjoy equal opportunity? If we knew that they would have a fair shot to obtain scarce social goods on the basis of their merits? I do not think so; or at least the drive would be very much less. It is only because we do not live in a meritocracy, and have not for so long, that we have such an affection for inheritance. This is the message sent when positions of wealth, prestige, and influence are obtained not on the basis of merit but on the basis of one's social circumstances. This is the message sent by Trump, whose successes—such as they are—were enabled by tens of millions of dollars in inheritance.

In a meritocracy, parents appreciate the injustice of providing their children with special advantages. They understand that these advantages perforce disadvantage other children. They identify their interest in their own children's welfare with other parents' interests. This produces a happy equilibrium among parents, all of whom are willing to protect the meritocratic structure of society through the inheritance tax.

For similar reasons, we must eliminate the passage of non-monetary economic influence. In addition to receiving millions upon his father's death, Trump also took control of his father's real estate empire. There is no moral reason to allow a child to succeed his mother or father in this way, except in the special case in which he happens to be the most meritorious candidate for the job. Otherwise, he does not deserve it.

The hereditary passage of corporate control is inefficient. Francisco Pérez-González has looked at how firms perform when their control is determined *via* inheritance versus meritocratic selection, concluding that "the costs of nepotism are large and that they are likely to be borne by minority investors who do not share in the private benefits of control" (2006: 1561). In a similar study, Bennedsen et al. find that "family successions are significantly negatively correlated with firm performance around CEO successions . . . family CEOs cause an average decline in firm profitability on assets of at least four percentage points" (2007: 651).

Perhaps the best approach to inheritance is the one suggested by D. W. Haslett (1986), who argues that the government should seize all of a person's assets upon his death and then auction them off. (Haslett makes an exception: that people specifically designated by the decedent, like his children, may purchase these assets before the auction at fair market value.)

Such a system would have to be developed with care. Suppose that the majority shareholder of WidgetCo dies, and his shares in the firm are put up for auction. The government would have to ensure that they are not bought up by Best Widgets, a competitor. And the government will have to ensure that anti-competitive practices do not arise subsequently (i.e. we can't have the owners of Best Widgets, barred from participating in the auction, simply buying those shares of WidgetCo from those who did participate in the auction).

Finally, to say we ought to implement a robust inheritance tax, as I do, is not to say that no exceptions to it should be made. There are plausible exceptions: for the intergenerational passage of a family home; for the perpetuation of a small family business between generations; and for the transfer of heirlooms of sentimental value. I support all of these exceptions. If you ask me where exactly the line should be drawn, I reply that that is a question which cannot be answered and which need not concern us. Let us eliminate 90 percent of inheritance—that part that is plainly anti-meritocratic and that does not fall under these special cases. Once that is done, I suspect we will find that our worries about the line-drawing problem will have disappeared.

8.5 Is All Unearned Income Undeserved?

Inheritance is undeserved, but is this true for all unearned income? Need we worry about the potential for injustice when we levy a tax on the dividends and interest a rentier receives? Or are these forms of unearned income, like inheritance, also undeserved as a conceptual matter?

This question is of practical importance in light of contemporary worries about wealth inequality and its possible remedies. Piketty (2014), for example, endorses a progressive tax on wealth, with the tax rates coupled to the rates of return within various wealth brackets. Such a tax will be rendered more or less viable depending on whether all unearned income is undeserved. I argue here that, unlike inheritance specifically, unearned income is not generally undeserved.

Again, the reason that a person has no claim of justice on an inheritance is that it is undeserved; if it were deserved, then it would be grounded in his contributions, but inheritance is grounded in one's father's or mother's contributions, or their fathers' or mothers' contributions, etc.

Some unearned income does not operate in this way. Suppose that I earn $100,000 through my labor, which I deserve, which I then deposit in an interest-bearing account which produces $4,000 annually. Observe, first, that I make a contribution to the economy not only with the labor that earned me $100,000, but with the $100,000 itself; when I invest it, I am making a direct equity investment in a company or loaning it money, or helping a bank to make loans to its customers, and so on. These activities lead to greater output. Thus, when determining my meritorious contribution for the purpose of reckoning my deserts, it is appropriate to consider not only the output created by my labor, but also the output created by my capital.

Second, there is no dispute over whether I deserve the $100,000—the dispute is over whether I deserve the $4,000 of interest from it which I receive annually. This is categorically different from the case of inheritance—there, the debate is centered on the justness of my coming to possess the principal itself. There is an asymmetry between inheritance and other forms of unearned income: In the case of inheritance, issues of justice may arise with (1) the receipt of the inheritance itself, and (2) the subsequent way in which it is invested. In the case of other forms of unearned income, only (2) arises.

Third, even if it were true that that $4,000 annually does not reflect a contribution to the economy—which is not the case—it reflects my possession of $100,000, which, in turn, does reflect my contribution. Unlike inheritance, where both the principal and the subsequent unearned income from it cannot be traced to one's own economic contributions, this $4,000 is part of a causal chain which is grounded in the relevant desert basis.

Fourth, the logic of regarding all unearned income as undeserved introduces injustice into cases of trade where there is none. Suppose I am awarded a prize, which I deserve on the basis of my performance but which I do not want. I convert the prize into money via a mutually beneficial trade with another person. But it was the prize, not the money, which was the proximate desert good—so must we conclude that I do not deserve this money? That seems wrong on its face, and it has the further, untenable implication that maintaining just control over my income means never consuming or investing it at all. But it seems to me that I deserve, say, the books that I bought with my deserved income, even though the proximate desert good was the income and not the books. In the same way, I deserve the benefits that my investments provide me.

Most economists oppose higher rates on capital gains and interest owing to the distortionary effect of these taxes on investment and entrepreneurship. The above analysis shows that there is no urgent demand of justice to level taxes on these. It remains true that desert-based taxation is efficient.

8.6 Desert-Based Taxation: Efficient and Progressive

The preceding policy prescriptions flow from a moral source of desert. If we think that justice is a matter of giving people what they deserve, then we ought, morally, to tax economic rents, negative externalities, and inheritance.

In conclusion, I wish to note, first, that desert-based taxation would go some ways toward rectifying salient worries about economic injustice. A tax on rents would flatten the income distribution, progressivity would be incorporated into the tax code *via* the public goods argument, and wealth would be redistributed away from rich families through new taxes on inheritance. Indeed, these policy results are not dissimilar to the ones that Piketty (2014) desires—and which have resonated with the public. But take care to note that the moral justifications involved are quite different: We do these things not because we are worried about inequality, but because we want people get what they deserve.

Second, a common feature of the tax policies I advance is that they are efficient. Moral considerations aside, we will be wealthier, as a society, if we tax rents and negative externalities (and subsidize producers of positive externalities, as described).

With an inheritance tax, things are less clear. There will be deadweight loss insofar as the prospect of passing wealth along motivates a person, at the margin, to work. I could find no conclusive data on this, although, as James Himes notes, "there is a part of the optimal taxation literature that can be taken to imply that the optimal tax rate is very high, possibly close to 100%, on windfalls received by unusually wealthy individuals" (2010: 196).

There is deadweight loss today owing to the *existence* of unrestricted inheritance. As I have described, receiving an inheritance is a disincentive to labor force participation. In short, there are arguments both for and against the efficiency of an inheritance tax, and of course the particulars of a proposed tax matter greatly. This is an open question.

The tax policies meritocracy calls for are, by American political standards, progressive. In this way, desert may be regarded as a conservative justification for progressive policy. The normative ideal is that citizens should be guaranteed an equal opportunity—not equal outcomes—and that each ought to receive the economic goods that he can achieve for himself, through the market, on the basis of his merit. In contrast to many philosophers, I don't think that there is anything distinctively conservative about this ideal. But insofar as there is, then the harbinger of just tax policy approaches not from the left but from the right.

Notes

1 Halliday's survey article (2013) and Murphy and Nagel's *The Myth of Ownership* are two exceptions.
2 See Mankiw (2010).
3 There are, in addition, a few efforts to adapt the optimal tax approach to accommodate normative goals other than utility maximization. See Fleurbaey and Maniquet (Forthcoming) and Saez and Stantcheva (2016).
4 The relevant papers are collected in Fleurbaey and Maniquet (2012). See also Fleurbaey and Maniquet (2011).
5 This allowance provides, in effect, a free human capital upgrade to some citizens. These citizens need not be leveled down, nor does the equal opportunity regime have to spend resources to compensate other citizens for their relative natural disadvantage. Keep in mind, though, that the advantage due to natural traits is quite small (§6.5).
6 Or a number of people are each receiving some fraction of r less than they deserve.
7 Lockwood, Nathanson, and Weyl (2017) have developed an interesting, albeit coarse, approach to externality taxation/subsidization through the income tax. Rates end up being highly sensitive to estimates of the prevalence of externalities. For example, under "Tea Party" estimates, marginal rates start at 0 and *decrease* so that highest earners end up receiving a subsidy of about 20 percent of their income. Under "Occupy Wall Street" assumptions, those making under about $40,000 receive a small subsidy, and then marginal rates rise rapidly, leveling out around 50 percent.
8 Weinzierl (Forthcoming) shows that the optimal tax model may be adapted to benefit-based taxation under the assumptions that (1) we measure benefit by earning power, and (2) earning power is a function of both individual ability and public goods.
9 See also Feldstein (1976).

8.7 References

Batchelder, L. L. 2009. What should society expect from heirs? The case for a comprehensive inheritance tax. *Tax Law Review* 63: 1–112.
Bebchuk, L. and Fried, J. 2004. *Pay without Performance: The Unfulfilled Promise of Executive Compensation*. Cambridge: Harvard University Press.
Bennedsen, M., Nielsen, K. M., Perez-Gonzalez, F., and Wolfenzon, D. 2007. Inside the family firm: The role of families in succession decisions and performance. *Quarterly Journal of Economics* 122: 647–91.
Bertrand, M. and Mullainathan, S. 2000. Agents with and without principals. *American Economic Review* 90: 203–8.
———. 2001. Are CEOs rewarded for luck? The ones without principals are. *Quarterly Journal of Economics* 116: 901–32.
Bourget, D. and Chalmers, D. J. 2014. What do philosophers believe? *Philosophical Studies* 170: 465–500.
Carnegie, A. 1891. The advantages of poverty. *Nineteenth Century* 29: 367–85.

Drucker, P. 1963. Managing for business effectiveness. *Harvard Business Review* 41: 53–60.

Feldstein, M. 1976. On the theory of tax reform. *Journal of Public Economics* 6: 77–104.

Fleurbaey, M. and Maniquet, F. 2011. *A Theory of Fairness and Social Welfare*. New York: Cambridge University Press.

———. 2012. *Equality of Opportunity: The Economics of Responsibility*. Singapore: World Scientific Publishing.

———. Forthcoming. Optimal income taxation and principles of fairness. *Journal of Economic Literature*.

Halliday, D. 2013. Justice and taxation. *Philosophy Compass* 8: 1111–22.

Haslett, D. W. 1986. Is inheritance justified? *Philosophy & Public Affairs* 15: 122–55.

Havens, J. J. and Schervish, P. G. 2014. A golden age of philanthropy still beckons: National wealth transfer and potential for philanthropy. *Center on Wealth and Philanthropy*, technical report.

Hermalin, B. E. 2005. Trends in corporate governance. *Journal of Finance* 60: 2351–84.

Himes, J. R. 2010. Taxing inheritances, taxing estates. *Tax Law Review* 63: 189–207.

Holtz-Eakin, D., Joulfaian, D., and Rosen, H. S. 1993. The Carnegie conjecture: Some empirical evidence. *Quarterly Journal of Economics* 108: 413–35.

Lockwood, B. B., Nathanson, C. G., and Weyl, E. G. 2017. Taxation and the allocation of talent. *Journal of Political Economy* 125: 1635–82.

Mankiw, N. G. 2009. Smart taxes: An open invitation to join the Pigou club. *Eastern Economic Journal* 35: 14–23.

———. 2010. Spreading the wealth around: Reflections inspired by Joe the plumber. *Eastern Economic Journal* 36: 285–98.

Mazumder, B. 2005. The apple falls even closer to the tree than we thought: New and revised estimates of the intergenerational inheritance of earnings. In *Unequal Chances: Family Background and Economic Success*, eds. S. Bowles, H. Gintis, and M. O. Groves, 80–99. Princeton: Princeton University Press.

McCaffery, E. J. 2000. A voluntary tax? Revisited. *Proceedings: Annual Conference on Taxation and Minutes of the Annual Meeting of the National Tax Association* 93: 268–74.

Mill, J. S. 1848. *Principles of Political Economy: With Some of Their Applications to Social Philosophy*. London: John W. Parker.

Mirrlees, J. A. 1971. An exploration in the theory of optimal income taxation. *Review of Economic Studies* 38: 175–208.

Murphy, L. and Nagel, T. 2002. *The Myth of Ownership: Taxes and Justice*. New York: Oxford University Press.

Nozick, R. 1974. *Anarchy, State, and Utopia*. New York: Basic Books.

Pérez-González, F. 2006. Inherited control and firm performance. *American Economic Review* 96: 1559–88.

Piketty, T. 2000. Theories of persistent inequality and intergenerational mobility. In *Handbook of Income Distribution*, Volume 1, eds. A. B. Atkinson and F. Bourguignon, 429–76. Amsterdam: Elsevier.

———. 2014. *Capital in the Twenty-First Century*, trans. A. Goldhammer. Cambridge: Harvard University Press.

Piketty, T. and Saez, E. 2013. A theory of optimal inheritance taxation. *Econometrica* 81: 1851–86.

Piketty, T., Saez, E., and Stantcheva, S. 2014. Optimal taxation of top labor incomes: A tale of three elasticities. *American Economic Journal: Economic Policy* 6: 230–71.

Railton, P. 2003. Locke, stock, and peril: Natural property rights, pollution, and risk. In *Facts, Values, and Norms*, ed. P. Railton, 187–225. Cambridge: Cambridge University Press.

Roemer, J. E., Aaberge, R., Colombino, U., Fritzell, J., Jenkins, S. P., Lefranc, A., Marx, I., Page, M., Pommer, E., Ruiz-Castillo, J., San Segundo, M. J., Tranaes, T., Trannoy, A., Wagner, G. G., and Zubiri, I. 2003. To what extent do fiscal regimes equalize opportunities for income acquisition among citizens? *Journal of Public Economics* 87: 539–65.

Rothbard, M. 1982. *The Ethics of Liberty*. Atlantic Highlands, NJ: Humanities Press.

Saez, E. and Stantcheva, S. 2016. Generalized social marginal welfare weights for optimal tax theory. *American Economic Review* 106: 24–45.

Sheffrin, S. M. 2013. *Tax Fairness and Folk Justice*. New York: Cambridge University Press.

Smith, A. 1776. *An Inquiry into the Nature and Causes of the Wealth of Nations*. London: Strahan and Cadell.

Tomasi, J. 2012. *Free Market Fairness*. Princeton: Princeton University Press.

Weinzierl, M. 2014. The promise of positive optimal taxation: Normative diversity and a role for equal sacrifice. *Journal of Public Economics* 118: 128–42.

———. Forthcoming. Revisiting the classical view of benefit-based taxation. *Economic Journal*.

Wolff, E. N. and Gittleman, M. 2014. Inheritances and the distribution of wealth or whatever happened to the great inheritance boom? *Journal of Economic Inequality* 12: 439–68.

Young, H. P. 1990. Progressive taxation and equal sacrifice. *American Economic Review* 80: 253–66.

9 Meritocratic Social Programs and Final Matters

9.1 On Schooling

I hesitate to write much about education policy, which is outside of my expertise. But given how important education is in a meritocracy—as a driver of equal opportunity above all else—I want to make two broad comments.

First, on this matter we must take special care to exercise epistemic modesty (§4.5). Education policy is complex and expertise-apt, but it is also a topic which makes people's blood run hot. Citizens tend to be highly confident that their opinions about education are correct, and they act on the basis of that confidence. But, lacking expertise, their confidence is unwarranted—and so their influence deviates from their merit. This reduces the probability that the right education policies, whatever they be, get selected.

Effective education might include smaller classes or larger ones; private education or outlawing charter schools; culling ineffective teachers or strengthening teachers' unions. There are no normative complications here. No liberties are violated if we tax to support public education; teachers have no right to organize if that's not in the interests of students; etc. I have no idea what the right policies are, but there are experts who do, and we should act in accordance with their guidance.

Second, research suggests that disadvantage that arises early in life—say, from birth until age six—persists and is difficult to neutralize. Thus, an effective and *efficient* equal opportunity regime will operate at this stage in young citizens' lives. The earlier an equal opportunity investment is made, the bigger the payoff. (Some late-stage investment remains necessary.)

But education can only go so far. From this fact, a normative problem arises. One possible way to establish equal opportunity is through transfers to poor parents. One-fifth of American children live in poverty,[1] which leads to long-term cognitive deficiencies.[2] Intuitively, there is a causal relationship here (impoverished children are malnourished, and so their development is stunted; parents who aren't worried about where their next meal will come from are more attentive to their children; etc.) And so a transfer payment to the parent might improve matters for the child, thereby aiding the equal opportunity cause. (And, indeed, it appears to have this effect—see Akee et al. 2015.)

But what if the parent doesn't deserve that money? When we make such a transfer, haven't we disrupted the just pattern of distribution?

Not necessarily. First, it is plausible that the average poor person today is getting less than he deserves (the just distribution is a proportional one (§6.3), and the rich, not the poor, are extracting rents (§6.4)). This suggests that these transfer payments could be undertaken without violating justice.

Second, the injustice could only arise to the extent to which these poor parents fail to spend the payment altruistically on their children. This mitigates the problem.

Third, we must remember that the achievement of justice has two parts—equal opportunity and merit-based distribution. These work in tandem, and in the long run they will reinforce each other. But in the short term, we might need to break the cycle of unequal opportunity through this kind of redistribution. This is an empirical conjecture; I do not know if it is true or not. If it is, then perhaps we should tolerate, for a generation or two, *modest* violations of the just distributive pattern in the name of equal opportunity. This is more defensible given that it is quite hard now to judge citizens' deserts because of unequal opportunity (§6.10).

Whatever policies we choose, citizens must have confidence that their government is taking *both* equal opportunity *and* judgment-based-on-merit seriously. If transfer payments like these were deemed an efficient way to establish equal opportunity, then extra steps would have to be taken to assure citizens that merit mattered. The elimination of affirmative action programs, which I shall now discuss, would be a sensible step.

9.2 (Most) Affirmative Action Is Unjust

"Affirmative action" refers to a range of policies which have quite different justifications and effects. Some of these policies are not controversial. Consider a college that makes special efforts to solicit applications from black high schoolers, by, for example, sending admissions counselors to inner city schools. The college might increase its black enrollment in this way—by increasing the number of black applicants and then discriminating on the basis of merit. This form of affirmative action does not tend to strike us as morally troublesome.

I want to focus on the form of affirmative action that *is* controversial—and by many people's lights, including my own, deeply unjust. This is the deviation from merit-based selection, such that race advantages or disadvantages an applicant. As of 2017, it is legal for American universities to prefer a less-qualified black applicant (lower SAT scores; worse grades and essays; etc.) over a more-qualified white applicant in the name of increasing diversity on campus. We wish to know if this is just or not.

Keep in mind that the college case is difficult (§5.4): It is unclear whether applicants to college should be considered (1) full moral agents beginning their plans-of-life, or (2) children entering the final step of the equal opportunity framework. If it's the latter, then there shouldn't be any competition for university in the first place; it should be available to all young citizens, just like quality secondary education. Our intuitions in the college case get confounded by this factor. A better case to consider is graduate admissions: This is plainly *not* part of the equal opportunity framework, and yet the arguments given in favor of affirmative action in college admissions, like the promotion of diversity, still apply.

If affirmative action is just, it must be because it is required for reasons of meritocratic discrimination or Fair EO.

One might think that affirmative action unambiguously violates merit-based discrimination. But that is too quick. Suppose we discover that some employers suffer from implicit bias against a group. That is, perhaps without any ill-will, they regard members of this group as less attractive than their resumes imply. Indeed, this appears to have been a problem in academia in the not-so-distant past—academics, male and female, rated the very same *curriculum vitae* higher when it had a male name on it rather than a female name.[3]

This is a threat to merit-based selection: A hiring committee might be bound by the rules to select the most meritorious applicant; it might in fact wish to do this; but because of implicit bias it does not.

Once recognized, implicit bias can and should be corrected by affirmative action-style assignment of extra "points" (the details to be settled here through empirical research) to relevant applicants. That ensures that everyone is chosen on the basis of her merit. The meritocrat encourages this form of affirmative action. It is important to combat non-merit-based discrimination wherever we find it.

There is a related argument for the use of race, gender, etc.—but this one is not compelling. It is sometimes argued that being a minority (e.g.) should be considered a merit *in itself*. If an admissions committee wanted to establish a racial pattern in their entering class, then to the extent to which an applicant contributes to that goal, their race is putatively a merit. If that were so, then extra consideration could be given to race, gender, etc. without violating meritocratic selection.

This idea is counterintuitive. While there are arguments to be made (I think bad ones) for the importance of diversity, their supporters typically concede that they require violating meritocratic standards. They do not maintain that being black is a merit in itself.

More important, we have already seen, in Chapter 5, why a line like this is untenable. First, it violates the meritocratic hiring principle. Second, it is analogous to taste-based arguments (§5.9): "Because my company is filled with racists who will produce less if I hire a black widget-maker, black applicants *really are less-qualified*, on account of their race." That is conceptually wrong. Race is irrelevant to one's merit as a widget maker, but it can be highly relevant when it comes to consequences. Race may induce effects, like reduced productivity in other workers and a more diverse university experience. Of course, one could call this "merit" or whatever else one likes—but that flies against the common usage of the term, and it is incompatible with the concept of merit.

This does not appear to be a controversial point within the affirmative action debate:

> The aims of real world affirmative action make race and ethnicity (and sometimes gender) salient, not personal desert or merit. The test of real world affirmative action lies in the urgency of its ends (preventing discrimination, promoting diversity or integration) and the aptness (moral and causal) of its means (racial, ethnic, and gender preferences).
>
> (Fullinwider 2017)

Therefore, the only way to justify an affirmative action program on grounds of meritocratic selection is to show that it nullifies anti-meritocratic bias. I am not aware of any affirmative action programs that purport to do this, although I am sure that there are some that have this as a side-effect in some cases (but which on the whole violate meritocratic selection).

We now consider whether affirmative action can be justified on grounds of Fair EO. Of course, we cannot provide equal opportunity to the graduate school applicant; he has already left the equal opportunity framework. But maybe by providing him an advantage now—an advantage on the basis of his race—we can improve opportunities for other members of his race. Ronald Dworkin has argued along these lines:

> Increasing the number of blacks who are at work in the professions will, in the long run, reduce the sense of frustration and injustice and racial self-consciousness in the black community to the point at which blacks may begin to think of themselves as individuals who can succeed like others through talent and initiative. At that future point the consequences of nonracial admissions programs, whatever these consequences might be, could be accepted with no sense of racial barriers or injustice.
>
> (1977: 11)

This is affirmative action justified on grounds of equal opportunity. It is possible that children must have "role models" (Allen 1990) whom they resemble in order to feel that the full range of jobs is in fact open to them. But do children require this? As Dworkin concedes, this is a positive claim, open to empirical confirmation or disconfirmation.

So far as I am aware, there is no empirical evidence that affirmative action benefits equal opportunity as described. In fact, the evidence that does exist suggests that just the opposite is true: Affirmative action puts people into competitive environments for which they are ill-equipped. This is known as the "mismatch theory".[4]

For example, being black is a powerful advantage when applying to law school, but academic outcomes for black law students are poor: 52 percent of black students find themselves in the bottom 10 percent of their class after their first year (only 8 percent find themselves in the top *half*). And for those blacks who do go on to graduate, they are *four times* more likely than whites to fail their bar exams (Sander 2004).

Affirmative action reinforces a sense of inferiority in young blacks: Even with these benefits, they think, we cannot succeed. Of course, that is untrue; but it is a predictable result of violating meritocratic selection criteria along racial lines. The solution is not to keep violating meritocratic selection on the basis of these tortuous arguments, but to provide *real, unambiguous* equal opportunity support. Not "role models", but education, health care, mentorship, maybe cash.

There is an added danger to affirmative action. When we promote racial "role models"—or gender "role models", or "role models" of a certain ethnicity, or religious affiliation, or whatever—we reinforce the division of society along racial, gender (etc.) lines. This undermines the meritocratic ethos necessary for economic solidarity. It foments resentment in the labor market and reinforces nasty racial stereotypes. It suggests to children that admiration is due to people not on the basis of their merit, but on the basis of superficial characteristics, like skin color.

Affirmative action has a further problem: Because it is a racial, not a socioeconomic, instrument, it provides unjust benefits to blacks born into social advantage. Consider a case in which a black child, *B*, is born into a wealthy and loving family. He enjoys excellent private schools and health care. A white child, *W*, is raised in a blue-collar household. He attends a lackluster public school and works full-time to support his family. Obviously, even if there is some type of disadvantage that only *B* experiences owing to his race, he—the black child—is the immensely privileged one.

Suppose that through hard work, *W* becomes more meritorious than *B*. When they apply to university, the young man who was on the losing end of unequal opportunity, yet *still* made himself the most meritorious applicant, is denied admission because of the color of his skin. There is little more unjust than that.

Let us consider one final justification for affirmative action: that it provides reparations to the descendants of slaves.

Note, first, that reparations are hugely unpopular and are regarded as a radical, left-wing idea. Fair EO, on the other hand, has always enjoyed wide support; conservatives support it in word, if not in action. At the same time, the redistribution necessary to effect Fair EO would *dwarf* the redistribution any plausible reparations program would require. The conservative ideal calls for the more radical policy.

Unlike Fair EO, reparations would have little effect on the long-term prospects of blacks. Most of the reparations payment would support present-day consumption; only a portion would be invested, and only a portion of that in black human capital. Black socioeconomic outcomes would not change much. At the same time, public sentiment would harden: "With these reparations payments, we are putting the slavery matter to bed forever". This would reinforce false racial stereotypes about black inferiority.

There are a host of other objections to reparations (metaphysical, legal, etc.) Desert levels its own. For one thing, what people deserve turns on facts about their character—not their ancestors'. The descendants of those who participated in the slave trade do not deserve to be punished for the sins of their fathers, and none of us deserves compensation for harms done to relatives long ago. All of these problems are avoided with Fair EO.

Finally, affirmative action provides cover for those unwilling to make the much deeper economic sacrifices necessary to establish Fair EO. For the economically dominant class in America, it is not much of a sacrifice to toss a few university slots every year to blacks. Nor would these elites find a one-time reparations payment terribly troubling. It *would* be a real sacrifice to eliminate the institution of inheritance; or to support massive public investment in education; or to implement a confiscatory top income tax rate. As we have seen, all of these measures are required by justice, and would be far more effective in achieving racial equality. Affirmative action is unjust—in itself, and in the change it precludes.

9.3 Structuring Social Spending

The newest *cause célèbre* in the fight against poverty, unequal opportunity, our stagnant labor market, etc., is *universal basic income* (UBI). Supporters—found on both the right and the left—say that the solution to our social ills is to provide every citizen with an unconditional, government-provided cash payment. Because of the attention that UBI has received in recent years, and because it has attracted philosophical defenders,[5] I wish to say a few words about why it is a bad idea.

The best-developed UBI proposal is Charles Murray's (2006), which calls for each adult American to be given $10,000 a year. It is critical to keep in mind that UBI *replaces* the current social welfare system. This is sometimes made explicit, sometimes not—but in any case it is necessary to make UBI even minimally plausible in light of the costs involved (Murray's proposal would cost ~$2.5 trillion/year). UBI would replace Social Security, Medicaid and Medicare, food stamps, and the other components of the current system.

Even so, this would leave a revenue shortfall; and so UBI proponents must explain whose taxes they are going to raise, and by how much (or whether they will borrow). It is impossible to evaluate any program, including UBI, independent of the tax regime that will fund it. The distributional effect of UBI is determined by *both* (1) whom it pays and how much it pays them, *and* (2) how it is funded. In light of this, it is not obvious that UBI will make the poor or the working class better-off, or indeed have a distributional effect that anybody would find appealing.

There are efficiency worries, too. We should not incur deadweight loss without a good reason. Establishing justice is an excellent reason. But I do not see what justification there is for providing an unconditional income to the wealthy. As we have seen, they probably have more money than they deserve. And a UBI will hardly affect their welfare. So whatever else we might want to do along these lines, we should certainly restrict payments to poor and middle-class Americans in exchange for lower taxes. But then it is no longer a UBI.

Meritocratic principles suggest that we should take a dim view of UBI. First, UBI rests on an unprincipled presumption of equality. Not everyone is equally deserving. It is wrong to give additional income to citizens who are making more than they deserve; it is wrong to give to the undeserving poor (§6.10).

Second, UBI will not help establish equal opportunity. It might even make things worse. This is because (1) unlike our current social welfare system, UBI pays no direct attention to the well-being of children, and (2) UBI (like reparations) would sap any public will for the badly needed economic reforms which I have described in this work.

Third, what are we supposed to do with deserving citizens who fall on hard times? Suppose Deborah is an industrious worker, a single mother, and a fine woman. She is terribly injured by a drunk driver. We're supposed to give her $10,000 a year and say, "that's the end of the matter, you and your child are on your own"? I'll buy that for the inveterate drug user, but for Deborah, no thanks.

Fourth, a UBI would reduce labor force participation and change social attitudes toward work for the worse. As I alluded to in §2.5, work is a fundamental part of the human experience: Producing goods and services, contributing to the welfare of others, and developing one's professional merits are important to realizing a full life. This is not to say that these experiences cannot be had outside of the labor market—a stay-at-home parent provides a good example of how they can be—but those are exceptions to the rule. For most of us, work provides necessary meaning. I fear that a UBI would promote mindless consumption, further isolate citizens from each other, and lead to a culture of low moral and aesthetic quality.

I also worry about the effects of any large cash transfers. There are good reasons to prefer the in-kind benefits (food stamps, health care, education, etc.) that comprise much of our current welfare system. This view flies against the accepted wisdom,[6] but I think it has much to commend it.

To begin with, we have seen that universal education is essential to a just society. But the state cannot give money to children to fund their education (or for any other reason, for that matter). The state can give money to parents, but many will not act altruistically toward their children. Universal public education, or perhaps a school voucher system, makes more sense.

Cash transfers to the poor perpetuate a cycle of poverty (Buchanan 1975). Because one receives the transfer only if one is poor, the incentive is to not develop one's human capital. But human capital development is what we should like most of all. Achieving equal opportunity requires that we subsidize human capital formation. Cash transfers, even large ones, are ineffective toward this end.[7]

We must also be attentive to the way that social spending affects preference formation (§6.7). A pure cash transfer more-or-less encourages the formation of whatever preferences prevail in the market. On the other hand, an education benefit (e.g.) increases citizens' desire to be educated. And a greater appreciation for education may redound to our collective benefit (§4.8).

If we do have pure cash transfers, we must ensure that they are connected to desert. An exemplar is the Earned Income Tax Credit (EITC), which redistributes wealth to poor and lower-middle class Americans—to the tune of $70 billion in 2015. What makes the EITC distinctive is that to qualify for it, one must have *earned income*, defined by the Internal Revenue Service as income gained through "purposeful effort". Effort is, of course, one of the classic bases for desert (§6.2), and the result is that the EITC strikes us, viscerally, as just. Despite its progressive nature, the EITC has always enjoyed bipartisan support: It was introduced during the Ford administration and expanded under Reagan, Clinton, George W. Bush, and Obama—and with strong support from both Democratic and Republican legislators.

Another admirable example comes from the Netherlands, which has in recent years reformed its social welfare system—which remains generous—toward the ideal of the "participation society". Welfare recipients must demonstrate that they deserve the benefits that other citizens' labor makes possible. For example, able-bodied Dutch must show that they have tried to find a job before obtaining unemployment benefits, and upon receiving these benefits, they must do unpaid work "for the benefit of society". The policy has been wildly popular, supported even by those "forced" to do community service in this way (Veldboer, Kleinhans, and van Ham 2015). In light of the empirical data surveyed, that is no surprise.

9.4 Positive Predictions of Meritocracy

I have endeavored to give a consistent and complete theory of justice. For justification, I have appealed primarily to intuition, and to the metatheoretical desiderata discussed in §2.3.

It is important that a theory of justice cohere with our intuitions, but it is also important that our theories be *bold*—to use Karl Popper's (1959) term—and make predictions. This provides reason to believe that the theory has explanatory power, and is not merely an *ad hoc* accommodation of known facts. Predictions are especially important if we want our theories to actually guide policymaking—as I think we should. The policymaker needs some objective means by which she can judge the correctness of a normative theory. Epistemic modesty (§4.5) tells us that the mere fact that she believes it to be true does not justify her acting on it. Predictions verified or falsified provide a measure of justification which can ground policy.

Rawls's theory is commendable in that it does make predictions. The most important is that contractors in the original position would elect the difference principle as their distributive rule. Unfortunately, this prediction appears to have been falsified (§3.5). As I discussed, this does not doom Rawls's broader normative project, and of course one might take issue with the relevant experiments. But surely, a policymaker who is aware of these experiments, if she is being rational, reduces her reliance on Rawls when choosing policy.

Libertarianism fares worse, in that its theory—at least in its Nozickian form—rests on principles that are not only unfalsifiable but unverifiable as well. I, at least, can think of no way to verify that we have natural rights to acquire and exchange goods. Of course, this unverifiability has led some philosophers to reject the very idea of natural rights; as Bentham puts it,

> that which has no existence cannot be destroyed—that which cannot be destroyed cannot require anything to preserve it from destruction. *Natural rights* is simple nonsense: natural and imprescriptible rights, rhetorical nonsense,—nonsense upon stilts.
>
> (1843: 501)

Nozick concedes that he can provide no "precise theory of the moral basis of individual rights" (1974: xiv)—a drawback tempered, he thinks, by the fact that Locke also "does not provide anything remotely resembling a satisfactory explanation of the status and basis of the law of nature" (p. 9).

To be sure, we should not afford verifiability and falsifiability the same deference in political philosophy as we do in the natural sciences. Nozick's theory is obviously legitimate in a way that astrology is not. Nozick may well be right. But *ceteris paribus* we should prefer theories that are bold enough to make claims about the way the world one day will be, as opposed to theories that cloak themselves in unassailable, unfalsifiable claims.

In order for fulfilled predictions to justify belief in a theory of justice, it must be that the world is becoming a more just place. In the sciences, we accept that the true laws of nature are fixed. But if the world is becoming *less* just, then the *wrong* theories gain support through fulfilled prediction.

I do not know what argument I can give to support the idea that we have made and are making moral progress; each reader must decide that for himself. By my lights it is plainly true, although progress is less a steady climb toward the ideal of justice and more a scamper across peaks and troughs. Jim Crow was better than slavery; police brutality toward blacks today is better than Jim Crow. Relations between the sexes have improved but remain imperfect. Our economic distribution is better than feudalism.

In contrast to science, philosophical prediction is imprecise. It is usually obvious when a scientific prediction has been falsified, but whether meritocracy fulfills or fails the below predictions—which involve imprecisely-defined social, cultural, and economic trends—requires interpretation. We must do the best that we can.

> **The First Positive Prediction of Meritocracy:** Well-ordered societies will be increasingly unwilling to discriminate on grounds irrelevant from the point-of-view of merit.

Recent years have seen increasing intolerance toward allowing race, gender, and sexual preference to play a role in hiring and similar contexts, like college admissions. (Except, of course, when positive preference is unjustly granted to blacks, women, et al.)

Meritocracy predicts that this trend will continue. Specifically, meritocracy predicts that this trend will continue until only those features that are relevant from the point-of-view of merit remain as legitimate grounds on which to discriminate. The next personal features which are likely to be found objectionable—and rightly so—are sexual behavior; beliefs about controversial moral issues, like abortion; and partisan identification.

> **The Second Positive Prediction of Meritocracy:** Affirmative action programs that violate meritocratic standards will be largely *ineffective* in achieving their desired ends. Affirmative action programs aimed at establishing equal opportunity will be largely *effective* in achieving their desired ends.

In §9.2 I provided theoretical grounds for believing this to be the case. In coming years, empirical work should tell us whether the conjecture is true or false.

> **The Third Positive Prediction of Meritocracy:** Welfare policies that are sensitive to citizens' deserts will become and remain law; welfare policies that are not, will not.

In the last section, I described the success of the EITC and some recent European moves toward a desert-sensitive welfare system. Meritocracy predicts that this idea will spread. Welfare policies that find their way into law will include mechanisms to ensure that the undeserving do not benefit from the efforts and the contributions of others. The ethos of the participation society should increase in appeal.

The Fourth Positive Prediction of Meritocracy: Pre-theoretical support for desert-based justice will persist.

In Chapter 3 I provided an overview of the empirical research on justice. This research demonstrates that there is strong, cross-cultural, nonpartisan consensus that justice is a matter of giving people what they deserve. Meritocracy predicts that this consensus will persist, and that research into the justice-feelings of yet-unexplored communities (to include, perhaps, non-humans) will reinforce the primacy of desert.

The Fifth Positive Prediction of Meritocracy: Social satisfaction will positively correlate with the presence of meritocratic institutions.

Since 1980, Americans have become unhappier with each passing year (Blanchflower and Oswald 2004). We do not know why. Possible reasons include (1) the changing pattern of income distribution; (2) the collapse of communism, which left us without a uniting mission; (3) our foreign policy decisions after 9/11 (e.g. the Iraq War), which deprived us of the moral high ground; (4) a decline in the traditional family structure, decreased religious participation, and the loss of close-knit ethnic communities; and (5) ideological and political partisanship, which has ruined friendships and family comity.

I think that there is truth in all of these. But I posit another, more important, factor—namely, that social satisfaction is highly correlated with the existence of a meritocratic social framework. A happy country is one in which citizens believe that (1) they enjoy equal opportunity to pursue the social goods they deem important, and (2) they will be judged strictly on their merits. In short, the healthier the American Dream, the happier citizens (of whatever nation) will be.

9.5 Justice in Our Lifetimes

As I have presented meritocratic justice, I have contrasted it with egalitarianism and libertarianism, explaining what it has in common with these two dominant theories of justice and what it does not. Once again: There is a sort of equality that should concern us—namely, equality of opportunity—but unequal outcomes are not only morally unproblematic but evidence that we are living under a just distributive system. And while we should embrace markets, we should do so instrumentally, as useful tools for giving people what they deserve.

Just as meritocracy is a third, better way of thinking about justice, so too is it an alternative to the partisan stand-off which characterizes contemporary American politics. Those on the political right complain about government bailouts of irresponsible homeowners; welfare programs that support drug users; and tax policies that punish the talented and hard-working. As we have seen, these arguments are not really about liberty. They are arguments against harming the deserving to reward the undeserving.

On the other side of the aisle, the left inveighs against exorbitant CEO salaries and racial and gender discrimination. And these are morally worrying features of our economy, but not because of any inequality involved. They are worrying because they violate desert.

Over the past few decades, the left has failed to win significant economic policy change, even as the economy has transformed in ways not to the advantage of most Americans. We now know the reason for this failure: The left has failed to use the language of desert, and has rested its arguments on egalitarian principles which are widely regarded as unjust. What meritocracy can do, and other theories of justice cannot, is advance progressive public policies through arguments that appeal to people on the political left, right, and center. As we have seen, valuing personal responsibility, merit, and economic efficiency means higher taxes, new anti-discrimination laws, and increased social spending.

Nevertheless, it is hard to effect lasting political change without a firm theoretical foundation. While I have tried to put down the most important roots here, there is much work to be done. The literature on equality and liberty is enormous. On meritocracy it is threadbare.

Empirically-minded scholars must turn ideals of merit-based hiring and equal opportunity into concrete policy proposals. What interventions are necessary to ensure robust equal opportunity? Clearly, education is one, but in what form should that be provided (§9.1)? How can we distinguish economic rents from returns to capital? What redistributive policies will move us closer to the just pattern of contribution-based income?

Normative questions remain, too: What is the precise extent of legitimate parental influence over children? Should the social safety net be extended to people who are neither unambiguously deserving nor undeserving? What are those cases? Should this kind of public support come in gradations, metered to desert?

Another normative question concerns the definition of "economic contribution": Should it be understood more broadly than I have defined it? For example, if a citizen rushes into a burning building to save another, isn't that an economic contribution that deserves remuneration? On a plausible theory of intergenerational justice, aren't stay-at-home parents making a *bona fide* economic contribution when they care for their children? Don't they deserve an income for that? I am inclined to say "yes", but the answer is not obvious.

These are debates for another time. I do not doubt that many thoughtful arguments can be made on behalf of the many perspectives therein. Our responsibility is to do the best that we can to get to the truth about justice, by judging these arguments, as of course we must, on their merits.

Notes

1 See Proctor, Semega, and Kollar 2016.
2 See, e.g. Hair et al. (2015); Hanson et al. (2013); and Noble, Norman, and Farah (2005, 2015).
3 Steinpreis, Anders, and Ritzke (1999). Clearly, in light of recent research (§5.1 n. 3), things have changed in academia—at the very least, bias against women has been eliminated.
4 See, e.g. Arcidiacono, Aucejo, and Hotz (2016); Sander (2004); Sander and Taylor (2012); and Williams (2013).
5 E.g. Munger (2015); van Parijs (1995); van Parijs and Vanderborght (2017); and Zwolinski (2015).
6 Cash benefits are putatively superior because, e.g. they reduce bureaucracy, are not paternalistic, and because individuals can make better choices about how to improve their welfare than the government can.
7 See, e.g. Bénabou (1994); Durlauf (1996); and Lundberg and Startz (2000).

9.6 References

Akee, R., Simeonova, E., Costello, E. J., and Copeland, W. Forthcoming. How does household income affect child personality traits and behaviors? *American Economic Review.*

Allen, A. L. 1990. On being a role model. *Berkeley Women's Law Journal* 6: 22–42.

Arcidiacono, P., Aucejo, E. M., and Hotz, V. J. 2016. University differences in the graduation of minorities in STEM fields: Evidence from California. *American Economic Review* 106: 525–62.

Bénabou, R. 1994. Human capital, inequality, and growth: A local perspective. *European Economic Review* 38: 817–26.

Bentham, J. 1843. Anarchical fallacies; being an examination of the declarations of rights issued during the French Revolution. In *The Works of Jeremy Bentham*, Volume 2, ed. J. Bowring, 489–534. Edinburgh: William Tait.

Blanchflower, D. G. and Oswald, A. J. 2004. Well-being over time in Britain and the USA. *Journal of Public Economics* 88: 1359–86.

Buchanan, J. M. 1975. The Samaritan's dilemma. In *Altruism, Morality, and Economic Theory*, ed. E. S. Phelps, 71–86. New York: Russell Sage.

Durlauf, S. N. 1996. A theory of persistent income inequality. *Journal of Economic Growth* 1: 75–93.

Dworkin, R. 1977. Why Bakke has no case. *New York Review of Books* 24: 11–15.

Fullinwider, R. 2017. Affirmative action. In *The Stanford Encyclopedia of Philosophy (Summer 2017 Edition)*, ed. E. N. Zalta. URL = <https://plato.stanford.edu/archives/sum2017/entries/affirmative-action/>, retrieved 21 August 2017.

Hair, N. L., Hanson, J. L., Wolfe, B. L., and Pollak, S. D. 2015. Association of child poverty, brain development, and academic achievement. *JAMA Pediatrics* 169: 822–9.

Hanson, J. L., Hair, N., Shen, D. G., Shi, F., Gilmore, J. H., Wolfe, B. L., and Pollack, S. D. 2013. Family poverty affects the rate of human infant brain growth. *PLoS One* 10: 1–9.

Lundberg, S. J. and Startz, R. 2000. Occupational status, education, and social mobility in the meritocracy. In *Meritocracy and Economic Inequality*, eds. K. Arrow, S. Bowles, and S. Durlauf, 269–95. Princeton: Princeton University Press.

Munger, M. 2015. One and one-half cheers for a basic-income guarantee: We could do worse, and already have. *Independent Review* 19: 503–13.

Murray, C. 2006. *In Our Hands: A Plan to Replace the Welfare State*. Washington: AEI Press.

Noble, K. G., Houston, S. M., Brito, N. H., Bartsch, H., Kan, E., Kuperman, J. M., Akshoomoff, N., Amaral, D. G., Bloss, C. S., Libiger, O., Schork, N. J., Murray, S. S., Casey, B. J., Chang, L., Ernst, T. M., Frazier, J. A., Gruen, J. R., Kennedy, D. N., van Zijl, P., Mostofsky, S., Kaufmann, W. E., Kenet, T., Dale, A. M., Jernigan, T. L., and Sowell, E. R. 2015. Family income, parental education and brain structure in children and adolescents. *Nature Neuroscience* 18: 773–8.

Noble, K. G., Norman, M. F., and Farah, M. J. 2005. Neurocognitive correlates of socioeconomic status in kindergarten children. *Development Science* 8: 74–87.

Nozick, R. 1974. *Anarchy, State, and Utopia*. New York: Basic Books.

Popper, K. 1959. *The Logic of Scientific Discovery*. London: Hutchinson & Co.

Proctor, B. D., Semega, J. L., and Kollar, M. A. 2016. Income and poverty in the United States: 2015, URL = <www.census.gov/content/dam/Census/library/publications/2016/demo/p60-256.pdf>, retrieved 20 August 2017.

Sander, R. H. 2004. A systemic analysis of affirmative action in American law schools. *Stanford Law Review* 57: 367–483.

Sander, R. H. and Taylor, S. 2012. *Mismatch: How Affirmative Action Hurts Students It's Intended to Help, and Why Universities Won't Admit It*. New York: Basic Books.

Steinpreis, R. E., Anders, K. A., and Ritzke, D. 1999. The impact of gender on the review of the curricula vitae of job applicants and tenure candidates: A national empirical study. *Sex Roles* 41: 509–28.

Van Parijs, P. 1995. *Real Freedom for All: What (If Anything) Can Justify Capitalism?* New York: Oxford University Press.

Van Parijs, P. and Vanderborght, Y. 2017. *Basic Income: A Radical Proposal for a Free Society and a Sane Economy*. Cambridge: Harvard University Press.

Veldboer, L., Kleinhans, R., and van Ham, M. 2015. Mandatory volunteer work as fair reciprocity for unemployment and social benefits? *IZA*, discussion paper 9111.

Williams, D. 2013. Do racial preferences affect minority learning in law schools? *Journal of Empirical Legal Studies* 10: 171–95.

Zwolinski, M. 2015. Property rights, coercion, and the welfare state: The libertarian case for a basic income for all. *Independent Review* 19: 515–29.

Index